READING ON THE EDGE

Reading on the Edge

*Exiles, Modernities, and
Cultural Transformation in
Proust, Joyce, and Baldwin*

Cyraina E. Johnson-Roullier

STATE UNIVERSITY OF NEW YORK PRESS

Published by
State University of New York Press, Albany

For information, address State University of New York Press,
State University Plaza, Albany, NY, 12246

Production by Cathleen Collins
Marketing by Fran Keneston

Cover Art: T-O Map, Isidore, Bishop de Seville, first printed 1472. Oldest western
European map of the world, the "O" representing the ancient belief that the world
was surrounded by water, the "T" dividing the world into the three known
continents, Asia, Africa and Europe. Photo courtesy of The Newberry Library,
Chicago.

Library of Congress Cataloging in Publication Data
Johnson-Roullier, Cyraina E., 1960–
    Reading on the edge : exiles, modernities, and cultural transformation in
Proust, Joyce, and Baldwin / Cyraina E. Johnson-Roullier.
        p.   cm.
    Includes bibliographical references (p.   ) and index.
    ISBN 0-7914-4541-0 (alk. paper.)—ISBN 0-7914-4542-9 (pb.)
    1. Baldwin, James, 1924—Criticism and interpretation.   2. Proust, Marcel,
1871–1922—Criticism and interpretation.   3. Joyce, James, 1882–1941—
Criticism and interpretation.   4. Homosexuality and literature—History—20th
century.   5. Literature and anthropology—History–20th century.   6. Difference
(Psychology) in literature.   7. Modernism (Literature).   8. Silence in literature.
9. Exiles in literature.   10. Canon (Literature).   I. Title.
PS3552.A45Z746   2000
820.9′112—dc21   99-37822
                                                                                CIP

10 9 8 7 6 5 4 3 2 1

For Cyndi, who listened, who cried, and who laughed
1959–1996

It is easier to register the loss of traditional orders of difference than to perceive the emergence of new ones.
—James Clifford, *The Predicament of Culture*

The job facing the cultural intellectual is therefore not to accept the politics of identity as given, but to show how all representations are constructed, for what purpose, by whom, and with what components. . . . Every society and official tradition defends itself against interferences with its sanctioned narratives; over time, these acquire an almost theological status, with founding heroes, cherished ideas and values, national allegories having an estimable effect in cultural and political life.
—Edward Said, *Culture and Imperialism*

Myths . . . have the function of founding and articulating spaces.
—Michel de Certeau, *The Practice of Everyday Life*

Contents

Preface

Around the world ethnic and cultural differences continue to produce, as they have from the beginning of the twentieth century, strife, violence, war and death. Refugees of genocide, poverty, oppression and political violence crowd neighboring countries. Workers seeking a better life leave their homelands far behind, contenting themselves on foreign soil among other nationals from their countries, with whom they form small cells of linguistic and cultural belonging. Sometimes, as language skills improve, and cultural differences grow less threatening, such individuals move beyond the borders even of these small communities, forging new paths in unknown and unfamiliar cultural territory. But such cultural change also comes very hard, more strife is often created as old ways are threatened, and true cultural understanding and tolerance between disparate groups is, as the twentieth century has proved time and again, often a distant chimera.

Our epoch has thus been one in which competing notions of cultural, racial and/or ethnic value, of authenticity, identity, and community, have made us increasingly—and globally—on edge. In what ways can literary representations of these competing notions, versions of what more than one critic has called the critique of Western hegemony, alter the critical landscape within which we have traditionally studied literary works? And, as they are read into new literary critical traditions, how can such newly recognized literary representations also serve to obscure, silence or render invisible the voices, perspectives and/or cultural representations of those whose more hybrid cultural identities are not recognized by any pre-existing nation-state or collective oppositional group—just as these newly authorized literary perspectives were traditionally obscured, silenced or rendered invisible by the literary traditions which came before them?

These are the overriding questions with which *Reading on the Edge* is concerned. By posing these central questions, however, I also mean to suggest that the act of criticism, which takes place in relation both to culture and to institutions (in this case the university), and by which literary traditions are constituted and formed, is not subject to the perspicuity of the individual literary critic alone. As Wlad Godzich writes, "interpretation, beholden as it is to the institutional framework that both authorizes and empowers it, finds itself indebted to the instituting act that enables it."[1] Thus, the act of criticism, necessarily linked to prior, institutionally sanctioned acts of criticism, also becomes a powerful arbiter of the way in which we articulate the cultures and cultural products that we "interpret." Often, it is precisely in the act of criticism that our own perspectives toward the cultural representations we read are rigidly policed.

When I began this book, I had intended to explore a number of issues along these lines that had frustrated me for quite some time. As a burgeoning cultural critic, I was initially troubled by two difficulties—first, the problem of studying international modernism within the context of a national literature, and second, the almost total separation of African-American literature from all other instances of Euro-American literature. Reflecting on these issues, it seemed to me that where there was the most cultural difference, there also should be the most turbulence, and where there was the most cultural similarity, there also should be the least turbulence. In these two instances, however, that did not at all seem to be the case. The present text, then, began with one overarching concern: what is the nature of the instability between the boundaries drawn by international modernism and those drawn by the national literatures, and, in spite of that instability, why do modernism and the national literatures share a racial homogeneity that would seem to belie the embattled border between them? This question derived from others that speak in important ways to the cultural complexities I have encountered while seeking to understand the complicated relation between race and modernity, and its significance in the field of modern studies. In all its celebration of cultural difference (defined primarily in national and linguistic terms), for example, why is Euro-American modernism traditionally represented by a group of authors who were overwhelmingly white and male? Why is the cultural space of modernity so hotly contested (between national and international perspectives on literary modernism and modernity, between the modern and the postmodern, between Euro-American and "other" modernisms), when the authors who comprised its canons were often equally white and equally male? These questions were complicated by the fact that although I could perceive the troubled relationship between national and international perspectives on Euro-American literary modernism, the shared origins of these two points of view prevented me from destabilizing that relationship enough to begin to analyze and understand it.

I was also, as aforesaid, very disturbed by the seeming total lack of turbulence on the border between African-American literature and Euro-American literature. Although African-American literature was, after all,

American literature, it was yet (and is still very much so) totally and neatly separated, as if it represented a life experience lived in another geographical space.[2] These two literatures seemed to inhabit two discrete categories, calmly differentiated, as if such differentiation were the outcome of a natural process.

Given the issues and problems I have outlined above, it was obvious that my work would need to take the form of a critique and a revision of Euro-American modernism. Thus, I began this task by researching the origins of modernity in Englightenment philosophy, in Hegel and Marx, and in the early literary criticism forming the institutionalization of Euro-American modernism as a cultural force in the academy. Yet it was soon evident that this track seemed also to take me further and further from my original goal, which was to examine the difficult relation between race and modernity. I watched my text grow larger and larger as the issues I would need to consider in this vein multiplied—too large, in fact ever to allow me the space even to begin to address the relationship between race and modernity.

This seemed an insurmountable impasse. However, as I continued to work with these issues, it finally occurred to me that since my initial intention had been to explore the relation between race and modernity by determining what would be the result if a text written by an African-American were introduced into the canon of international modernism, perhaps I had actually been on the wrong track in trying to do a more conventional study and critique of the origins of Euro-American modernism. Studying this problematic relation by considering instead a variety of racially disparate texts would, I felt, not only provide the possibility of testing the limits of international modernism—it would at the same time allow for the interrogation and critique of the historical separation of Euro-American literature into racially determined categories. From this perspective, it suddenly became clear that studying the work of Euro-American modernists and their "others" together in seeking to examine the relation between race and modernity was itself the critique I was trying to describe. As a result, I abandoned the effort to analyze the origins of modernity, decided to change direction completely, and set out to discuss the significance of intertextuality in the work of a number of racially, culturally and ethnically disparate modern authors. It was a relatively simple task to determine which works to choose from the Euro-American modernist canon. If what was to be attempted was to test the limits of international modernism, it was clear that this could only be done by examining its foundations, in the form of some of its central proponents. I chose, then, to work with Marcel Proust and James Joyce, because these authors were among the most revered in traditional critical formulations of Euro-American modernism.

At about this time, I also happened upon the idea of the chiasmus as an originary form of thought,[3] and decided to try using it as such in order to determine where a possible intersection between international modernism and African-American literature might be, if one existed at all. On examination, two intersections presented themselves, one with the Harlem Renaissance, and the other with James Baldwin. Although choosing an author from the Harlem Renaissance would have been consistent with the time period of international modernism's heydey, I chose instead to work with James Baldwin, and slightly stretch the length of the period. This was because, in my analysis of Baldwin, I discovered the same disciplinary instability that I had found with regard to the relation between international modernism and the national literatures, by virtue of his problematic relationship with the African-American literary tradition. In order to explore this very interesting similarity further, I decided to test my ideas by working more closely with the three authors, James Baldwin, James Joyce and Marcel Proust.

Having chosen the authors, I then needed to determine which of their works would be suitable for this study. The central texts by Proust and Joyce in traditional formulations of Euro-American modernism were Proust's *A la recherche du temps perdu* (*Remembrance of Things Past*) and Joyce's *Ulysses*. However, the first major difficulty with which I was confronted in trying to discuss in the same text the three quite disparate authors I had chosen—reading their works in relation to each other, through each other, even—was how to handle in microcosm the racial divide by which the received literary tradition has been traditionally characterized and within which their work was necessarily ensconced. Since I knew that all three authors had been in some sense exiles, Joyce and Baldwin in terms of their long sojourns in France, and Proust in terms of his lengthy and eccentric seclusion, it quickly became clear that the best way to handle this difficulty would be to focus on the significance of the autiobiographical aspect of their texts, supporting this part of my work with a historical/biographical approach. This made Joyce's *A Portrait of the Artist as a Young Man* a much better choice for the particular examination of Euro-American modernism expounded in *Reading on the Edge*, since it is more directly autobiographical than is *Ulysses*, even though *Ulysses* is the more important Euro-American modernist text.[4] In the case of Baldwin, *Giovanni's Room* immediately presented itself as the most interesting of his works to examine in relation to the issues to be studied here. As Baldwin's second novel, it was written during his long exile in France, and makes use of his experience there. In addition, through its treatment of homosexuality, it problematizes the issue of race.

The primary goal of this book is to strive toward the potential for cultural transformation, opening the possibility for new modes of cultural understanding, such as that suggested by the emergent field of "border writing." In her book, *Border Writing: The Multidimensional Text*, D. Emily Hicks describes a type of writing that cuts across cultural boundaries in order to represent a multiple cultural experience. She writes:

> Border writing emphasizes the differences in reference codes be-
> tween two or more cultures. It depicts, therefore, a kind of realism
> that approaches the experience of border crossers, who live in a
> bilingual, bicultural, biconceptual reality. I am speaking of cultural,
> not physical, borders.[5]

While Hicks is discussing here a form of *writing*, I would like to expand her idea to encompass a method of *reading*, in order to describe the method by which *Reading on the Edge*, in its analysis of literary modernism and moder-nity, reads the texts of Marcel Proust, James Joyce, and James Baldwin. Be-cause reading "a border text is to cross over into another set of referential codes," Hicks suggests, any "reader of border writing will not always be able to perceive the 'logic' of the text at first."[6] Thus, a quick flip through this book could give the impression of its being, at best, a comparative study of works from three different literary traditions and, at worst, a hodge-podge of assertions that could not possibly be sustained. Yet if *Reading on the Edge* is considered itself as a form of "border writing" and, as such, sub-ject to its own inner logic very different from that suggested by traditional notions and forms of literary study, it follows, then, that its *reading* of Proust, Joyce, and Baldwin should also be subject to its own inner logic.

The type of cultural situation and experience here discussed in relation to literary modernism and modernity and each of the three authors with which it is concerned is that of the "border crosser," the individual who "is both 'self' and 'other,'" whose "'subject' emerges from double strings of signifiers of two sets of referential codes, from both sides of the border."[7] In other words, it fo-cuses on the articulation of identity in the context of multiple cultural referents and associations. Such cultural associations need not be described only in terms of two different cultural codes, but may include three, perhaps four, or even more, depending on the individual situation. The cultural circumstances of the "border crosser" can encompass all types of intercultural experience, from the worker who spends six months out of the year in one or more differ-ent countries, to the second-generation immigrant who must cope not only with the culture of his or her ancestors, but also find a way to adapt to a new one,[8] to the experience of partners in an intercultural marriage.

Chapter 1 discusses the issues I have outlined above from the perspec-tive of what I have called the "politics of cultural space," or the complex in-teraction between authors, their work, their critics, the cultures that shape it and them, and their relation to the university, which exerts great influence over the way their work is received. By analyzing this process, I suggest that our cultural understanding is characterized by authorized and unauthorized "cultural spaces" engaged in a battle for legitimacy, represented in literary modernism by canonical Euro-American modernism and the neglected modernity of literary representations from traditionally excluded cultures.

Chapter 2 re-reads Euro-American modernism as one cultural instance in a broader vision of modern culture, and reconfigures its central trope of exile as the key to understanding the unauthorized modernist cultural spaces explored in the following three chapters.

Chapter 3 re-reads Marcel Proust's *A la recherche du temps perdu* for its textual articulation of the hidden cultural space of homosexuality. By reconceiving the *Recherche's* central character, Marcel, as a double narrator made up of the heterosexual Marcel who is the novel's protagonist, and Marcel Proust, the novel's author, this chapter sheds light on the complicated narrative tapestry by which Proust writes the experience of homosexuality without the need for public admission of his sexual preference.

Chapter 4 re-reads James Joyce's *A Portrait of the Artist as a Young Man* not as a work of pure aesthetic genius, but as an exploration of the cultural politics of late nineteenth-century Ireland. Through analyzing the complex interrelationship between fear and shame and religious and secular reality in the text, this chapter shows how the novel's protagonist, Stephen Dedalus, creates a new relationship to language that enables him to begin the journey toward the development of a clearer understanding of late nineteenth-century Irish identity.

Chapter 5 re-reads James Baldwin's *Giovanni's Room* to reveal its central focus not on race, but on the problems of self-deception and sexual ambiguity. Through this, it identifies Baldwin not specifically as an African-American writer, but as one who comments meaningfully on many of the larger issues of modern identity.

Chapter 6 describes the new and transformative cultural possibilities latent in modernity, and their significance for ongoing literary study.

I have described in detail a few of the permutations of the journey that has been the writing of this book in order to lay bare some of the difficulties of "reading on the edge"—experimenting with new intellectual frameworks within prior modes of thought, testing conventional borders and boundaries and, perhaps, seeking to draw these lines anew. While many may focus their work on the new alone, I believe that the interplay between the old and the new is a much more fruitful path. In emphasizing dialogue, it sparks intellectual exchange which, whether positive or negative, is not only healthy, but it is the lifeblood of critical and scholarly endeavor. Life on the border—even over the edge—is perhaps more risky, but exhilarating; perhaps more dangerous, but challenging; and perhaps more difficult, yet potentially illuminating. As D. Emily Hicks writes, border writing, writing about the problems often presented by the clash between cultures, "offers a new form of knowledge: information about and understanding of the present to the past in terms of the possibilities of the future."[9] *Reading on the Edge* is only a tiny step in this direction—edging toward the transformative cultures of a world yet to come.

Acknowledgments

No book can come to fruition without the aid of many others along the way. *Reading on the Edge* is no exception, and I would like to offer my heartfelt gratitude to all of those who have helped, sustained, nurtured, encouraged, critiqued, pushed or even just listened during its writing.

I would like first to thank Henry Sussman. He has gone so far beyond the call of duty that such thanks, though gratefully given, can only fall far short of the mark. Without his faith, support, encouragement and sincere interest in my work, I could never have accomplished so much. His contribution has been invaluable, and I am forever in his debt.

My thanks to the English Department at the University of Notre Dame for two very generous leaves that released me to devote myself full-time to this project. My thanks also go to the Institute for Scholarship in the Liberal Arts at the University of Notre Dame, for a Summer Research Grant to complete its introductory chapter.

Through the writing of this book, I have had the opportunity to present large portions of it in various venues. My sincere thanks to Susan Stanford Friedman for organizing the MLA 1994 conference panel on "The New Modernisms," which provided a challenging forum for testing my ideas. Her long-time interest in my work, conscientious reading and challenging criticism have all been invaluable assets.

I would also like to extend many thanks to the various universities where I was invited to lecture, and their audiences. I thank Diane Elam and Robyn Wiegman for an invitation to visit the University of Indiana at Bloomington; my heartfelt thanks to Hazel Rowley, for organizing my visits to Melbourne University, Monash University, Deakin University/Toorak, Griffith University, Australian Defence Force Academy and University of Technology in Australia; thanks to Lydia Thompson, for an invitation to Virginia Commonwealth University; thanks to Aoi Mori for organizing my visit to Japan as Keynote Speaker to the Kyushu American Literature Society in Fukuoka; and most important, I would like to thank my colleagues at the State University of New York at Buffalo—their tough and challenging questions were an honor that went a long way toward helping me to shape the final product.

I would like to thank Patrick McGee for organizing the panel "Joyce, Postmodernism, Postcolonialism," and for taking an interest in my work. This panel was pivotal in the development of some of the key premises of this book.

I would also like to thank Richard Brown. His interest in my work, timely suggestions, support and encouragement came at just the right time.

I remain very grateful to Wlad Godzich for his careful and perspicacious reading of my work, his tough criticisms and pertinent suggestions, as well as an invitation to spend a semester at the University of Geneva in Geneva, Switzerland as a Visiting Scholar. I thank him for a singular and extremely enlightening opportunity.

Warm thanks go to James Peltz and Cathleen Collins, my editors at SUNY Press. I thank James for providing sanity in a difficult process, for prompt, detailed and concerted attention to issues as they arose, and for patience and a great sense of humor! I thank Cathleen for her patience, prompt responses, and useful suggestions. No author could have had a better team.

I am especially grateful to Rhonda Pretlow, for her consistent and conscientious work with the technical and administrative details concerning this project. The value of her contributions is inestimable.

A shorter version of Chapter 5 appeared in *Modern Fiction Studies* in December 1999. I thank the editors for permission to reprint.

Many friends and colleagues have also been especially helpful as I have worked on this project.

I would like to thank my colleagues at Notre Dame for providing an intellectually stimulating environment in which to continue my scholarly growth and development. I remain very grateful to Joseph Buttiegieg, and I thank him for the interest in my work which initially brought me to Notre Dame. I am greatly indebted to Steve Fredman, for many conversations, for his continued and unflagging interest in my work, and for timely suggestions. His support has been indispensable. I wish to express also my keen appreciation for the efforts of Jacque Brogan, who initially smoothed the way for me, and whose continued interest in my work has been of great help. I thank Ewa Ziarek for interesting and thought-provoking conversations, and for pertinent and much-needed advice. Thanks to Kathy Psomiades for wise counsel about the publishing process. And to Barbara Green, thanks for sharing my interest in revisionary approaches to Euro-American modernism.

To Kim Flint Hamilton, my thanks for a ready ear and unstoppable optimism; to Dr. George Dedes and Alexandra Dedes, thanks for being there at just the right time.

To Fritz Senn, thanks for knowing as much as you do about Joyce, and for sharing in a pinch!

And finally, I would like to acknowledge the invaluable contributions of several members of my family. To my cousin Earl S. Glass, thanks for unfailing confidence. To my mother, Wanda R. Johnson, my deepest gratitude. Her faith, confidence and loving and constant support were the lifeblood of this project. I save my warmest thanks, however, for my husband, Thierry Roullier. His daily sacrifices for this project, his continued support, his interest and intellectual and technical contributions have all been truly exceptional. Without them, this book could not have been written.

* * * *

Toutefois, je réserve mes remerceiments les plus chaleureux pour mon époux, Thierry Roullier. Ses sacrifices quotidiens pour ce projet, ses encouragements continus, ses contributions intellectuelles et techniques ont été véritablement exceptionnels. Sans eux, ce livre n'aurait pas été écrit. De Clamart, à San Francisco, jusqu'à Chicago, tu as été la flamme constante derrière ce projet. Pour ton support, pour les conversations sans fin, et pour tes rêves imaginaires, je te remercie, Thierry, de tout coeur.

PERMISSIONS ACKNOWLEDGEMENTS

Grateful acknowledgement is made to the following for permission to reprint previously published material:

Excerpt from Gottlieb Gaiser, "Joyce and Joyceans: A Critical View on the Problem of Institutionalization," in *International Perspectives on James Joyce*, copyright 1986, Whitston, Troy, New York. Reprinted by permission of Gottlieb Gaiser.

Excerpt from Colin MacCabe, "Preface," in *James Joyce: New Perspectives*, ed. Colin MacCabe, Harvester, Sussex, 1982. Reprinted by permission of Prentice-Hall Europe.

Excerpt from Patrick Parrinder, "The Strange Necessity: James Joyce's Rejection in England (1914–1930)," in *James Joyce: New Perspectives*, ed. Colin MacCabe, Harvester, Sussex, 1982. Reprinted by permission of Prentice-Hall Europe.

Excerpts from Marcel Proust, *A la recherche du temps perdu*, eds. Jean-Yves Tadié, Florence Callu, Francine Goujon, Eugene Nicole, Pierre-Louis Rey, Brian Rogers et Jo Yoshida, Bibliothèque de la Pléiade, 4 Tomes, Editions Gallimard, Paris, 1987.

Excerpts from *Remembrance of Things Past*, Vol. III by Marcel Proust, trans. By C. K. Montcrieff and T. Kilmartin. Copyright 1981 by Random

House, Inc. and Chatto & Windus. Reprinted by permission of Random House, Inc. and the Estate of Marcel Proust.

Excerpt from Joel Rudinow, "Representation, Voyeurism, and the Vacant Point of View," *Philosophy and Literature* 3.2 (Fall 1979). Reprinted by permission of The Johns Hopkins University Press.

Excerpts from "Ireland, Island of Saints and Sages," from *The Critical Writings of James Joyce* by James Joyce E. Mason & R. Ellman, editors. Copyright 1959 by Harriet Weaver and F. Lionel Monro, as Administrators for the Estate of James Joyce, renewed © 1987 by F. Lionel Monro. Used by permission of Viking Penguin, a division of Penguin Putnam Inc.

Excerpts from James Joyce's *A Portrait of the Artist as a Young Man* and *Critical Writings* are reproduced with the kind permission of the Estate of James Joyce.

Excerpts from *A Portrait of the Artist as a Young Man* by James Joyce. Copyright 1916 by B. W. Huebsch, Copyright 1944 by Nora Joyce, Copyright 1964 by the Estate of James Joyce. Used by permission of Viking Penguin, a division of Penguin Putnam Inc.

Excerpt from Lyall Powers, "Henry James and James Baldwin: The Complex Figure," *Modern Fiction Studies* 30.4 (Winter 1984), pp. 651, 653, 656 © 1984). Purdue Research Foundation. Reprinted with permission of The Johns Hopkins University Press.

Excerpt from Morris Beja and Shari Benstock, "Introduction," in *Coping with Joyce: Essays from the Copenhagen Symposium*, copyright 1989, Ohio State University Press, Columbus. Reprinted by permission of the Ohio State University Press, Morris Beja and Shari Benstock.

Excerpt from Fritz Senn, "Joyce the Verb," in *Coping with Joyce: Essays from the Copenhagen Symposium*, copyright 1989, Ohio State University Press, Columbus. Reprinted by permission of the Ohio State University Press and Fritz Senn.

Excerpt from Cornel West, "Minority Discourse and the Pitfalls of Canon Formation," *The Yale Journal of Criticism* 1.1 (Fall 1987). Reprinted by permission of the The Johns Hopkins University Press.

Excerpts from Mark D. Guenette, "Le Loup et le narrateur: The Masking and UnMasking of Homosexuality in Proust's *A la recherche du temps perdu*," *Romanic Review* 80.2 (March 1989). Reprinted by permission of *Romanic Review*.

Excerpts from Craig Werner, "Bigger's Blues: Native Son and the Articulation of Afro-American Modernism," in *New Essays on Native Son*, ed. Kenneth Kinnamon, copyright 1990, Cambridge University Press, Cambridge. Reprinted by permission of Cambridge University Press.

Excerpts from Linda Hutcheon, "Circling the Downspout of Empire: Post-Colonialism and Postmodernism," *Ariel*, A Review of International

English Literature, 20:4 (Oct. 1989), copyright 1989. Reprinted by permission of The Board of Governors and The University of Calgary.

Excerpt from "Race and Gender in the Shaping of the American Literary Canon: A Case Study from the Twenties," in *Canons and Contexts*, ed. Paul Lauter, copyright 1991, Oxford, New York, 1991. Reprinted by permission of Oxford University Press.

Excerpt from Patrick Brady, "The Present State of Studies on Marcel Proust," *Claudel Studies* 16.1–2 (1989), copyright 1989. Reprinted by permission of Moses Nagy, editor, *Claudel Studies*.

Excerpt from Richard Johnson, "What is Cultural Studies Anyway?" *Social Text* 16, Winter 1986/7, copyright 1986/7. Reprint by permission of Duke University Press.

Excerpts from *Giovanni's Room* by James Baldwin. Copyright 1956 by James Baldwin. Used by permission of Doubleday, a division of Random House, Inc. and the James Baldwin Estate.

Excerpt from Adrian Marino, "Modernity and the Evolution of Literary Consciousness," *Diogenes* 77 (Spring 1972), copyright 1972. Reprint by permission of Berghahn Books.

Excerpt from *Newsweek* 5/11/92, copyright 1992, Newsweek, Inc. All rights reserved. Reprinted by permission.

Excerpt from Johnson-Roullier, Cyraina, "(An)Other Modernism: James Baldwin, Giovanni's Room, and the Rhetoric of Flight," *Modern Fiction Studies* 45. 4 (Winter 1999), pp. 932–956. Copyright 1999. Purdue Research Foundation. Reprinted by permission of the Johns Hopkins University Press.

Cover image from Isidore, T-O Map, photo courtesy of The Newberry Library, Chicago.

CHAPTER 1

Introduction

Borders, Cultures, and Spatial Politics

> The question is . . . what social effects effects are produced
> by the knowledges disseminated in the university, and by
> the manner of their dissemination.
> —John Guillory, *Cultural Capital*

Since the 1987 publication of Houston Baker's ground-breaking study, *Modernism and the Harlem Renaissance*, and other equally seminal works on modernism and gender, such as Bonnie Kime Scott's *The Gender of Modernism* (1990), modernist scholarship has been increasingly characterized by revision, to an extent that threatens to bring about nothing short of a revolution in the field. Followed by such studies as James de Jongh's *Vicious Modernism* (1990), Paul Gilroy's *The Black Atlantic* (1993), Walter Kalaidjian's *American Culture Between the Wars* (1993), and Michael North's *The Dialect of Modernism* (1994) among others, the exploration of the complex interrelationships between race and modernity begun in Baker's challenging work has become an important and challenging avenue in modernist studies, opening many new doors to cultural understanding of this time in literary history.

While all of these works have provided invaluable engagements with the glaring lacunae in modernist studies regarding the literary contributions to modern culture of both African-Americans and other black diasporic cultures, as well as other traditionally excluded and/or neglected groups, those that deal with race are largely limited to the study of black authors alone. Those among such studies that are not limited in this way also do not substantially explore the interrelationships between black and Euro-American cultural contributions, or investigate what such an analysis could bring to our understanding of roughly the first half of the twentieth century: a time of great upheaval and massive technological and cultural change, that would

1

seem radically to contradict the neat borders and boundaries by which it is commonly described.

In this book, I seek to broaden the cultural frame within which it is possible to study and understand modern culture, through expanding the examination of race and modernity beyond conventional borders. By reading the work of Marcel Proust, James Joyce and James Baldwin outside the traditional parameters within which their work has been primarily understood in relation to their nationality and/or race, I hope to establish the foundation for a larger vision of modern culture, one that would recognize the significance of instances of cultural multiplicity and hybrid identity in any more complete understanding of modernity. Reading James Baldwin's work in this context becomes, then, not an effort to prove that it has "modern" characteristics, or that it is "good enough" to be considered as such, but the endeavor to discover more directly what its *in*clusion can tell us about the processes of its *ex*clusion. Such discussion must also, inevitably, raise the issues of canon revision and the proper and/or most efficacious means of bringing it about.

But approaching these issues from the oppositional perspective often put forward by conventional views of canon revision not only predetermines the avenues by which such issues may be investigated; it also leaves unexplored an underlying assumption of incommensurable cultural difference that exists on both sides of whatever issue, and by which "canonical" and "non-canonical" authors have often traditionally been separated. This assumption is difficult to examine, as it is naturalized because masked by the presupposition that the only way to address these issues is through analyzing them within a paradigm of inclusion or exclusion with regard to a seemingly self-evident canon of established authors. Thus, one of the most important concerns this book will explore is the way in which the problem of difference, as it is made manifest in this paradigm of inclusion and exclusion, actually figures as a hidden obstacle in canon revision. When the notion of cultural difference is articulated as incommensurable, it becomes nearly impossible to discover an equitable way to address the interpretive and epistemological difficulties raised by the act of canon revision, which is also often intimately concerned with the vagaries of cultural difference.

Reading on the Edge is concerned with precisely this issue, and its implications for the study of literary modernism within a broad vision of modern culture. In this study, I argue that although the recent revisionist trend in modern scholarship broadens our understanding of cultural possibility in the roughly first half of the twentieth century, it often fragments, rather than expands, our understanding of the modern, because it does not analyze the significance of intertextuality among modern works from disparate cultural contexts. This book asserts that in order to apprehend the true complexity of modern experience, we must read modernity "on the edge," that is, against the critical trends and institutional structures that have not only engendered modernism as primarily a Euro-American cultural movement, but which have also encouraged the development of these various new and largely disconnected "modernisms." I suggest that more profound connections between modern works from disparate cultural contexts do indeed exist, but that because they represent a cultural excess that is not easily assimilated to existing disciplinary classifications, these connections are often lost as we "read" modern experience into more conventional contexts. While the separate and distinct "modernisms" that reflect these contexts may certainly allow us to recognize the multiplicity of modern experience on the surface, they also simultaneously deny us the opportunity to examine its deeper implications for our understanding of modern culture as a whole. In its analysis of the problem of difference, then, this book thus moves beyond the binary opposition of inclusion/exclusion (by which efforts at canon revision are typically characterized)—goes over the edge, so to speak—in advancing a notion of cultural difference that deconstructs the traditional, oppositional understanding of "self" and "other" upon which Western culture has historically been based.[1] In doing this, it also explores a cultural construction that does not attempt to transcend cultural difference, subsuming that difference into what some might call a "culture of the same" which would deny any possibility of traditionally conceived authenticity. Rather, the concept of culture elaborated in this book does not participate in this oppositional framework at all.

Here, "reading on the edge" suggests the exploration and analysis of representations of cultural experience that exist beyond those to be found in conventional articulations of collective, ostensibly ethnically and/or racially pure, nationally-defined notions of identity. This book discusses instead the significance of racial and cultural hybridities whose intermixture places individual authors—in this case, Marcel Proust, James Joyce, and James Baldwin—and their cultural representations in various contexts more or less outside of preconstructed traditional paradigms of authorized subjectivity and/or identity. Representations of such cultural experiences, if they are to be considered at all, must be (and, historically, have been) *read* into more conventional contexts, and all excess simply filtered out—in other words, silenced.

In studying the implications of this for our understanding of Proust, Joyce, and Baldwin, this book reconceives the notion of exile in modern culture by redefining and then positing it as a new interpretive ground upon which to reconfigure conventionally accepted aesthetic and cultural differences their work in order to retrieve their previously unexplored similarities, silenced as part of that cultural excess that cannot easily be read within more narrowly defined cultural and linguistic disciplinary constraints. Exile is here broadly defined to include the alienation often brought about by the experience of oppression and/or exclusion as a result of, for example, race or sexual preference. Pictured as exiles—Joyce and Baldwin as expatriates, Proust as a long-term recluse, Joyce as a colonial subject, Proust and Baldwin as homosexuals—all three of these authors share, and evidence in their work, what I identify as an important yet neglected and distinctly modern characteristic: that of hybrid and/or multiple cultural identity. By focusing on the silenced and submerged intertextual meaning of the markers of such hybrid and multiple identity in these authors' work, *Reading on the Edge* disrupts the traditional divide between Euro-American modernism and its "others," thereby enlarging our understanding toward a more comprehensive, and transformative, vision of modern experience and culture.

This book thus reads culture "on the edge" because it delves into the voiceless silence of cultural excess—into those cultural locations of identity that are, for the most part, voiceless because not centered in constellations of authorized group identity,[2] and which have, therefore, remained culturally unauthorized, unsanctioned, and illegitimate, and, above all, mute; or, if such an identity participates in more than one authorized collective group identity by virtue of multiple cultural locations,[3] its voice is often fractured along the fault lines that differentiate and divide these collective identities. To "read on the edge" in this instance means to risk the denial of fracture— to derive concepts of "self" and "identity" from a ground characterized by multiplicity, hybridity, changeability and instability, as opposed to what Paul Gilroy would call a kind of "ethnic absolutism,"[4] or the positing of a solid, often essentialized, ostensibly stable ground upon which readings of singular, racially and/or ethnically pure notions of "self" and "identity" may be constructed. This is not to say that the present text's reading of "self" and "identity" is the "right" one and the other (or any other) reading the "wrong" one. It is to say, however, that the powerful attraction of the latter type of reading is often so forceful as to utterly silence notions of "self" and "identity" derived from any other type of ground. To "read on the edge" is thus to read the cultural significance of that silence.

Such cultural experiences and representations as those described in relation to the three authors to be studied here might necessarily be perceived as individual and particular from a more conventional cultural perspective. Yet, in terms of their mutual silencing, they may also be perceived as very much collective—albeit not in the traditional sense of collectivity—if viewed from a non-conventional cultural perspective that would recognize the existence in multiple cultural contexts of a cultural level such as this one. Using the metaphor of a cliff, then, this book suggests the cultural and interpretive limit beyond which it is no longer "safe" to go—beyond which, epistemologically, there is, seemingly, nothing but the open air—or, perhaps, in the eyes of many cultural conservatives, beyond which there is only a form of pluralist anarchy, confusion and dangerous amalgamation, in which true "culture" becomes an anomaly and what some would call the multicultural onslaught erases all possibility of collective historical identity.[5]

In this book, I am interested specifically in the way in which these issues relate to the articulation of cultural difference found in the twentieth-century notion of modernity through its transformation into those knowledges I have identified as the interpretive readings that have served, from the late 1980s to the present time, to create numerous "modernisms"—each its own separate, culturally distinct modern understanding—rather than a comprehensive rearticulation of the modern experience itself. My primary interest is in the process by which such readings are then disseminated in the university, becoming the sanctioned mode by which our understanding of the modern is apprehended (or the production of culture).[6] I have called this process the "politics of cultural space." This notion encompasses the cultural "spaces" created by sanctioned "readings" of texts, yet it also encompasses an important, yet largely hidden aspect of silencing within such readings: underlying assumptions of incommensurable difference located in the geographical, national, racial, ethnic and gender foundations of conventionally defined collectivities, which then become the authorized objects of study around which literary canons are produced, canonicity determined, canon formation achieved and legitimized, and knowledges about them thus disseminated through the university. This book is, then, also largely about how the problem of incommensurable difference figures in cultural understanding, as well as how this has functioned in the production of our notions of literary "culture" itself, in the formation, legitimization and dissemination of the canons by which such cultural understanding is normally apprehended. In the case of literary modernism and modernity, this has resulted in a fracturing of our understanding of the modern along strictly drawn lines of cultural difference that deny and/or distort the pervasiveness of modern experience and its inherent propensity to bulge across such borders.

Through examining this cultural process, or the politics of cultural space, it becomes possible to analyze much more closely the significance of the aforementioned assumption of incommensurable difference that often lies silently at the heart of both sides of the debate on canon revision. Within the production of culture, an activity that lies at the heart of the politics of cultural space, there exist a number of actors: the scholar-critic, the reader (both professional and ordinary), the text, and the university. Traditionally, the production of culture in English studies has focused on the meanings generated by the text and fleshed out in our readings of particular texts: in the national literature context this has focused on the linguistic permutations of the text alone; in the context of comparative literature, it has focused on this in addition to the particular problems of polyglossia and translation, and the cultural frameworks of texts from several languages. Each context, however, has traditionally ignored the potential influence on our readings of the political, historical, sociological, and/or psychological contexts of the text, viewing these as a substantial deemphasis on the specifically "literary" value of whatever text in question, which should be able to stand on its own.

In this book, I study this process, the politics of cultural space, as it relates to literary modernism and modernity from these two perspectives—that of the national literatures, and that of comparative literature. This double-edged point of view is necessary for three reasons. First, the problem of "difference" figures differently in each of these two contexts. While the national literatures (in this case that of English) have in large part excluded cultural difference by the singular nature of their object of study,[7] comparative literature has traditionally embraced such difference, in its emphasis on multilingual, multicultural study across disciplinary boundaries, and in its advancement of the notion of *Weltliteratur*, or "world literature," in which such difference is to be transcended in seeking to achieve the broader goals of unity and human understanding.

Second, the process that I have identified as the politics of cultural space is particularly conflictual in the subfield of literary modernism and modernity. Here, in addition to the conflicts represented in the debate on canon revision, the national literatures and comparative literature meet and clash in a more pointed conflict concerning how each will articulate the cultural space of modernity—something to which we will return in more detail in chapter 2.

The third reason for discussing the problem of difference from these two perspectives has to do with how it figures more generally in twentieth-century literary studies. The twentieth century saw the professionalization first of English literature, then, in the 1920s, that of American literature, then after World War II, that of comparative literature.[8] In the early part of the century, the institutionalization of mainstream Euro-American literary modernism[9] in North American universities created a number of interpretive and epistemological difficulties that are still being debated today, as we shall discuss further in chapter 2. In the early 1970s, the institutionalization of African-American literature and of women's literature and feminist theory in North American universities helped to bring about an unprecedented change in the way in which the role of literary studies in the production of culture is perceived, the way in which those involved in it do their work, and the range of cultural representations available for consumption to the ordinary reader, and for study to the scholar-critic. The early and mid-nineteen-nineties have brought an even greater challenge—the pressure to re-create comparative literature's traditional notion of *Weltliteratur* on a truly global scale, as the need to make sense of the influx of literatures and epistemologies from previously colonized countries and the literary voices of oppressed or marginalized peoples within the borders of what have traditionally been represented as culturally homogeneous nation-states began to demand a radical alteration of the traditional map of literary studies in all fields and languages.[10]

This explosion has had (and will have) the effect of opening up an even broader array of literary materials to the ordinary reader, but in the discipline of English literature, it has also only heated up the intensity of the ongoing debate on canon revision. For both comparative literature and the national literatures, the issue has now become the proper place of a relatively new literary approach, that of cultural studies,[11] both in their fields and in the university. The debate on cultural studies, which hinges very closely on that of canon revision, is extremely wide-ranging, far too expansive for sustained analysis in the present discussion. It will suffice here to suggest the most important points of differentiation between comparative literature and the national literatures with regard to the issue, as well as how each perspective is currently approaching it, before continuing to elaborate on the scope of this book.

"CULTURAL" STUDIES/"CULTURE" STUDIES

Broadly, cultural studies[12] is a critical construct that arises from the desire to bring the external cultural context, long held at loggerheads with the study of literature, back into its purview. It has its origins in the Birmingham School in Britain, influenced by such scholar-critics as Stuart Hall and Paul Gilroy, but in its North American form it is substantially different from the British one. While in Great Britain "cultural studies" grew out of the analysis of the cultural representations of the British working class, the American version, which some are calling "culture"[13] rather than "cultural" studies, seems to be a conglomeration of a number of approaches, most of them theoretical—among these are feminist theory, black studies, deconstruction, psychoanalytic theory, Marxist theory, gay and lesbian theory, postcolonial theory, and discourse analysis. As the great variety of perspectives listed here would suggest, there are potentially any number of culture/cultural studies approaches at any given moment (one of the most important problems many more traditional critics may have with this burgeoning area of literary study), focusing on any number of cultural representations in any number of literary historical periods.

They are all, however, united in the commitment to studying literary texts as involved in complex and interrelated social systems, consisting of authors and their texts, readers, teachers, students, and culture and its institutions.[14] Those who adopt culture studies approaches "maintain that literary texts are always cultural texts and that readers read differently according to the cultures from which they derive their identities."[15] This suggests, however, a very important shift in the way in which the object of literary study is perceived, as those involved in teaching, studying, and considering literature from this perspective would also primarily "see themselves . . . as interrogating cultural phenomena rather than elucidating literary masterpieces."[16]

CULTURE STUDIES AND NEW CRITICAL CULTURE

Viewed from a literary historical perspective, it becomes very easy to understand how an approach such as that of culture/cultural studies might seem especially problematic from a traditional point of view, one that would perhaps emphasize an understanding of literature as the revered repository of national cultural heritage. When English literary studies was still in the process of being professionalized in the early to mid-twentieth century, its institutionalization in the university took place in tandem with just such a view as this—that of the New Criticism—which, in its focus on the formal properties of the text (although it did not in itself espouse the development of a nationally defined culture) also lent itself very well to the endeavor to create a notion of homogeneous national culture through literary understanding.[17] In emphasizing "close reading" and the separation of literary art from socio-historico-political concerns, the New Criticism "provided an attractive model for studying literature because it concentrated on single works (usually a poem), seemed to require no knowledge of historical context or of an author's biography or other works, and did not force readers to consider complex, ambiguous relations between literature and social experience."[18]

It is important to note here that the institutionalization of Euro-American literary modernism in the North American university also came about at this fortuitous moment. Although at first it took a somewhat different tack in terms of its relation to established literary culture,[19] nevertheless, its arcane language and obscure forms lent themselves quite easily to the classroom endeavors of the New Critical scholar-critic. With his or her superior literary and cultural knowledge and New Criticial techniques, such a scholar-critic was invested with the sacred task of explication, of helping students through the painstaking and laborious process of deriving meaning from difficult texts, guiding them through the experience of epiphany. From its advent never understood to possess the potential to instill traditional, collective cultural values, Euro-American literary modernism was viewed askance in the university until nearly midcentury, surviving until then largely through the critical efforts of many of its own proponents, such as T. S. Eliot, Ezra Pound, Ford Madox Ford, and Virginia Woolf.[20]

But in the framework of the New Criticism, Euro-American literary modernism offered a different kind of cultural value than that established in and for the traditional role of literature—one of near reverence for the "genius" of the modern author, and the seemingly superhuman erudition of the scholar-critic who could so skillfully unlock the doors to the endless and profound pearls of meaning hidden deep within the modern text (an issue to which we will return in both chapters 2 and 4). However, as concerns the institutionalization of Euro-American literary modernism in connection with the New Criticism, I also want to suggest something else: that these two literary phenomena linked so well precisely *because* the New Criticism helped to separate art from society at a very problematic and war-torn era in world history, when it could indeed have seemed that analysis of the socio-historico-political events and conditions behind modern texts could bring nothing but the knowledge of a worldwide and seemingly permanent exodus from the aesthetic, nationalistic, and/or moral values that literature had historically been construed to represent. Euro-American literary modernism is thus often put forward as a moment when salvation was sought through art, when Euro-America looked at its troubled cultural history and retreated into a utopic world of aesthetic beauty, in which artistic experimentation would serve not only to make sense of the horrors of modern society, but would also restore some of the moral values that it had lost.[21]

NEW CRITICISM AND THE SOCIOCULTURAL ROLE OF THE UNIVERSITY

Outside of its relation to Euro-American literary modernism, however, the New Criticism was, as previously mentioned, quite instrumental in helping to bring about some of the larger cultural goals of literary study within the university, most importantly those having to do with cultural homogenization, and its underlying emphasis on national affiliation.[22] Thus, literature could be studied in the form of nationally defined "canons," each text included on whatever canon having gained that status as a result of its having withstood the test of time and thereby proving itself deserving of such honor, or due to the degree of its "national representativeness"—its representation of the values considered important to the formation and cultural establishment of the national identity in question. Each text in this framework would be considered a literary masterpiece, as Jonathan Culler describes in a recent book:

> One [must] . . . [consider] the models by which universities operate and how they may affect critical writing. The first makes the university the transmitter of a cultural heritage, gives it the ideological function of reproducing culture and the social order. The second model makes the university a site for the production of knowledge. . . . The New Criticism succeeded as well as it did, one could argue,

> because it could function as a way of making the literary heritage
> accessible to a growing and more diversified student body entering
> universities. . . . It gives criticism the role of interpreting the canon,
> elucidating the 'core' knowledge to be conveyed.[23]

Although I would add here the consideration of critical *reading* in this regard as
well, it would seem that this is precisely one of the most pressing difficulties in
the debates on canon revision and culture studies, in all concerned fields and
disciplines, one which is also not often articulated in conjunction with arguments either pro or con on either of these issues. If the controversy surrounding culture/cultural studies and its concomitant emphasis on canon revision is
really a discussion of the cultural function of the university in literary studies, as
well as its larger role as a societal institution, then the issues at the core of the
debate must certainly be understood as going much deeper than simply the
question of whether or not literary canons are (or should be) culturally representative. These two perspectives not only describe radically different notions
of the cultural significance of the university.[24] They also describe radically different processes of cultural production, whose effects filter down into all aspects
of critical, cultural, and educational endeavor: research and analysis, reading
and interpretation, critical and pedagogical methodology. In light of Culler's articulation of the role of the university in this context, those whose attitudes fall
on either side of the debate are, in effect, working and reading—producing culture—side-by-side in two symbolically different universities.

   Thus any in-depth discussion of these issues, in whatever context, cannot
easily proceed without specifying its goals and methodology at the outset. Although not in entire agreement with every aspect of the culture/cultural studies model, the present discussion adheres more closely to this model of the
university and its processes of cultural production than it does to the traditional one, particularly in terms of its reading of literary modernism and
modernity, which seeks to widen the range of cultural consideration in that
context.[25] As such, this study is also concerned specifically with the way in
which the debate on canon revision and culture studies impacts the role of
comparative literature in its study of the modern. This is demanded not only
because of the comparative nature of much extant literary analysis of modernism and modernity, but also because of the increased emphasis on comparatism within the culture studies paradigm.

   This focus points again to one of the central premises of this book: that
the literary profession is currently undergoing a radical transformation,
what Gilroy has called a politics of transfiguration,[26] that seems to center on
an impasse in literary critical endeavor, between the study and analysis of
"literariness," or the particular properties that pertain expressly to "literature," and that of culture itself. Comparative literature, its goals and

methodology, lies at the nexus of this change. Although many of its proponents are very much in disagreement with the alterations sought in the field at the behest of cultural studies approaches, many others find such change invigorating, and believe it can only give the field a renewed vigor and added importance in the literary critical profession.[27]

The traditional model of the university and its processes of cultural production would, however, seem to uphold this particular notion of value, not just with regard to texts, but also with regard to notions of national and cultural identity. Those comparatists who would uphold this value, who would respect and revere the authority of tradition above all else, would perhaps also find any attempt to view the situation from a different perspective iconoclastic and subversive, and those involved in putting forward such perspectives rude despoilers of cultural and national heritage, whatever that cultural and national heritage may be. Yet for many others who find themselves increasingly presented with the need to engage in comparative endeavors, the refusal to consider the full significance of these new perspectives also seems to make of the traditional model a somewhat closed system, one which would continue on into the future in a seemingly timeless stasis of almost nostalgic belief.

The cultural "representativeness" of the literary canon, in this instance, comes to pose a glaring question: Representative of what, and of whom? Beyond comparative analyses, those who would uphold the traditional model of the university have often viewed this question as an attack or as a threat to their integrity and beliefs, and have rightfully sought to defend them. Those who would react against the loud and angry backlash, would equally as staunchly defend their right to be heard. But those who would stand apart from either of these poles, whether in- or outside the domain of comparative literature, would also pose a related and still equally important question—and one to which no attention has been given in the current debate. What cultural space should those authors, readers, educators, and students inhabit whose cultural representations and/or cultural backgrounds do not fit completely within the framework of values that the traditional model of the university, and the traditional sides in the polarized debate on canon revision and otherness within it, would represent?

THE POLITICS OF CULTURAL SPACE

The conflict between this question and the bifurcated debate on canon revision and culture studies (which is conflictual enough in itself) forms the crux of this book's elaboration of what I have called the politics of cultural space and its particular reading of literary modernism and modernity.[28] Space, in the form of geography, is one of the silenced aspects of the knowledges of literary culture disseminated in the university. The national literatures maintain a symbiotic relationship to geography through their connection to geographical spaces or territories in the form of recognized nation-states, whose political cohesion and territorial boundaries serve to authorize them as legitimate entities. It is also this recognized division that forms the foundation of comparative literature, something to which we will return in more detail below.

Although ethnically, racially, and/or gender-determined constellations of group identity do not always adhere perfectly to the more traditional model of cultural knowledge about a nation-state, they imply this structure through their emphasis on a single aspect of cultural identity, the fact of "blackness," or the fact of "femaleness" or "genderedness" in various cultural contexts. Part of the traditional argument on canon revision is that there is at the present time implied geographical space in the university for the literary representations of only certain politically authorized entities, while a vast range of others remain outside its purview. Traditionalist arguments counterposed to this view would maintain that it is not possible to teach everything without sacrificing quality, depth and/or breadth of knowledge. Therefore there are, necessarily, some things that we just will not be able to teach.[29] Nontraditionalist arguments would maintain that this is not an answer to their overriding question. And while the oppositional debate continues on, each side firmly entrenched in its own position, the voices of those whose cultural experiences and cultural representations do not fit in *either* camp are muffled in the din.

CULTURE STUDIES, CANON REVISION, AND CULTURAL TRANSFORMATION

The impetus for a reconsideration of the deeper cultural significance of this debate is not hard to find, and it is also what has formed the major impetus toward change on both sides of the issue. The world is changing before our very eyes. Changing too slowly, perhaps, for some, but changing just the same. In the course of the 1990s, we saw the demise of old worldviews, the fall of old dividing lines, the redrawing of national and territorial boundaries, the birth of new nations and the disintegration of old ones. In *Reading on the Edge*, I am primarily interested in the sociocultural implications of this world-change, in terms of how the increasing proximity of individuals to those whom they would traditionally have considered "other" can alter (and is altering) the social and cultural constructs in which the social identity projecting the notion of "otherness" is formed. In other words, the significance of these changes is that as the boundaries between cultures become increasingly blurred, what happens to our notion of "culture"[30] itself? How must our traditional conception of "culture," of what it means to be "cultured," change in keeping with the changing social realities of our world?

James Clifford explains this situation in terms of an alteration in our understanding of what Stephen Kern has called "geopolitical"[31] space, a perceptible shrinkage caused in large part by the twentieth-century's technological onslaught:

> This century has seen a drastic expansion of mobility, including tourism, migrant labor, immigration, urban sprawl. More and more people "dwell" with the help of mass transit, automobiles, airplanes. In cities on six continents foreign populations have come to stay. . . . The "exotic" is uncannily close. Conversely, there seem no distant places left on the planet where the presence of "modern" products, media, and power cannot be felt. An older topography and experience of travel is exploded. One no longer leaves home confident of finding something radically new, another time or space. Difference is encountered in the adjoining neighborhood, the familiar turns up at the ends of the earth. . . . "Cultural" difference is no longer a stable, exotic otherness; self-other relations are a means of power and rhetoric rather than of essence. A whole structure of expectations about authenticity in culture and in art is thrown in doubt.[32]

Here Clifford identifies the second of the present text's major premises: that the relationship between power and our traditional notions of literary culture is not effaced, but palpable, and that it replicates, on a symbolic level, imperial relations of power and cultural dominance in the material world. Through "reading on the edge," through unearthing and examining how power is operative in the critical act, we can begin to understand more clearly the impasse represented by the problem of difference in canon revision, and, perhaps, even begin to move beyond it. Polarized, the debate on canon revision makes only one advance possible: the substitution of nontraditional, revised canon B for traditional canon A, something that would simply serve to re-create the whole systemic difficulty all over again, albeit from a different perspective. This threat of substitution also underlies much of the backlash against revision. It would seem, then, that this becomes perhaps the most important question with regard to the cultural problems facing literary study at the birth of a new century. How are we to avoid the problem of substitution in the act of revision? This is a truly vexed problem, and one that also throws the operations of power in cultural production, or the politics of cultural space, into bas-relief.[33]

In this book, I argue that it is precisely this problem of substitution that not only covertly impedes the process of revision, but it also obfuscates and/or silences alternative ways of being and knowing, new and different perspectives on culture and cultural experience from which much could be learned about the cultural complexities now facing us in contemporary life. By analyzing the underlying processes of cultural production in terms of the notion of the politics of cultural space, we can gain a clearer understanding of why the debate on canon revision seems to be caught in a never-ending seesaw of pushing and pulling wills, and how perhaps to avoid simply substituting a new cultural problematic for an old one. To "read on the edge" in this instance is to read *beyond* cultural difference as an oppositional framework, and to read instead how this oppositional framework functions. It is to read for an understanding of "difference" itself not as incommensurable, but as the necessary ground for the creation of new constellations of group existence, and for beginning to understand the cultural locations of many of the new and often multiple identities (as revealed in their cultural representations) currently clamoring for recognition. It is to seek knowledge and understanding in the potential evidenced within cultural transformation.

CULTURE STUDIES, CANON REVISION, AND THE TRANSFORMATION OF CULTURE

In the cultural framework that Clifford describes, new understandings of the distinction and relation between "self" and "other," new conceptions that would rearticulate difference in ways that would open possibilities for cultural rapprochement, rather than closing them off before they have a chance even to begin, become increasingly necessary. The difficulty facing the development of such possibilities is that, as an important factor in many articulations of imperial ideology, culture—specifically, literary culture—comes to represent (viewed through the politics of cultural space) one of the ways by which that ideology, as contained in written form, may be inculcated into the dominated masses[34]—and thereby close off possibilities for cultural knowledge and exchange that might otherwise exist. But, as aforementioned, one of the most important aspects of this often ideological use of culture is also the assumption of a certain kind of racial and cultural purity,[35] something which, in Clifford's new world, is also becoming more and more difficult to assert, as proximity threatens to reduce the traditional distinction between "self" and "other" to a mere play of words. By this, however, I do not mean to suggest that culturally, all are slowly becoming slightly differing versions of the "same"; rather, the traditional means of differentiating "self" from "other" no longer has the same credence as before, and is not always applicable in each and every cultural situation.

   This book asserts that the ideal of "culture," at least of literary "culture" as we have come to define it, may not only be to represent the inviolate repository of "the best that is thought and said" of a given people—something that has conventionally been taken as the most important arbiter of "canonicity," or the way in which eligibility for canonical inclusion is determined. Rather, in examining the traditional idea of literary "culture" in the university by analyzing the very terms on which its existence is founded, that is, notions of "canon," "canonicity," and "canonization"—in "reading on the edge," exploring such culture in terms of the politics of cultural space and thereby moving beyond its canonical foundational structure—I seek to reveal our traditional conceptions of such "culture" as potentially problematic—especially in the current cultural climate. This is not intended to suggest that there is nothing useful and/or valuable about the traditional boundaries established in literary studies and the knowledges produced within their domain. But when such knowledge becomes the only *acceptable* knowledge, when new pathways are ignored, negated or closed off because they do not substantially contribute to knowledge in a given, preestablished discipline or field, then these boundaries become quite unsettling because in this scenario, they may be seen to inhibit, rather than to facilitate, the ongoing process of intellectual discovery.[36]

What I am describing here is precisely the situation with which this text's reading of Marcel Proust, James Joyce, and James Baldwin is confronted. Because it crosses a number of established disciplinary boundaries, this book cannot automatically be categorized as a study that contributes solely to any one of them. As a result, it must be characterized, if it is approached from a traditional point of view, as a comparative study. On close examination, however, this book will resist attempts to classify it as such, at least not in the traditional sense, largely because it does not express as its primary goal the desire simply to provide a study of contrasts, comparisons, and/or interrelationships, nor does it posit itself as a study of influences. Most important, it does not focus on the historical Eurocentric emphasis of comparative literature. Though it does compare and contrast the work of Proust, Joyce, and Baldwin, its examination of the interrelationships between these three authors not only broadens (as would a comparative study) our horizon of cultural understanding with regard to their literary achievements, but produces at the same time a subtle critique, one of the relation to literary modernism and modernity of those disciplines established as the national literatures, as well as that established as comparative literature.

This critique is evidenced in what may be discovered by "reading the edge" between traditional conceptions of the national literatures and comparative literature and the problem of difference as articulated within them, as revealed in (1) the present text's examination of culture; (2) the way each of these domains has read Euro-American literary modernism; and (3) the relation between this text's revision of literary modernism and modernity and traditional conceptions of the same.

In its reading of literary modernism and modernity, this book posits Euro-American modernism as an early twentieth-century artistic and intellectual movement which, in its comparative aspect, is in direct conflict with the goals and premises of the national literatures and which, in terms of its cultural excess, or all that has been read (interpreted) out of it, is also at odds with the traditionally Eurocentric goals and premises of conventional comparative literature. Traditional formulations of Euro-American literary modernism have articulated it in two ways, as will be discussed in greater detail in chapter 2. The first is as a short period of time in a much larger, national literary tradition, which is how it is inscribed in relation to the national literary traditions; the second is as a sort of subcanon of early twentieth-century literature called "international modernism,"[37] whose works are largely disconnected from local or national affiliation, existing in an almost timeless state of "transcendental homelessness," in which capacity it has also been necessarily linked to comparative literature.[38]

In this study I presume the canon of international modernism—basing this, to be sure, on a comparatist assumption of the role of influences, cultural and or literary, on the authors whose work comprises this canon. Though this assumption (as one of this text's core foundations) could, however, be characterized as comparative, its relation to comparative literature proper is uneasy, because due to its emphasis on the multiple ground of "self" and "identity," the position of this book on the question of nationality and its relation to the literary product is incompatible with accepted notions of nationally conceived identity,[39] while more traditional notions of comparative literature view the question of such identity in nationality as a founding premise, as Claudio Guillén points out:

> La Literatura Comparada es un proyecto plausible desde el momento en que, por una parte, hay una pluralidad de literaturas modernas que se reconocen a sí mismas como tales y, por otra, la Poética unitaria o absoluta cesa de ser un modelo vigente. Nos hallamos entonces ante una fecunda paradoja histórica. El nacionalismo ascendente es lo que cimentará un internacionalismo neuvo.

> Comparative literature becomes a plausible project when two events occur: one, when a large number of modern literatures—literatures that recognize themselves as such—come into existence; and two, when a unitary or absolute poetics ceases to be an accepted model. We then find ourselves before a fruitful historical paradox: the rise of nationalism will lay the foundation for a new internationalism.[40]

Guillén is writing in the context of what he describes as the complete disintegration of the notion of a cultural concept that was based on the idea of literature as representing one whole sanctified by a consensus erecting a "cluster of masterworks."[41] By the end of the eighteenth century, this notion of literature had entirely collapsed, leaving behind what Guillén identifies as a "multiverse," composed of all of the cultural elements previously denied by the notion of literary culture as a representation of a single unified tradition.[42] In this sense, then, traditional formulations of comparative literature as a discipline needed to posit a certain kind of nationalism at its base, if only in order to justify the comparative mode; the only way to escape this reliance on nationalism and yet remain within the bounds of the discipline has been to suggest, as Guillén does in the first part of his book, that comparative literature "involves the systematic study of supranational assemblages."[43] What he means by this is that he desires, within comparative literature, "to go beyond cultural nationalism, beyond using literature in nationalistic ways, out of narcissistic instincts, for ideological ends."[44] "I dream," he writes, ". . . of a 'world literature.' (But what world? what worlds?)"[45] By disconnecting the "national" and therefore "ideological" from the "comparative," Guillén is able to approach a level of "supranationality" that will, he feels, enable him to write about literature with more general, more wholly humanist goals in mind.

Yet in so doing, Guillén also removes the literary from the material and the social, going beyond the world itself in his desire to achieve another world on the higher level of literary communion. While this traditionally comparative, utopic view certainly had its place in the devastation that represented the aftermath of World War II, when comparative literature was first instituted as a field in North America, it is also problematic, as is to be seen in Guillén's questions, "But what world? what worlds?" Whose worlds have been and will be represented in that higher world of literary communion? While the multiple and polyglot emphasis of traditional comparative literature has subtly critiqued the singularity and monolingualism of the national literatures, it has yet, in its reliance on those self-same national literatures in the act of comparison, traditionally emphasized the same overtly Euro-American purview of many of those literatures. As a result, it also, in its traditional form, puts forward much the same perspective as do the national literatures on the issues of canon revision and culture studies.[46]

By contrast, this book assumes an alternative cultural space that is authorized neither by a relation to a single geographical territory nor a relation to any single collective identity because having simultaneous existence in multiple cultural circumstances, existing within multiple geographical territories, in multiple temporal frames. Thus, the cultural space asserted here is largely symbolic, at least in traditional terms. Its principle characteristic is multiplicity, rather than singularity—yet a certain similarity[47] of cultural experience.[48] Therefore, it does not transcend difference, and it does not create from difference a utopic unity of cultural understanding that completely effaces it in the pursuit of general humanitarian goals. Rather, it views difference *itself* as the common denominator, as opposed to understanding *differentiation* as a necessary condition to deriving commonality, for example, a and b are not x, therefore, counterposed to x, a is equal to b.

Viewed from this perspective, it becomes obvious that canon revision in this instance can no longer be about inclusion or exclusion, but, rather, must be about our understanding of "culture" itself—in terms of its production and dissemination as knowledge in the university. In this broader context, it also becomes clear that discussion of "inclusion" and/or "exclusion" can reveal only half of the picture with regard to the cultural implications of the debate on canon revision and culture studies. The other half has to do with what lies beyond that discussion, the cultural locations that yet exist in the silent (and silenced) cultural space(s) masked by that more visible debate, and the institutional processes by which this masking is itself institutionalized. This book is an attempt to understand this hidden, silent, and/or silenced half as it relates to literary modernism and modernity.

Doing so will necessitate a certain transformation in our cultural understanding not only of literary modernism and modernity, but of its relation to the work of Proust, Joyce, and Baldwin. Through exploring this hidden and silenced half in relation to these three authors by rereading the traditional Euro-American modernist notion of exile and establishing it as a new interpretive ground on which to reconfigure conventionally accepted aesthetic differences in their work, this book seeks to reveal their previously unexplored similarities, and their silent (and silenced) cultural locations.[49] Here, exile is broadly defined to include the voiceless alienation often brought about by the experience of oppression as a result of, for example, race or sexual preference. Accordingly, this discussion puts forward a reading of literary modernism and modernity that provides the possibility of understanding the work of these authors from a perspective other than that offered by a prior assumption of their separation by an essentialized, incommensurable cultural difference.

What I am describing, however, is not simply a reelaboration of the commonplace themes of the "artist in exile" or the alienated Romantic hero. The situation of the authors in question and their relation to the concept of exile here expounded is far more complex than that of the alienation experienced by either of these traditional literary and artistic figures. The "artist in exile" may be viewed as rebellious and nonconformist, but he or she is still basically a creation derived from the status quo, because resentment against it forms the basis of his or her antitraditional leanings. The latter might be described as the alienation of a child who threatens to run away from home, not heeding, at the moment the threat is made, the reality of the situation, which is that he or she has the means neither to go far nor to stay away long. A child in such a situation will also nurture his or her feelings of resentment in order to fuel the escape, and must therefore continually invoke, in his or her imagination, the home from which he or she is alienated. Thus, rather than being truly alone, he or she is accompanied by a presence which, though rejected, is yet a presence.

In both of these situations of alienation, resentment is a strong motivating force. Yet this is not the case for any of the authors under consideration here. While these authors might seek to represent previously unexplored aspects of cultural experience, it is not done with resentment. It is done more with a sense of separateness, from a sense of self that is solipsistic, derived from being fully aware of having gone beyond any sense of connection with conventional norms, as Marino explains:

> The modern creator searches for himself by explaining himself and explains himself by self-analysis. Way back, Rivarol accused Rousseau of writing "without consciousness." It is certain that the Romantic writer does not know his own secret. For him the mystery of creation is still whole and impenetrable. It is precisely this enigma, felt to be a serious insufficiency, that the modern spirit eliminates, and extirpates by the roots. It *knows* what it is doing.[50]

What is important here is this quality of "consciousness"—moreover, in the case of these authors, each creating his art in the crucible of his own form of exile, the quality of *self-consciousness*. Unlike the Romantic hero, who experiences his alienation from society as a thing apart from him- or herself, the traditional Euro-American modern hero is often a narcissistic rendering of aspects of the modern writer's life, discovered through and created by the author's encouragement, and embracement, of such alienation. As a result, such writers become linked by a shared condition of both artistic and social exile. Thus, it is here that traditional readings of Euro-American modernism and the rereading of literary modernism and modernity here undertaken converge: in the fact and implications of exile.

This still does not, however, fully explain the importance of the issue of self-consciousness in the texts to be considered in this study, or the full significance of the concept of exile as it is here presented, something that may only be understood through a discussion of the way in which the two are related. First, it is necessary to view the concept of exile not just as something in which the authors here discussed participate, but as something that is also descriptive of their individual lifestyles. While it is easy to understand how one might consider James Joyce an exile under the definition of the term as explained to this point (his problematic relationship to the political situation in Ireland near the beginning of the twentieth century caused him to choose to spend most of his life in France and Italy), what of the other two authors?

This argument requires a willingness to understand exile as an instance of rupture with the social group into which an individual was born, whether voluntary or involuntary. Such rupture does not have to be defined solely as a physical rupture involving geographic relocation, but must, however, be radical. Physical rupture, for example, may also be described simply as a withdrawal, as in the case of Proust who, after the death of his mother in 1905, became a recluse in his cork-lined room while writing *A la recherche du temps perdu.*

James Baldwin represents a life situation of exile resulting both from involuntary and voluntary rupture. Endowed from birth with intellectual capabilities that surprised many of those by whom he was surrounded, Baldwin found himself unable to adjust to the condition of being black in America (a circumstance that served to alienate him from the mainstream of both black and white cultures) during the first half of the twentieth century, and he subsequently left the country for France before the beginning of the Civil Rights Movement, where he lived for much of the remainder of his life.

In each of the above situations, it is clear that social and artistic exile had a major impact on the lives of these authors, and it is only through this impact that the significance of the relation between exile and self-consciousness in their literary works may be properly comprehended. Thus, it may be seen that these authors are linked in two ways: (1) through a voluntary act of commitment toward a type of artistic representation that embraces a number of nontraditional cultural ideas and (2) through a shared life situation of voluntary or involuntary exile. Though the first type of linkage is certainly important to an understanding of the significance of exile in modern literature to be examined in this book, it is, finally, the second type of linkage that forms the crux of the matter. Because this study describes a new cultural space within which to consider the notion of literary modernity, as well as both old and new texts to be considered its representatives, it also becomes possible to introduce within it alternative ways of thinking about the notion of "value" and how it relates to literary texts in institutional contexts. Through this, I argue, social value in "modernist" literary representation is determined not solely as the evidence of a text's contribution to a nationally defined culture or to a Euro-American "high" (international) modernist tradition, but by the relation of self as represented in the text to what it *perceives* as valuable, and the way in which the self and such perceived value interact with the larger social world of which the protagonist(s) is (are) a part.

This new consideration of the notion of "value" takes place in terms of what I have called the "romance of exile." The notion of romance here brings to the fore the divided, seemingly unreal nature of reality in exile, a reality that is perennially hybrid because always intertwined with another, perpetually questioned because constantly compared, and never fully assimilated. In romance, where anything is possible, the almost surreal nature of this more fluid experience of reality finds its natural context. In romance, because objective reality lacks the hard edges of fact and necessity, subjective reality takes on exaggerated importance. As such, the "romance of exile" describes a particular relationship between the individual and reality, one that also remains full of possibility because never fully objectified.

On this new basis, the reconfiguration of literary modernism and modernity to encompass the work of James Baldwin in relation to that of Marcel Proust and James Joyce, both traditionally considered Euro-American "high" (international) modernists, is made possible. Conventional readings of Euro-American modernism such as that put forward by Bradbury and McFarlane, often highlight (as the organizing principle of its literary canon) its authors' shared participation in aesthetic innovation. The present rereading of literary modernism and modernity, by contrast, emphasizes what may be revealed by reconsidering the relation between modernity and exile in terms of the multicultural potential of the cultural condition of exile (experienced by many in different cultural contexts for different reasons), using this as an alternative organizing principle around which a new, more culturally and ethnically broad understanding of literary modernism and modernity may begin to take form.[51]

In this new context, the way in which we read the work of all three authors is necessarily changed. On the one hand, the effect of studying Baldwin's work in this way is that its social and political aspects are deemphasized as it is shifted out of the traditional category of race (i.e., African-American literature), because it is read in terms of its similarities[52] with the work of two Euro-American high modernist authors. On the other hand, the aesthetic aspects of the work of Proust and Joyce (recognized in isolation in the Euro-American context) are repoliticized, because read in terms of their similarities with that of an author (Baldwin) traditionally excluded from the Euro-American literary canons within which their work has commonly been read. Thus, reading these three authors' work in a "canon" organized around the principle of their shared participation in exile enlarges our understanding of the cultural possibilities inherent in literary modernism and modernity, and forces us not only to rethink the way in which we have read, but consequently, how we will reread each of these authors. In so doing, we discover those aspects of their work that were previously hidden and/or neglected, pointing toward previously silent and/or silenced cultural locations that bring them together in unprecedented ways.

For example, the innovations of Joyce's work, "canonized" as purely aesthetic and prototypically "modern," may be read instead in relation to his position as an exiled Irishman using an alien language to write within an alien tradition, and what this might tell us about a specific instance of the cultural politics of modernity. Similarly, Proust's work, "canonized" in the same way, may be viewed instead in terms of the cultural significance of his covert homosexuality, while Baldwin's work may be read for what it itself reveals, as opposed to seeking conformity with a set of racially defined circumstances that may be external to the work itself.[53] And, finally, in this new context, the work of all three authors together takes on an entirely different cultural significance.

In emphasizing this perspective then, the present text critiques Euro-American modernism as a cultural construct whose traditional canon artificially limits and narrows the scope of those cultural phenomena by which literary modernism and modernity may potentially be understood, while eliding the range of influences from which such understanding may be derived. By separating the idea of Euro-American modernism from the phenomena the term has historically been used to designate, this book emphasizes a new understanding of literary modernism and modernity themselves, rather than simply a reconfiguration of Euro-American modernism alone. As such, this perspective suggests that the role played by the processes of canon formation[54] in the creation and institutionalization of Euro-American modernism hides its paradoxical reality as a cultural construct whose "otherness" (i.e., "modernism" established as "other" largely in opposition to British and/or French realistic literary traditions) negates its own social and political sources in becoming the "high culture" (traditional) standard by which such "otherness" is often culturally determined, understood, and excluded.

The implications of this are that the emphasis placed in Euro-American modernism on "modernist" aesthetics may be seen to camouflage a deeply political character translated as specifically "modernist" literary representation. What has been traditionally articulated as "modernist" aesthetics may be understood, then, to play a double role in the process of Euro-American modernist canonization and/or legitimation: it represents the voice of the (Euro-American) "other," but it also forms the foundation of Euro-American "high" modernism, which "traditionalizes" (assimilates, periodizes) that voice by denying its "otherness," and rereading it as the genius of aesthetic innovation.

But in order to understand how this occurs, it is necessary to examine Euro-American modernism itself in more detail, and thus, to assume, as a place to begin, the legitimacy of the Euro-American canon of high, or, as Hugh Kenner would call it, "International Modernism."[55] As we shall see, this canon operates in terms of a different organizing principle than that pertaining to the traditional canons of the national literatures. To the extent that it challenges traditional notions of canon formation based on shared nationality, the Euro-American international modernist canon may already be viewed as potentially revisionary. Yet even as it challenges the more firmly established Euro-American national modernist canons, the Euro-American canon of international modernism remains only selectively inclusive. And it is so in a way that has traditionally not only excluded cultural "others" such as minorities and, for the most part, women (along with those belonging to the silent and/or silenced cultural locations with which this text is primarily concerned), but has effected this by camouflaging its resistance to the full assimilation of their cultural products through its openness to the consideration of cultural, that is, national, difference, by virtue of its inherent internationality. In other words, it excludes, while seeming to embrace, cultural difference, through a very subtle determination of "acceptable" versus "unacceptable" cultural "otherness."[56]

But, as will be explored in more depth in chapter 2, the battle for legitimacy between Euro-American modernism both nationally and internationally defined also provides the only starting point from which a satisfactory understanding of the difficulty posed by the paradigm of inclusion/exclusion in revisionary analyses of literary modernism and modernity may be derived. If there is to be any possibility at all of moving beyond the polarized paradigm of inclusion/exclusion in such analysis, what has been termed Euro-American modernism's exclusionary nature must be examined, and this must be done in terms of a rereading not only of this aspect of literary modernism as a movement, but of each fictional text to be analyzed in relation to it, as well as the critical readings through which these texts have been engendered as "modernist"—or not—and through which our understanding of the cultural significance of literary modernity has been developed. The next four chapters will read Euro-American modernism from this perspective, as one cultural instance within a broader reconceputalization of literary modernism and modernity. And as we shall see, reading Proust, Joyce, and Baldwin together as modern writers in such a new conception of literary modernism and modernity underscores the silent (and silenced) cultural locations that they share, and that also celebrate their similarity in difference—thus widening our perception, and deepening our understanding, of one aspect of the cultural possibility always latent in modernity, yet never quite brought to light.

CHAPTER 2

(An)Other Modernism

"A conscious internationalism is possible only in opposition
to a conscious nationalism."
—Claudio Guillén, *The Challenge of
Comparative Literature*

EXCLUSIONARY MODERNISM AND THE POLITICS
OF CULTURAL SPACE

In 1931, Edmund Wilson published *Axel's Castle*,[1] later considered a seminal critical work contributing to the foundation of the early- to mid-twentieth-century literary movement we now know as Euro-American modernism. In writing this work, Wilson's goal was to make more palatable to the average reader what could be described at the time as some rather disturbing nontraditional artistic trends in literature, represented in the work of such authors as Marcel Proust, James Joyce, and Gertrude Stein.

Locating their work in a tradition originating with the symbolist movement in nineteenth-century French poetry, Wilson's text focuses more on the aesthetic qualities of these authors' artistic endeavors than on the disparate national traditions to which their efforts could be said to contribute. Yet while this aestheticizing trend was taken up by other early literary critics, such as Harry Levin,[2] it did not succeed in creating a dominant literary canon of what, as mentioned in chapter 1, Kenner has called "International Modernism,"[3] comprised of an international set of Euro-American authors whose work, though they come from different countries, espouses many of those artistic and aesthetic goals that have traditionally been identified as distinctly "modernist." Instead, Euro-American international modernism became a sort of subcanon, a contested site of cultural signification where a number of professionally unsettling questions reigned (and, I contend, still reign) supreme: What is the role of literature in culture and society? How is it to be studied, and to what end? How does literature help (or not) to determine the nature of cultural identity? To whom, after all, do cultural products, such as literature, belong? The answers to such questions were asserted

25

with confidence by the national literatures during roughly the first half of the twentieth century: literature was, of course, one of the most important arbiters of the temper of the times in the life of any given nation; literature and art were the highest cultural achievements possible for any people to attain; as one such achievement, then, a literary text should rightfully belong to whichever nation had given birth to and nurtured its author.

Thus, while the integrity of the canon of international modernism was maintained on a highly abstract, highly aestheticized, theoretical level, those texts of which it was comprised were at the same time appropriated by each author's national literary tradition—as representative of a modernist "period" in the literary history of that tradition—one of various other "periods," depending on the tradition in question. In this context, then, the primary emphasis was taken off the aesthetic achievement of "modernist" authors per se, and placed instead on the way in which the work produced by individual authors during this modern "period" contributed to the cultural heritage overall of that author's nation. But even though the national literatures sought through periodization to locate such texts within their frameworks, this endeavor has, with Euro-American modernism, been less than successful.

This is evidenced by what has been for some time a heated debate in English literary studies over what have up to now been accepted notions of what literary modernism and modernity, after all, are. This debate is exacerbated by another, equally vociferous debate (within which the debate on modernism and modernity is ensconced)—that on canon revision and culture studies, as was elaborated in chapter 1. The intensity of the debate suggests that the meaning of modernity has by no means been digested in literary studies, and that there are still many contested issues within its ken. Two of the most important strands in this debate concern first, the time period during which the modern moment is supposed to have taken place, and second, the works and authors to be considered its representatives.

The debate over the issue of periodization in literary modernism and modernity has been motivated largely by the advent of postmodernism. The elaboration of its own premises demands that postmodernism reach some final conclusions about the demise of Euro-American modernism, if only in order to take these as a place from which to launch itself.[4] Yet what has been described as "postmodern" can also be found as early as Kafka, and certainly in the later Joyce. Such overlap suggests that the distinction between the two is in fact quite blurred, and that, as a result, the traditionalizing tendency of periodization in the academy may here become quite problematic, particularly where Euro-American modernism is concerned. How, for example, do we account for the "postmodern" in what has been previously identified as a "modern" work? If this "modern" work was written long before the agreed upon beginning of the "postmodern" (whatever that may be), how then, are the boundaries of either "period" to be ascertained?

This is one of the reasons why debate over the range, content, and significance of Euro-American modernism remains deeply contentious. Postmodernism's demands that modernism and modernity become settled issues and quietly take their place in the history of literary tradition only exacerbate the problem. The "settled" (traditional) formulation of "international modernism" would primarily include the work of Marcel Proust, James Joyce, T. S. Eliot, Ezra Pound, Ford Madox Ford, Joseph Conrad—the list continues in like manner. They are all men. But they are also all white, and this brings us to the second strand in the debate over Euro-American modernism—the point at which it converges with the debate on canon revision and culture studies—its legacy of exclusion.

Even a cursory glance at the range of cultural production during the first fifty years or so of the twentieth century reveals that the attempt to settle the critical articulation of modernism and modernity with these well-known authors must necessarily leave out a wealth of unexplored material. Critics such as Frederic Jameson[5] have recognized this, in suggesting that our accepted notions of Euro-American modernism need redefinition, not just in terms of the influence of political forces such as imperialism on early twentieth-century literature, but also in terms of how it has handled the artistic contributions of cultural "others," such as women and minorities. To the present, Euro-American modernism has (often begrudgingly) encompassed the contributions of women such as Virginia Woolf or Gertrude Stein, but it has recognized those of other women and of minorities barely or not at all. Many of these were writing and publishing during the same period of time, yet few or none ever attained the status of "modernist."

It is here, then, that the notion of "reading on the edge," as elaborated in chapter 1, becomes quite useful in seeking to rearticulate our understanding of literary modernism and modernity. Merely noting the absence of the literary representations of women and minorities in conventional critical articulations of Euro-American modernism allows us only to draw the conclusion that it has been, traditionally, exclusionary. But this can tell us nothing about why and how it came to be so, or about how we can substantially change our present perceptions of literary modernism and modernity as a whole. By examining the underlying operations of this exclusion through exploring its relation to the politics of cultural space, we can perhaps begin to gain a clearer perspective on Euro-American modernism in particular, and begin as well the difficult task of rearticulating its ascendancy within a broader, more comprehensive vision of literary modernism and modernity in general. To do this, Euro-American modernism must first be considered from the perspective outlined in chapter 1, as signifying a clash over the cultural space of the modern, which then becomes the nexus of a number of conflicting interests and claims in twentieth-century literary studies: the conflicting perspectives of the national literatures and comparative literature over the definition of literary modernism—whether as one period among others in a number of national literary traditions, or as a "high" culture, international, multimedia phenomenon; the articulation of "difference" from both national and international (comparative) perspectives; and the debate over what is to be studied in relation to the modern (canon revision) and how it is to be studied (culture studies).

But it is in the "high" culture or comparative mode that conventional articulations of Euro-American modernism become most complicated in this regard. To investigate this, we must begin, as outlined in chapter 1, with the cultural significance that Euro-American *international* (as opposed to periodized, nationally defined) modernism has come to bear. This has always been described as the domain of "high" as opposed to "low" culture, the land of artistic excellence, the world of genius, as Kalaidjian points out:

> Until recently . . . the diversity of this cultural production has been overshadowed by the more sanitized canon of high modernism. The academy's classic definition of "high" or "great" culture—the domain of its "intellectual and especially artistic activity"—is founded on a logic that denies another cultural model: what Raymond Williams has described in terms of "a particular way of life, whether of a people, a period or a group."[6]

When traditional notions of "high" or international Euro-American modernism are viewed through the alternative "cultural model" of which Kalaidjian speaks, we can begin to make telling and important discoveries about its cultural significance. As the repository of all that is "great," the traditional category "modernist" acts as a screen by which all that it encompasses may take on an artistic aura of almost otherworldliness. Texts designated as such cannot therefore really be reduced to the status of mere contributions to the understanding of a "particular way of life." Texts such as these are above life—they are not just representations of the supreme heights of aesthetic excellence to which human beings may aspire—they *are* that height of aesthetic excellence.[7] As a result, when those texts that may be included on the canon of Euro-American international modernism are appropriated by the national literature of a given author's country of origin, they are never completely assimilated into that framework. They always retain a subtle residue of added greatness, a carryover from their connection with that cultural space of aesthetic perfection which has traditionally been that of Euro-American international modernism.

The division between these two cultural models is perhaps nowhere so stark as in the context of American literature, where what Kalaidjian identifies as "high modernism's pledge of allegiance to a transhistorical canon, founded on the subordination of gender, race, and class differences to what T. S. Eliot idealized as the universal 'mind of Europe,'"[8] is most evident. Traditional American modernism has relied heavily for its articulation on the work of Henry James, T. S. Eliot, Ezra Pound, Gertrude Stein, Ernest Hemingway, and F. Scott Fitzgerald. Yet as the work of recent critics (such as Kalaidjian and others)[9] makes clear, such a scope is much too narrow a way to describe the culturally vibrant period between the two world wars in America. To stop here is to seriously limit the range of intellectual possibility in this regard by valorizing, as Kalaidjian writes, a "mainly Caucasian and androcentric outlook" over a "plurality of transnational, racial, sexual, and class representations."[10]

But it is not just this type of valorization that makes any discussion of Euro-American international modernism within a broader context very difficult. Such difficulty is also brought about by its cultural significance as somewhat "larger than life," as somehow so far removed from everyday life as to eradicate any possibility for rapprochement between it and any literary product falling outside its domain. Not only do the texts written by canonized Euro-American modernist authors remain encircled by the special significance held by the appellation, "international modernism," but this aura acts as a type of force field, keeping a select few texts in, and those unselected out.

"SERIOUS FICTIONS"/FICTIONAL REALITIES

The question, then, becomes, what is the nature of this "force field," and how may it be described? We might begin by calling it Euro-American international modernism's "ideological effect"—the peculiar significance that the cultural space of Euro-American international modernism has come to have in contemporary literary criticism.[11] I am calling it an "ideological effect" because as a literary critical cultural construct, Euro-American international modernism possesses a strange, almost mythical and/or metaphysical presence,[12] one that powerfully replicates itself even as it is subjected to the process of critique. It is as if its mere mention operates to reinscribe it in an almost timeless stasis, untouchable and indestructible because so far removed, in its aesthetic perfection, from the time-ridden decay of the temporal world. And it is this elusive power, the fact that it may be described as a "power" at all, which also suggests that any discussion seeking to open up new avenues in the study of this moment in literary history is useless without a concomitant analysis of the way in which our traditional notions of literary modernism both relate to and articulate a politics of cultural space, from which perspective we may also begin the reading of literary modernism and modernity—on the edge.

In his book, *The Practice of Everyday Life,* Michel de Certeau describes the notion of "space" in general as something that is always defined by difference:

> It is the partition of space that structures it. Everything refers in fact to this differentiation which makes possible the isolation and interplay of distinct spaces. From the distinction that separates a subject from its exteriority to the distinctions that localize objects . . . from the functioning of the urban network to that of the rural landscape, there is no spatiality that is not organized by the determination of frontiers.[13]

If de Certeau's definition is taken in the most general sense, then any type of space, in order to be understood as such, must always be defined by both itself and its "other." Without this recognition of "otherness," if we follow de Certeau's line of reasoning, the notion of particularity in space would disintegrate, and the possibility of deriving a concept of space would disappear along with it. This is because everything would then be itself, and nothing would be "other." Thus, the first thing that must be ascertained about the notion of space, whatever type of space is under discussion, is that it presumes some sort of frontier, some borderline, or edge, on the other side of which it is no longer itself. Consequently, in the context of the above discussion of Euro-American international modernism, this borderline would be represented by what I have identified above as the "force field" by which certain texts are contained in its canon and "other," unselected texts excluded.

In the same instance, however, what we are discussing in the case of Euro-American international modernism is a particular type of cultural space, one that is, for the most part, imaginary, as opposed to concrete. We might say, for example, that the notion of "cultural space" refers to that social space described by the language, ideas, values, customs, and/or traditions of a given national culture. As such, it implies an interconnection between place or, in other words, geography, and social and/or national identity, as mentioned in chapter 1. But with regard to our present discussion of Euro-American international modernism, this more generalized notion of cultural space must be immediately understood as far more complex. How can the cultural space of Euro-American modernism be defined? Constructing such a definition is not, as it might initially seem, a simple task. This is because first, in its traditional form, Euro-American modernism (as elaborated above) represents not one cultural space, but two—an international, broad-based artistic phenomenon with literature as just one of its manifestations, and an isolated literary period occurring chronologically in a long, nationally defined tradition of other literary developments and events. But what these two notions also represent is two conflicting narratives of the role and importance of the modern in literary history. They are, in effect, stories,[14] each possessing a different goal with regard to the way in which the significance of literary modernism and modernity to literature and literary history is to be articulated.

On the one hand, the narrative of Euro-American modernist periodization views "modernism" as a period no more important than any other period in the long progression and development of a literary tradition. What is important in this narrative is the valorization of literature's national character, of the way in which each literary work contributes to the exfoliation of a national identity, through emphasizing its literary tradition as a whole. Expounded by this narrative, literature and nation are two manifestations of the same cultural idea: as the representative of the highest thoughts and values of the nation, literature becomes its spokesperson, the means by which the most important qualities of a nation's identity as a people may be known and understood.

By contrast, the narrative of Euro-American international modernism denies not only the importance of a national character in literature, but the need for discussion of the nation in relation to literature at all, except where it concerns the way in which the literature itself might refer to it. In this sense, the narrative of Euro-American international modernism seems even to deny the very existence of the nation, at least in terms of viewing literature as a representation of national character. This narrative tells a story of influences, whether these be social and political, in terms of technological development or the effects of world war; artistic, in terms of interdisciplinary intellectual exchange; or strictly literary, in terms of the way in which many literary artists of the time were affected by each other's work. Because this narrative seeks to link the work of those artists it deems "modernist" in an international context, crossing national borders and disciplinary boundaries, it must, if viewed in traditional terms, necessarily focus on the study of influences. Thus, it is this necessity, along with its disregard of national constraints, that must also (at least in traditional terms) categorize the narrative of international modernism as a comparative practice, as elaborated in chapter 1.

In view of these two narratives, traditional notions of Euro-American modernism may be understood as being automatically inscribed with a sort of semantic confusion, continually produced at the level of signification. Discussions of Euro-American modernism are thus always covertly concerned with questions such as what does "modernism" actually mean, in the context of literary history? Which modernism is being discussed? For which ends? I say covertly because these questions are never brought to the fore. Rather, they are submerged within the confines of Euro-American modernism's two narratives, lurking just below the surface, never actually confronted and analyzed. Part of the difficulty caused by the existence of these unexpressed questions is the fact that they are engendered by an inability on the part of the two narratives of Euro-American modernism actually to come to terms with the significance of the dichotomy between the national and the international at this time in history, and literary history in particular, which they themselves identify.

In suggesting this, I am touching again on the epigraph with which this chapter began: Guillén's assertion that "a conscious internationalism is possible only in opposition to a conscious nationalism." This paradox lies at the heart of these two narratives of Euro-American modernism, making them to a large extent irreconcilable. A "conscious nationalism," informing the Euro-American modernist narrative of periodization, would necessarily seek to claim those authors possessing whichever nationality was in question no matter what history of influences lay behind the production of their texts, while a "conscious internationalism," that which informs the narrative of Euro-American international modernism, would need to assume a plurality of nationalities in order to constitute itself as international. In the narrative of Euro-American international modernism, a spatial difference based on considerations of geography and nation is already inscribed in the concept "international," whether it chooses to emphasize these or no. The two narratives of Euro-American modernism are thus, even while opposed to each other, inevitably linked, as de Certeau suggests:

> Stories are actuated by a contradiction that is represented in them by the relationship between the frontier and the bridge, that is, between a (legitimate) space and its (alien) exteriority.[15]

If in the context of de Certeau's assertions, these narratives of Euro-American modernism are to be viewed as two separate "stories" about one powerful way in which we should understand this time in literary history, then we might also describe the deeply imbedded paradox discussed above as both the "frontier" and the "bridge," the edge by which they are simultaneously differentiated and linked. Consequently, this point of contact[16] must also be rearticulated as the locus of the semantic ambiguity that is inevitably produced in traditional formulations of Euro-American modernism. The intensity of this ambiguity is what lies behind Euro-American international modernism's linguistic assertion of power. It is also this ambiguity that informs the "force field" that imbues its canonical texts with that power, and by which those texts not designated as such are judged lacking—and, thereby, excluded. Thus, the semantic ambiguity seen through the "frontier" and the "bridge" by which the two traditional "stories" are linked becomes also the endpoint of these stories—the edge beyond which it first becomes possible to approach those silent (and silenced) cultural representations existing outside the "force field" of signification created by these stories—and by which a more comprehensive vision of the cultural significance of "otherness" in literary modernism and modernity may begin to be gained.

What is of primary importance with regard to this "force field" is that it is a secondary effect of a particular way of *reading* literary modernism and modernity—a manner of reading that, in determining the meaning and significance of those traits it deems "modernist" engenders, even as it describes, our notions of the movement and its relation to literary culture. In this sense, such "readings" may also be viewed as a sort of mythmaking *process*,[17] one by which Euro-American modernism is not only inscribed within literary history, but also given a particular status within it that, by virtue of the cultural significance it acquires *because* of its "mythical" status, is not easily altered and/or dislodged.

It is here that this book's emphasis on the importance of reading and "readings" in the consideration and/or reconsideration of literary texts becomes most important in this context. But although such readings may be understood as forming part of the subjective experience of each reader, it must also be recognized that there is another, more important site where "significance" and "meaning" are publicly determined, one in which they are produced, rather than simply experienced—that is, the university, as touched on in chapter 1.[18] Under the auspices of the university, "meaning" and "significance" become interpretations that are institutionally sanctioned, and, thereby, invested with the authority of truth. As such, the university also becomes a place where "serious fictions" can be clothed in the garments of reality, and begin in this way to inform the manner in which we view the world, as Guillory explains:

> The objective history of canon formation, if the latter is an effect of syllabus construction and revision . . . can be recovered only in the history of the school, whose invariant social function is the distribution of knowledge by means of techniques of dissemination and rituals of credentialization. . . . The forms of cultural capital are . . . determined within the whole social order as arenas of both certification and contestation, because the social totality is structured by the multiple and relatively incommensurable distinctions of class, sex, race, national status . . . distinctions produced and reproduced in a system that never closes upon its objective of homeostasis.[19]

What Guillory identifies here is the particular "ideological effect" of literary tradition as it has been articulated to this time, what he calls its "objective of homeostasis." But, however, when this objective is understood in terms of the fact that, for just one example, American literature was not considered as an academic discipline until the 1920s, and that those who developed it as such were, as Paul Lauter points out, "college-educated white men of Anglo-Saxon or northern European origins" who "came . . . from that tiny, elite portion of the population of the United States which, around the turn of the century, could go to college,"[20] it becomes much easier to understand how and why such an objective could have been established. When this is considered in terms of the present discussion, in which the university is posited as a system of exchange that transforms critical and scholarly texts by endowing them with an institutionally sanctioned authority that simultaneously invests them with the power of truth, it also begins to become clear how traditional Euro-American formulations of literary modernism and modernity could have been associated with notions of "high" as opposed to "low" culture, and how such associations could, concomitantly, imply the exclusion and/or silencing of cultural voices deemed "other" from this perspective.

For Guillory, the canon, as represented by the academic syllabus, symbolizes the reproduction of this process of textual transformation, which also mirrors existing cultural relations in the social world.[21] But while Guillory finds the most important locus of ideology in the university, as the site of knowledge-dissemination, and the syllabus as the mode by which such dissemination is accomplished, I am arguing that it is even more significant to locate such ideology in the institutionally sanctioned *readings* by which literary tradition is and has been constituted—the "serious fictions" by which culturally dominant ideas are given voice, while other cultural representations derived from outside that context are often silenced, obfuscated, and/or erased, *read* (interpreted) out of literary and cultural existence.[22]

Because this discussion has centered on the "cultural space" of Euro-American modernism, it has from the outset focused on the way in which the cultural effects of certain phenomena occurring at a particular point in literary history can be or have been interpreted. But since these phenomena can only be subsumed by culture through reading and interpretation, and since the act of interpretation is connected in a fundamental way with the subjective understanding of the interpreter, we must perhaps also conclude that if the pool of interpreters is limited to a certain type of individual, then the readings these individuals produce, as well as the ideology contained within them, will be limited as well—not by intent, but rather, by virtue of actual circumstance.[23]

This established, the question of ideology (with regard to the way in which a politics of cultural space might be understood to inform our understanding of Euro-American international modernism) becomes no longer an abstract possibility very difficult to isolate, but a concrete reality characterized by the interplay between the ideological content of literary texts and the ideological content of the institutionally sanctioned responses such textual ideology may engender. What is significant here is the way in which these two types of ideological content interact, particularly in relation to power and the way it is articulated in cultural spaces.

In his book, *The Interpretation of Cultures*, Clifford Geertz suggests that ideology often represents the most repressed aspects of a given social consciousness, stating that while "ideologies may be . . . projections of unacknowledged fears, disguises for ulterior motives, phatic expressions of group solidarity . . . they are . . . [also] maps of problematic social reality and matrices for the creation of collective conscience."[24] Within the institutional framework, or knowledge production, such ideologies are, in Geertz's view, "shaped as is all thought by the overall values of the society within which [they are] . . . contained" and "[where they are] . . . selective in the sort of questions [they ask] . . . the particular problems [they choose] . . . to tackle, and so forth, ideologies are subject to a . . . pernicious 'secondary' selectivity, in that they emphasize some aspects of social reality . . . and neglect or even suppress other aspects."[25] What is suggested by this is that when ideology is understood as an important, unavoidable factor in *all* textual undertakings, we must also begin to recognize as necessary a certain amount of digging before a clear picture of the way in which it may be operative in the cultural spaces it inhabits is revealed. If ideology is, as Geertz suggests, a means of creating group solidarity and collective conscience by selectively emphasizing certain aspects of social reality over other, less desirable ones in a given context, then its significance with regard to the politics of cultural space, as pertains specifically to literary culture and tradition, is broadly evident: it has also been operative traditionally in the silent exclusion, marginalization, and/or complete obfuscation of "other" cultural voices.[26] When we consider this notion with regard to Euro-American literary modernism's two narratives, we discover that not only is ideology a very important aspect of each, but that this ideology is also operative in each in very different ways, something that is ultimately quite illuminating with regard to the present discussion of the relation between Euro-American literary modernism and the politics of cultural space.

POST-ING MODERNISM IN THE "OTHER"

To continue our analysis of the politics of cultural space and its significance for our readings, traditional and nontraditional, of literary modernism and modernity, it is imperative to examine more deeply the notion that ideology is, as has been suggested above, not only a kind of "map" of problematic social reality, but a matrix in which the creation of collective conscience may take place. If this assertion is taken at face value, then one of the issues with which we would want to come to terms is precisely what kind of social reality such ideology serves to map.

In order to explore this difficulty, we must return once more to the epigraph with which this chapter was begun: "a conscious internationalism is possible only in opposition to a conscious nationalism." As stated above, this is the paradox with which the two narratives of Euro-American modernism cannot come to terms and which, as a result, produces a semantic ambiguity in all explorations of this aspect of literary modernism and modernity. On closer examination, however, this ambiguity may also be described as a sort of power play between two opposing views of the same subject, each one desiring to achieve ascendancy over the other.[27] And beyond this internal power play lies yet another: between canon revision and culture studies, as was described in chapter 1.

In *The Field of Cultural Production*, Pierre Bourdieu describes such a situation as that of the politics of cultural space in Euro-American modernism as a battle over control of the production of "meaning" and "significance" or, in other words, over the determination of reality with regard to a particular subject, that is, the way in which it is to be identified, referred to, and culturally understood:

> The fundamental stake in literary struggles is the monopoly of literary legitimacy, i.e. . . . . the monopoly of the power to say with authority who are authorized to call themselves writers; or, to put it another way, it is the monopoly of the power to consecrate producers or products (we are dealing with a world of belief and the consecrated writer is the one who has the power to consecrate and to win assent when he or she consecrates an author or a work—with a preface, a favourable review, a prize, etc.).[28]

In Bourdieu's formulation, the type of power and/or control authorized to make determinations of reality is called "legitimacy," a term that implies the sanction and authority of law—in this case, the law of accepted standards. Thus, each of the two narratives of Euro-American modernism identified above is locked in the struggle to attain the status of legitimacy, or the ability to determine the way in which our conceptions of literary historical reality will shape the phenomena that have come to be called "modernist."[29] Silenced within these two conflicts is the cultural space of "otherness," and, buried within this, the cultural space of hybridity, of multiplicity, and protean cultural identity. Unless yet another struggle is undertaken in this instance, one that reaches beyond the more limited cultural possibilities offered by the polarized debate on canon revision, this very important part of the cultural significance of literary modernism and modernity will remain, for the most part, hidden—and, as such, voiceless and impotent.

Yet, ironically, it is precisely the articulation of the politics of cultural space in Euro-American modernism that also makes this aspect of literary modernism and modernity all the more visible. Without the struggle between the internal conflict of Euro-American modernism (between its national and its comparative, or international, manifestations) and the polarized debate on canon revision and culture studies, there would also be no break in the "force field" by which Euro-American modernist texts are surrounded, therefore no possibility of examining its relation to the politics of cultural space, and thus no means of reading beyond the edge this reveals, into the silenced significance of modern cultural representations derived from unauthorized and multiple cultural locations.

The semantic ambiguity we have been discussing with regard to traditional formulations of Euro-American modernism is evidence that this struggle has been, and continues to be, a stiff one. The stronger of the two narratives, at least institutionally, seems to be that of modernist periodization, which is more easily assimilated into the academic structure of the more traditional English departments, while the narrative of international modernism is more clearly, at least in traditional terms, assimilated into the academic structure identified by the discipline of comparative literature.[30] Assimilated as such, however, its international aspect is subjected to a mode of study enforced by a discipline, rather than by the field of study itself, and as a result, this assmilation is only partial. Thus, while the framework of comparative literature may perhaps allow the scholar-critic studying literary modernism and modernity more leeway in terms of the types of and relationships between the influences he or she may want to explore, the demands of the discipline preempt the greater potential, in terms of intellectual terrain, that might be offered by the larger context of modernity itself—a potential that is often interdisciplinary, multinational, and multimedia, and, increasingly, multiethnic. The demands of the discipline, in its traditional form, preempt the unhampered exploration of such influences and engagements, which are often suggested by modern literature and/or the condition of modernity themselves. It is also through such examinations that the silenced cultural excess within the field is most likely to be apprehended. But in either case, assimilation not only does not eradicate competition between the two narratives—it also impedes any attempt toward study of the confluence, within literary modernism and modernity, of both its national/international quality independent of disciplinary constraints (as, e.g., a study emphasizing the interrelationships between American and British texts and artists) and its concomitant manifestations in races other than white, and genders other than male. While both narratives of Euro-American modernism are engaged in a struggle for legitimacy, neither one completely succeeds in achieving it; and while each one has achieved a legitimacy of sorts in different domains, neither of these domains adequately offers the possibility of studying literary modernism and modernity in its entirety.

This has largely been due to the fact (as previously stated) that, through their institutional connection, both the domains of English and comparative literature have traditionally reproduced a coventional form of social relations, what Guillory describes as "a structure of complex and ramifying inequality"[31]—what was described in chapter 1 as their traditionally Eurocentric emphasis. Yet when these social relations are re-created through the production of literary canons that mirror them (as do those forming the canonical foundations of Euro-American modernism), they are reified in a way that often serves also to reproduce (albeit in microcosm), in the form of the knowledges or critical interpretations they undergird, the power relations of the social world.[32] The reification of these power relations is then solidified by the extension of these canons into the notion of "tradition," as Guillory explains:

> The canon achieves its imaginary totality . . . not by embodying itself in a really existing list, but by retroactively constructing its individual texts as a *tradition*, to which works may be added or subtracted without altering the impression of totality or cultural homogeneity. A tradition is "real," of course, but only in the sense in which the imaginary is real.[33]

It is in this way that Bourdieu's notion of legitimacy becomes important with regard to the current discussion of literary modernism and modernity and the politics of cultural space. The battle over the achievement of legitimacy, as represented in the two narratives of Euro-American modernism, is a symbolic battle over the way in which the cultural significance of modernity and its relationship to the burgeoning socio-historico-political concepts of nationalism and internationalism, of which it was the literary representative, are to be conceived and understood. Each narrative struggles in its own way with the paradoxical relationship between these two concepts, and each one seeks to "consecrate" its own particular view of that relationship. Bourdieu's use of this specific term in his analysis of legitimacy is significant: in its religious connotations, it is suggestive not only of the tradition of religious authority (one of the age-old arbiters of authority) but also of canonized authority, both scriptural and literary, as well as the complicated early relationship between Euro-American modernism and Christianity, one of the origins of the notion of such literature as being in some way transcendent.[34] As Bourdieu suggests, the relationship between the writer and the notion of consecration serves to move his or her ideas into the world of belief; literary legitimacy confers the "power to consecrate" writers, both critical and creative, and their products; and "consecration" implies the attainment of another level of reality through the transformative process of institutionally conveyed authority. This new level of reality is similar to the "imaginary totality" engendered by the embodiment of a literary canon into a tradition, something that occurs as various readings and interpretations, which determine the "meaning" and "significance" of various works, begin to cohere around a substantial body of literary texts.[35] Once this has occurred, attempts to alter the literary canon itself (whatever canon is in question) become extremely difficult. The addition and subtraction of new texts and/or new subjects of study takes place on the periphery of the "tradition," which continues to give an impression of "cultural homogeneity," remaining almost impervious to pressures introduced by the implications of such new areas. When this happens, the "imaginary" reality of which the "tradition" is representative is reified around the already reified literary canon, and a new, almost seamless worldview is born.

When the literary "tradition" of Euro-American modernism is contextualized in this way, it becomes, by virtue of its two narratives, a sort of conflicted myth, a story that cannot seem to find its end. This is because, as we have seen, the worldview that is born with the consolidation of the Euro-American modernist canon is not seamless, but rather, fissured and unstable. We can, however, begin to gain a clearer picture of the larger significance of this instability through examining the implications of the way in which the traditional, Euro-American "modernist" worldview has developed—in other words, by looking at what its ongoing transformation into postmodernism might have to say about Euro-American modernism itself. Because there is no space here to digress into definitions of postmodernism, this discussion will assume a familiarity with the subject.[36]

If postmodernism is viewed, as Jameson suggests in his influential text, *Postmodernism, or the Cultural Logic of Late Capitalism*, as a "periodizing hypothesis,"[37] then what is most important in an analysis of the relationship between it and Euro-American modernism are not only the questions of when the period of Euro-American modernism can be said to have ended and that of postmodernism begun, but also how, in terms of the way it articulates itself, postmodernism is to be considered different enough from Euro-American modernism itself to warrant a periodizing break. Even if sketching only the barest outline, postmodernism must be viewed as a challenge to Euro-American notions of literary modernism and modernity. There is, however, one important way in which it is very much the same—that is, in its silencing of the "other," or those cultural influences it defines as not originating in itself. Here, what postmodernism silences is the conventional, racially, and/or ethnically defined "other." But, as I am arguing, behind this lies the even more deeply silenced threat of another, more amorphous and less containable "other"—that whose common denominators are hybridity, heterogeneity, and multiplicity, whose existence is to be fully recognized here only through analysis of its relations to the politics of cultural space. Postmodernism, too, participates in the politics of cultural space, in the silent, unintended significations of its linguistic articulation, that connotative excess that is always the ineradicable baggage of language, but which in this case, read through the politics of cultural space, is given voice. To illustrate this, I will quote four brief passages from Jameson's text. The first of these reveals a subtly articulated but powerful struggle between postmodernism and what it identifies as its "other":

> One of the concerns frequently aroused by periodizing hypotheses is that these tend to obliterate difference, and to project an idea of the historical period as massive homogeneity. . . . This is precisely why it seems to me essential to grasp 'postmodernism' not as a style, but rather as a cultural dominant: a conception which allows for the presence and coexistence of a range of very different, yet subordinate features.[38]

Here, in expressing concern over the "homogenizing" bent of periodization, its tendency to create a sense of cultural "totality," Jameson not only recognizes the struggle that is the politics of cultural space: seeking in this passage neither to "obliterate difference," nor to establish cultural hegemony, he does, however, precisely that. This is evident in the fact that while presenting the aims of postmodernism as coterminous with those of cultural heterogeneity, Jameson inevitably uses the language of power: he seeks to establish postmodernism as a cultural *dominant* that will *coexist* with other "different, yet *subordinate features*" (emphasis mine). Yet, we must ask, is not the notion of coexistence, which as a mode of shared being implies a modicum of equality, compromised by that of postmodernism as a cultural *dominant*? Is true *co*existence really possible in such a situation? Further, in Jameson's formulation, the problem of "difference" is overrun, assimilated, becoming nothing more than a *subordinate feature* of postmodernism itself. Outside of this definition, all that would signify in terms of "difference," both traditionally and nontraditionally defined,[39] falls into the silence of cultural and linguistic excess. Jameson's explanation of this articulation of postmodernism is framed in the same rhetoric of power, in its positing of cultural difference as a very real and potential threat:

> The postmodern is . . . the force field in which very different kinds of cultural impulses . . . must make their way. If we do not achieve some general sense of a cultural dominant, then we fall back into a view of present history as sheer heterogeneity, random difference, a coexistence of a host of distinct forces whose effectivity is undecidable.[40]

Here again, Jameson envelops postmodernism in images of control and dominance, in describing it as a "force field" through which "other" cultural representations must attempt to come into being. His articulation of the postmodern as a "force field" implies resistance (the same difficult relationship that pertains between Euro-American modernism and the debate on canon revision and culture studies), suggesting that postmodernism and "other" cultural representations exist in an oppositional relationship that denies any real possibility of coexistence. How can there be *"coexistence"* when "existence" itself is described by struggle alone? Postmodernism in this formulation is singular, while that which is described as "other" in relation to it is plural, "random." While such difference, too, possesses a certain "force," that force as it is described here is ultimately ineffective, especially in the face of the singular power that is postmodernism. What is particularly interesting to note is that while Jameson identifies the postmodern as linked to a type of cultural power resembling a sort of "force field" (just as I noted previously a similar cultural power with regard to modernism) there is a subtle difference between the way in which the two types of cultural power are operative in the cultural spaces they inhabit. While the "force field" defined by Euro-American modernism is one that provides a type of aura that distinguishes those texts it considers "modernist" from those it does not consider so, the "force field" of postmodernism operates here more as a defensive posture, one that, perceiving a threat, offers a powerful and counteractive rhetorical resistance. The difference between the two is suggested more clearly by this third passage from Jameson:

> It is not surprising to find the extraordinary flowering of the new postmodern architecture grounded in the patronage of multinational business, whose expansion and development is strictly contemporaneous with it . . . this whole global, yet American, postmodern culture is the internal and superstructural expression of a whole new wave of American military and economic domination throughout the world: in this sense, as throughout class history, the underside of culture is blood, torture, death and horror.[41]

In this passage, however, the "otherness" that is submerged and seemingly nonexistent in traditional formulations of Euro-American modernism is, in postmodernism, openly confronted. Here Jameson describes postmodern culture as not only global, but specifically American, and not only a *"cultural* dominant," (emphasis mine) but an economic one as well. In this formulation, what is deemed "postmodern culture" is only possible as the cultural expression of a powerful economic force, that is, the manifestation of what Jameson identifies as "late capitalism." Jameson uses here again a rhetoric of power—only this time, that power is overtly expressed, in terms of a necessary dominance and submission to be obtained by the clear and present threat of military force. But why, we may ask, is this rhetoric of power so prevalent in postmodernism? Why does it articulate itself in such clearly oppositional terms? What, after all, is postmodernism so violently articulating itself against?

The answers to these questions are to be found, paradoxically in Jameson's definition of postmodernism, as the "cultural logic of late capitalism." Jameson identifies this "logic" as the natural consequence of multinational capitalism, which has, in effect, produced what he calls a "bewildering new world space."[42] In this new and material world space, there are countless "others," and through this new stage of capitalist development, such "others" have been brought, on all levels, be it social, political, cultural, and/or economic, into closer and closer contact with the cultural experience of the West and Western ways of thinking. Thus, it is because of the sheer heterogeneity of difference and its influence on modes of signification that postmodernism is articulated in such terms of opposition, resistance, and defense. From a postmodernist perspective, "culture" has evolved from a singular, homogeneous idea into the province of the many—the effects of which postmodernism seeks to mitigate by reestablishing and reinforcing the notion of "culture" as a singular, dominant (and dominating) totality:

> What we must ask ourselves is whether it is not . . . [the] 'semi-autonomy' of the cultural sphere which has been destroyed by the logic of late capitalism. Yet to argue that culture is today no longer endowed with the relative autonomy it once enjoyed as one level among others in earlier moments of capitalism . . . is not necessarily to imply its disappearance or extinction. On the contrary: we must go on to affirm that the dissolution of an autonomous sphere of culture is rather to be imagined in terms of an explosion: a prodigious expansion of culture throughout the social realm, to the point at which everything in our social life—from economic value and state power to practices and to the very structure of the psyche itself—can be said to have become 'cultural' in some original and as yet unauthorized sense.[43]

Yet again, Jameson describes a situation in which "culture" is pitted against an obscure, indistinct, and *plural* threat which, as it is articulated here, is the end result of the "logic of late capitalism," a menace that could also, but need not, suggest the end of "culture" once and for all. In describing this difficulty in terms of culture's "disappearance" and/or "extinction," however, Jameson also suggests that the battle he is articulating, of "us" against "them,"[44] is one of life or death.[45] One or the other *must* conquer, or be destroyed. To approach this existential struggle from the strongest position possible, then, Jameson argues that "culture" as he understands it must be reimagined, and that this reimagining will function to affirm that notion of

culture. Because it is only through Jameson's idea of "culture" that the transformative process offered by the imagination takes place, that "culture," in
peforming it, yet succeeds in articulating itself as separate and distinct from
those it has defined as "other," even as it recognizes the effect of such "otherness" on its own processes of self-definition.

Through *reimagining* itself, Jameson's notion of "culture" stretches itself into that world of "belief" and "consecration" discussed above in relation to Bourdieu's notion of legitimacy. It is through this reimagining that
postmodernism seeks not only to differentiate itself from those cultural impulses it designates as "other," but to legitimize itself as a "cultural dominant." This is only reinforced by the fact that Jameson also identifies those
"other" cultural representations as "as yet unauthorized." Because these cultural representations will not, at least as Jameson has articulated the cultural
situation here, be subjected to any kind of *legitimizing* transformative
process, they will also, it seems, *remain* "unauthorized," lacking any external markers of legitimacy. Here, what is culturally "unauthorized" is not
only the conventionally defined identity of difference, but also that defined
by multiplicity and hybridity, discovered here through analysis of its impli-
cation in the politics of cultural space.

It is in this sense, then, that postmodernism is most directly related to
earlier Euro-American modernist practice, as it has been previously outlined.
Postmodernism, while discrediting the older Euro-American modernist "narrative" of a singular, hegemonic cultural worldview,[46] subtly posits itself as
what I will call a "metanarrative" because it serves, paradoxically, to transform the discreditation of the older Euro-American modernist narrative into
a new singular narrative of cultural understanding that is yet in many ways
still based on the demise of the old one.[47]

Thus, in postmodernism the two conflicting narratives of Euro-American modernism may be understood to become one—albeit uneasily—in a
sort of consolidation against an even greater cultural threat than that posed
in the earlier Euro-American modernist paradigm by the paradox between
nationalism and internationalism—a threat that Jameson "reimagines" as a
cultural "explosion." This fact, that "culture" as Jameson understands it has
"exploded," also suggests yet another kind of break than that implied by his
"periodizing hypothesis," one that this hypothesis actually serves to occlude
or obscure: that is, the true cultural impact of the "other" voices against
which postmodernism's notion of culture is opposed. And it is in the significance of this break and its implications in the politics of cultural space that
we may begin to discover very important implications for our understanding
of traditional formulations of Euro-American modernism.

This is because what Jameson identifies as an "expansion of culture
throughout the social realm" (brought about, in his view, by the develop-

ment of multinational capital) is also represented by another, and vocal, cultural representation, skeptical of postmodernism's stated goals and aims, and cognizant of its theoretical contradictions: that is, the burgeoning critical practice of postcolonialism, within the more broad context of culture studies. The emergence of this new frame of reference has produced what might be termed a broad-based cultural critique, yet one that has very specific implications for the aims and concerns of postmodernism. But this new frame of reference, along with the force of culture studies, is also a cultural force in its own right, one by which the contemporary politics of cultural space not only becomes immensely more complicated than was that of the cultural space inhabited by Euro-American modernism, but by which we may also begin to understand that a radical modification of traditional notions of literary modernism and modernity, as well as our understanding of the significance of the politics of cultural space in relation to these notions, must inevitably be the result.

In her essay, "'Circling the Downspout of Empire'": Post-Colonialism and Postmodernism," Linda Hutcheon asserts that what has been identified as "post-*colonial* is . . . as implicated in that which it challenges as is the post-*modern.*"[48] In this, Hutcheon emphasizes the role of history in the way in which each critical practice has been articulated and how that history must necessarily influence our understanding of both contemporary critical postions, as well as that of the earlier Euro-American modernism. But more important, Hutcheon identifies (quoting Frank Davey), the relationship between the postcolonial and the postmodern as a shared position toward "the predominant non-European interpretation of modernism as 'an international movement, elitist, imperialist, 'totalizing,' willing to appropriate the local while being condescending to its practice."[49]

It is, then, by examining the implications of linking both "*post-s*" (postcolonial and post-modern) through their shared concerns that the operations of the politics of cultural space in traditional formulations of Euro-American modernism become most evident. Hutcheon makes clear that while these two critical theories are joined in the political position they take with regard to the past, they are radically different in terms of the form that politics takes in their present practices. Postmodernism's critical practice is often contradictory and for many politically suspect, while that of postcolonialism often presents, for equal numbers, a clearer focus with regard to social and political agency.[50]

But the linkage of postmodernism and postcolonialism through their shared attitude toward the past is important in yet another, and even more subtle, way. If postmodernism's silent cultural resistance to the significance of "otherness," as established above, is viewed in relation to the idea that the development of postcolonial critical discourse is a counter, rather than a concomitant, development, the implications of considering them in relation to each other suggest a new, largely unexplored yet extremely important way of viewing that past. The significance of this is that we may then understand postcolonialism as representative, in opposition to postmodernist cultural formulations, of a vocalization of cultural impulses that were *previously silenced*. What this means is that, while such cultural impulses did indeed exist during the period identified by Euro-American modernism, they were also effectively prevented from giving voice to their various and different modes of perceiving and understanding culture. And along with many of the more conventionally defined locations of "otherness" found within the postcolonial framework come many others more deeply silent (and/or silenced), not so strongly articulated within this framework, yet, nevertheless, to some extent given by it the same possibility of expression. Since Jameson identifies the postmodern as the superstructural representation of the cultural and geographical expansion of multinational or "late" capitalism, it follows that the "modern," in the Euro-American sense, may perhaps also be viewed as the superstructural representation of the cultural and geographical expansion that was the economic system of colonialism. The difference is that while postmodernism must take the voice of the "other" into consideration, Euro-American international modernism, considered as the representation of colonial and imperial power and influence over cultural interpretation, could deny the "other," and whatever may be defined as "other" in relation to it, its very cultural existence.

In an analysis of Canadian critiques of this "double tethering" of Euro-American modernism and colonialism to postmodernism and postcolonialism, Hutcheon suggests that the only way to create a discourse that will nullify the power of colonialism to silence "other" cultural perspectives is to begin by "deconstructing existing myths which support the discourses of colonialism (including modernism) and constructing different ones to take their place."[51] In this regard, then, if Euro-American modernism and postmodernism are viewed as "myths" or narratives, "stories" that serve to engender or create a particular worldview, then the power they possess over the cultural spaces they inhabit can only be challenged through the construction of alternative myths or, in other words, alternative narratives (stories) that represent "other" ways of knowing. By revealing this problematic through examining the significance that the two *post-s* (of post-modernism and post-colonialism) hold for our understanding of Euro-American modernism and the politics of cultural space, we may, then, "post-" Euro-American modernism into its Other. And, in so doing, perhaps the beginnings of such alternative myths, narratives, or stories may be found.

THE CULTURAL AND SPATIAL POLITICS OF MODERNITY

To initiate such a new perspective of literary modernism and modernity, I would like to suggest that it be viewed from a perspective prior to its inscription (as examined above) in a canon of Euro-American high or international modernism. This more traditional perspective would loosely designate the time from about 1910 to about 1940, when the notion of literary modernism and modernity as we now know it did not exist, since those avant-garde tendencies it later described as typically "modernist" had yet to be given the iconic status they currently hold in critical formulations of this time in literary history. However, it also leaves open the possibility of shifting these traditional temporal boundaries, the need for which is plainly suggested by the intensity of the debate on modernism, as previously elaborated. Yet because it requires us not only to rethink the institutional origins of literary modernism and modernity, but to reformulate our understanding of it in a way that acknowledges its relation to the politics of cultural space, such a perspective effectively negates that "transcendent" power (which has been described as "colonial" or "colonizing," or even "imperial"), by which Euro-American modernism controls the cultural space it has traditionally inhabited.

It also negates this power in another, more specific way. The emphasis on such an articulation provides the initial and radical disruption through which a separate, and oppositional, semantic space is created, one whose primary significance is that it remains uncontaminated by the significatory power of the term "modernism" in its Euro-American designation. It is in this way that this oppositional perspective becomes a necessary, and effective, disruptive force in a discussion seeking to critique Euro-American modernism as a cultural construct. Because it causes not only a spatial, but a temporal disruption (in that it considers the time before the establishment of the literary canon by which Euro-American modernism was instituted) it escapes the repetitive need to describe why contemporary rearticulations of modernism and modernity are different from traditional, Euro-American conceptions of it, as are often found in postmodernist critiques of modernism—critical formulations that must be continually justified in relation to the cultural significance of Euro-American modernism itself. Since the prefix "post-" in this case may often be viewed more as an addition than anything else, and because as such, the semantic power of Euro-American modernism has been neither nullified nor dismantled, there is in this term a continual shifting back and forth of semantic power and control. Which aspect of the term is more important? The fact that it designates something that follows Euro-American modernism, or its role in the origination of the term itself?

Thus, centering a critique of Euro-American modernism in a perspective that is both spatially *and* temporally oppositional introduces a powerful semantic counterforce that prevents the traditional articulation of Euro-American modernism from endlessly replicating itself and all that it implies, as it may do even in the process of critique. But in order to fully explore such "other" ways of knowing with regard to this literary critical moment, it will also be necessary, as Edward Said points out in his influential work, *Culture and Imperialism*, to consent to a dramatic, and transformative, alteration in the current knowledges by which literary modernism and modernity have until now been articulated.[52] The spatiotemporal perspective here outlined is, then, one way to open the door to the investigation of such new ways of understanding this time in literary history. In the chapters that follow, the act of reading will now take center stage, just as rereading has in this one: reading literary modernism and modernity, rereading Euro-American modernism—on the edge—between what it has been, and what it can be, beginning with Marcel Proust and his masterwork, *A la recherche du temps perdu*.

CHAPTER 3

Marcel *mondain*, "Marcel," and the Hidden Diaspora

Author, Voyeur, or Both?

THE CRITICAL/CULTURAL PERSPECTIVE

So much has been said in Proust criticism about the apparent ambiguities and contradictions in Proust's nature that, as Guy Michaud observes, it is today "banal" even to set up these dichotomies in oppositional terms.[1] In 1973, when Michaud wrote his essay, the influence on Proust criticism of the New Criticism[2] made such juxtapositions superfluous at that time, and it continues to exert a similar influence over contemporary Proust criticism.[3] This is particularly true of criticism concerning Proust's massive work *A la recherche du temps perdu*, whose 2,000+ pages have stimulated an endless stream of commentary from the printing of *Du coté de chez Swann* until the present day. The sheer bulk and complexity of the *Recherche* seems enough of an invitation to regard the text as capable of producing its own meanings, independent of historical, cultural, or biographical information, and it is from this aspect of the novel that the familiar description of its world as the "Proustian universe" is derived.

But while the text does possess a rich abundance of thematic significance in its own right, nevertheless, the nature of those themes and their relationship to Proust's actual life have represented a perennial fascination for its critics. The idea that the *Recherche* is merely an autobiography or, at best, an imaginative autobiography, has dogged Proustian criticism since the appearance of Proust's first works in *Le Figaro*, when his critics denounced him as a social climber and dilettante artist more interested in the snob appeal of his associates than in true friendship or art.[4] Those critics who have been fascinated by the autobiographical aspects of the *Recherche* find their support in George

Painter's classic biography,[5] which addresses the dichotomy between Proust's life and art by showing, through an analysis of the way in which certain biographical events correspond to and explain particular incidents in the novel, how Proust's life possesses an inestimable value in the interpretation of his art:

> The biographer's task . . . is to trace the formation and the relationship of the . . . two selves which Proust distinguishes. He must discover, beneath the mask of the artist's every-day, objective life, the secret life from which he extracted his work; show how, in the apparently sterile persons and places of that external life, he found the hidden, universal meanings which are the themes of his book; and reveal the drama of the contrast and interaction between his daily existence and his incommensurably deeper life as a creator. *A la recherche*, of all great works of art, cannot be fully understood until the life in time of which it is a symbolic reconstruction in eternity is known.[6]

Thus, it may be seen that Painter's distinction between Proust's life and his art forms the fundamental opposition in discussions of his work, while all other oppositions become variations on the theme of this general rubric.[7]

The danger with any critical study that purports to discuss the relationship between author motivation and creative work, and one to which Painter's study is not immune,[8] is that one can never truly know what an author intended in his work. Often, a creative work ends by being something totally different from what an author *did* intend. It is, however, possible to create, using biographical information, a *context* of understanding for any given text, something that is, after all, the goal of any theoretical construct used in literary interpretation. Still, the autobiographical approach to the *Recherche* has come under fire in contemporary criticism of the novel, which finds the biographical connection too straightforward and uncomplicated to serve adequately in interpretations of it, and too glib a representation of a connection that is, as Milton Hindus described it, "of gossamer-like delicacy and subtlety."[9]

While the autobiographical approach to the *Recherche* is now thought to be one of the "naive assumptions of years gone by,"[10] it has, however, found a revival in relatively recent studies of its pervasive theme of homosexuality. Such studies continue to collapse, more often than not, into analyses of the relationship between Proust's actual experience of homosexuality and the way in which that experience is represented in the text.[11] It is quickly discovered that even when a study of homosexuality in the *Recherche* does seek to remain within the framework of the text in the attempt to interpret the theme only in relation to its various characters, one question always lingers in the background, a question fueled by Proust's many remarks on the subject of homosexuality, and in particular by the oft-quoted passage in André Gide's *Journal* regarding his dicussions with Proust concerning it: Why did Proust write in such graphic terms about homosexuality at a time when any public accusation of homosexuality was injurious enough to require a duel in order to repair the injury?[12] If the accusation by another were such a slur, one wonders how Proust could risk public self-accusation, which does not offer the possibility of restitution through the virility and courage represented by the willingness to fight a duel, and leaves the self-accuser naked and defenseless before the unforgiving eyes of the world.

In his book *Homosexualities and French Literature*, George Stambolian identifies homosexuality as "an instrument for analyzing a cultural and linguistic context extending in all directions." In his opinion, the French have perceived in homosexuality's "otherness" a privileged instrument for analysis, a question to raise questions, because homosexuality is something that "perpetually questions the social order and is always in question itself . . ."[13] In this respect, homosexuality becomes the construct within which a discussion of the relationship between Proust's life and his art may be revived, through this, its relation to the politics of cultural space in literary modernism and modernity explored, and a broader understanding of its contribution to modern culture derived.

Yet it must be observed that homosexuality, as a submerged theme in the *Recherche*, embraces only one aspect of the relationship between Proust's life and his art, and not the most important one. It does, however, through its thematic significance, bring to light not only another, more crucial, question concerning this relationship, but in demanding that question, yet another critical controversy surrounding it. That question is—as evidenced by Proust's famous statement to the author André Gide, "You may tell all . . . but on condition that you never say I"[14]—What is the relationship between Marcel Proust, Marcel *mondain*, or Marcel the public figure, and "Marcel," the narrator of the *Recherche*?

But such discussions already have a problematic status in Proust criticism. Patrick Brady, writing in 1989, sums up the contemporary critical controversy regarding this issue with comments on both the autobiographical aspect of the *Recherche* and on discussions concerning narration in the text:

> It is depressing to find that as late as 1984, in a book entirely devoted to precisely this question, Paul Jay totally confuses Proust himself with the narrator, who moreover is referred to as "Marcel": and the work is classed simply as an "autobiographical novel." . . . In narration, an effort has been made to distinguish between protagonist, narrator, author and Marcel Proust, and to face

the fact that in first-person narration the reader, like the psychoanalyst listening to his patient, registers no "facts" but merely a tissue of claims and allegations. Rigorous immanence is the key.[15]

Brady is here discussing what he views as a simplification of a work too sophisticated for such easy answers, yet it is also possible that his total rejection of the idea of a relationship between Proust and his narrator, and between Proust's life and his work, is somewhat hasty, and not altogether well-founded.

Brady's citation of "the now classical work on point of view,"[16] an article by Louis Martin-Chauffier, "Proust and the Double "I" of Four Persons" published in 1943 in the review *Confluences*, both admits the importance of this article while criticizing it for its participation in the act of "confusing protagonist, narrator, author and everyday man, and referring to the protagonist as 'Marcel.'"[17] Brady cites Proust's *Contre Sainte-Beuve* as evidence from the author himself that an artist's life and his work are, and should be, separate. But, as previously stated, authorial statements regarding artistic work are often not reliable guides in the interpretation of such work. In addition, it must be remembered that not long before Proust began writing *Contre Sainte-Beuve*, he had reached a point in his artistic development when he needed to free himself of the homage he had paid to John Ruskin, and of his slavish devotion to the artistic beauty others had found within, as opposed to outside of, themselves. Painter's discussion of Proust's essay "Sur la Lecture" details Proust's thrust toward creative independence through his indictment of reading, a sort of artistic liberation through writing, as his work *Contre Sainte-Beuve* was to be as well.[18]

When viewed in the context of Proust's hidden homosexuality, the function of "Sur la Lecture" and *Contre Sainte-Beuve* become clear: if Proust's essential artistic problem is not only the authentic representation of homosexuality but the authentic representation of homosexuality without the risk of self-accusation, there are a number of major obstacles to his freedom of speech that must be overcome before he may do so. One of these obstacles is, of course, his family—and it is pertinent to note that Proust does not begin *Sodome et Gomorrhe* in earnest until well after the death of his father in 1903, and his mother in 1905.[19] The other obstacles are literary: his lack of confidence in his own artistic abilities, and the pitfalls of the confessional form, already evidenced by the example of Gide, whose use of the "I" narrator in his work is easily viewed as a frank and public avowal of his personal preferences. Painter justifies his particular use of the biographical method, described above, in a way which is also pertinent to the present argument regarding Proust's statements in *Contre Sainte-Beuve*:

> Proust himself was concerned at this time to vindicate his future novel as a work of creative imagination, and to forestall the philis-

tine critics and readers who would mistake it for a *roman à clef*. But in different contexts, and particularly in *Le temps retrouvé* itself, he was ready to admit a much closer relation between the self that wrote his novel and 'the one we manifest in our habits, in society, in our vices,' and so conceded some truth to Sainte-Beuve's belief that 'an author's work is inseparable from the rest of him.'[20]

Any substantial reading of criticism concerning Proust's relation to society and his reputation in society would serve to validate this claim. But a stronger support for such an assertion is found in the relationship of Proust's work to his homosexuality: for if his novel would seem too factual a representation of the social world he inhabited at the time, how much more credence would such factuality lend to the idea that its treatment of homosexuality was a public self-disclosure of his own homosexual tendencies, if he did not pave the way for its artistic significance through his insistence that his work was not autobiographical? *Contre Sainte-Beuve* may thus be understood to function, as did his essay "Sur la Lecture," as a means for Proust to position himself artistically in such a way that he could begin his novel without fear of disclosure. Thus, Brady's assertion, based on *Contre Sainte-Beuve*, that it is wrong to analyze the relationships that may pertain between Proust (both as author and as man) and his narrator, is no longer satisfactory when the representational problem presented in the text by the issue of homosexuality is addressed.

In the essay by Martin Louis-Chauffier mentioned above, the narrative strategy of the *Recherche* is divided into four "consciousnesses": Marcel Proust, the man; Marcel Proust, the author; and an "I" narrator that is itself, if closely observed, double—there is the "I" narrator (called "Marcel"), one of whom tells the story, and one of whom the reader observes as living within the text—that is, "Marcel" the narrator and "Marcel" the hero.[21]

Though the present argument follows somewhat closely the lines of that of Martin-Chauffier, the two are quite different when it comes to the discussion of the narrator. In Martin-Chauffier's essay, the double "I" narrator, in tandem with Marcel Proust, the man, acts as a "screen"[22] behind which Marcel Proust, the author, hides while controlling the story. This is described as follows by Martin-Chauffier:

Marcel the narrator, who says "I"; Marcel the hero, who is "I"; Proust, the author, who never says "I," but intervenes unceasingly, even in the narrative itself, directing all, understanding all (. . .) and never losing sight of the goal to be attained. Marcel Proust finally, whose snobbery, kindness, urbanity, hypersensitivity, sickness, vices provide for Proust, lucid, indifferent and pure, the screen behind which he weaves his tale.[23]

Marcel Proust is, in Martin-Chauffier's view, the everyday man, and Proust the author, an omniscient being who hides behind him by using his "I" narrator, who is also double. But is it really the urbane and socially conscious Marcel Proust, as he is described above, behind whom Proust the author hides? Or is this urbane "Marcel Proust" someone else, someone whom I shall call Marcel *mondain*, who does not at all serve in the capacity of a "screen" behind which Proust the author operates in secret, but is, rather, a symptom of the social problem that lies at the heart of the *Recherche*, and forms its primary representational problem as well? This problem is the issue of homosexuality, both as a social reality and as a representational conundrum. While there is indeed a "screen" in the *Recherche*, that "screen" is not and cannot be partially composed of Martin-Chauffier's "Marcel Proust," as everyday man—it is, rather the narrator, "Marcel," alone. And it is the relationship that pertains between Marcel Proust, or Marcel *mondain* as he shall hereinafter be termed, and "Marcel," the fictional narrator, that, with this discovery, takes on a singular importance in the *Recherche*, and reveals the narrator "Marcel" as double in quite a different way from that described by Martin-Chauffier.

The significance of "Marcel" in this regard is suggested in a brilliant essay by Mark Guenette, titled "Le Loup et le narrateur: The Masking and Unmasking of Homosexuality in Proust's *A la recherche du temps perdu.*" Guenette here discusses the issue of homosexuality in precisely its relationship to narration in the *Recherche*, identifying its primary instance of homosexuality as "that of the novel's own narrator."[24] In revealing the hidden homosexuality of "Marcel," Guenette opens up a new dimension in the text, and introduces a new set of oppositions—hidden/revealed, danger/safety, exile/acceptance. These new categories suggest that the exploration of sexual deviation in the *Recherche* be extended to "Marcel" himself, whose sexuality is seemingly clearly heterosexual. What I am suggesting here is that this exploration must go yet one step further—not to assert the silent (and silenced) homosexuality of "Marcel," but rather, to assert the homosexuality of Proust himself—as filtered through the narrative voice of "Marcel."

As such, it may be seen that Proust the author slips between Marcel *mondain* and "Marcel," rather than hiding behind them, as in Martin-Chauffier's view. This is done in order to accomplish the one moment in the *Recherche* when Proust can say "I," with the triumph of not seeming to say "I." In this way, he achieves a moment of authenticity in which he reveals the silent, naked truth before all the world, yet reveals it with such subtlety that it is not readily apparent, and thus solves the representational problem that impeded the *Recherche* from its inception.

But in order to understand how and why this is so, it remains to answer the question posed above, first in terms of the critical territory, later in terms of the text itself: What is the relationship between Marcel *mondain* and "Marcel"? One must begin, however, by first asking what is the relationship between Proust the author and Marcel *mondain*? If this question is asked with regard to the present discussion of Proust's treatment of the theme of homosexuality in the *Recherche*, a number of unconsidered issues come to the fore. These issues point to Marcel *mondain* as being part of not only Marcel Proust, the man, but also as an important aspect of Marcel Proust the author, and, with regard to the *Recherche*, perhaps the most important aspect, as will be seen.

However, a discussion of Marcel *mondain* raises yet another critical controversy, one which, this time, may be understood to be so old, so worn-out, that the scholar-critic who revives it subjects him- or herself to the risk of general disdain on the part of the critical audience. This is the controversy surrounding Proust's relationship to society.[25] The general character of this controversy is that of the question of whether or not Proust was a snob. Since this question has already been elaborated in critical discussions from Rivière to Diesbach,[26] I will not reiterate their arguments here. For the purposes of this discussion, it is not the question per se of whether or not Proust was a snob that is important, but rather, *why* might he have been a snob? Further, what is the relationship between snobbism in the text and homosexuality, and how might the two interact to lend a new understanding to the place of society and the social in Proust's text? This is, in a sense, coming at Proust from the outside in. Rather than choosing society and the social as topics of critical interest simply because Proust wrote about them, they become important because a known aspect of Proust's life—his actual or attributed snobbism—is used to stimulate questions about its deeper implications in his work.

In considering these questions, it is useful at the outset to note the way in which snobbism functions in the *Recherche*. Roger Shattuck finds that "for Proust, snobbery is the great cohesive force that holds society together," and that "he studies it tirelessly at every social level."[27] Though there are hundreds of incidences of snobbery in the text, one of the most important, and one which will be of use later on in this discussion, is that of Swann's acceptance and Odette's exclusion from most of what is considered "respectable" social interaction throughout a good part of the novel. This acceptance-exclusion is a paradigm for the uncompromising severity of the social world that Proust depicts, which would require the social separation of a married couple because one of its halves cannot meet its rigid social requirements.

The most revealing aspect of the way in which snobbery operates in the *Recherche* is found, however, in Proust's ironic criticism of the very society within which he spent much of his time for a good portion of his life, the very pastime by which he is here given the appellation of "Marcel *mondain*."

E. F. N. Jephcott offers an interpretation of the situation with regard to society in the novel, which identifies the concept of subjectivity in terms of the way in which individual desire functions as a primary motivating factor in the text:

> The driving force in social life as depicted by Proust is the desire of individuals to achieve a higher position in the social hierarchy, a desire which is frustrated by the exclusiveness of the social circles above them. The inaccessibility of these circles heightens their attraction; the individual becomes obsessed by the need to penetrate the *salons* closed to him.[28]

Thus, the idea of subjectivity (the lowest common denominator by which the individuals who participate in the social world may be described) in the *Recherche* is one which is, invariably, a subjectivity suffering from the pain and stigma of exclusion. In this respect, the concepts of exclusion and of social acceptance based on exclusion form the essential fabric of the novel. As such, the idea of exclusion also becomes a necessary element in the text, without which the central themes that the novel attempts to communicate would be meaningless. But this idea becomes even more useful in an interpretation of the text when it is applied to Proust the man, as Kopp suggests:

> Even the exceptions who cast him [Proust] as a judge who condemns society still view his condemnation as a necessary step toward his eventual withdrawal from society into the world of art.[29]

What is interesting about Kopp's observation is that he identifies Proust's attitude toward society as oppositional, and connects this antagonistic position with his voluntary exile into illness and solitude in order to write the *Recherche*. But while Proust's almost total withdrawal from the world of normalcy[30] might seem merely a response to his desire to devote himself to the writing of his novel, it is possible that this action is indeed motivated in a far more complicated way.

It is through the underlying complexity of Proust's personal life *before* he became a part of "high society" that both the motivations for that ascent and the scaffolding on which Marcel *mondain* was created are revealed. For Marcel *mondain* is nothing more than a creation of Proust himself, created by himself. Marcel *mondain* is the man who was listed as having attended a social function in society columns such as that in *Le Gaulois*, and the writer of reviews and sketches for *Le Figaro*. He is the image offered by the printed name, "par Marcel Proust"—not the author himself, but that mysterious and ineluctable figure, the Author. He was a figment of Proust's and other people's imaginations, a mysterious, sought-after figure, a public image. The reasons for Proust's desire to create that public image begin early, and have been well-documented by Painter and other critics: the birth of his brother Robert, the denial of the maternal good-night kiss which forms the beginning of the *Recherche*. But there are other, more pressing causes for this desire which, when all are taken together, form a rigid, almost insurpassable barrier for Proust to the social acceptance that all ordinary human beings desire to partake in and that he, in particular, craved.

In any discussion of Proust, however, the idea of exclusion from society must be clarified. It is not simply an exclusion based on a recognized class distinction, the exclusion felt by one who envies those of a higher social order and desires to possess, as his or her own, their worldliness and what is imagined as their more perfect world. His sense of exclusion came from many and disparate causes, most of which can be seen to derive from loss or stigma. Proust was to feel all his life his separation from his past, from his beloved garden at Auteuil; late in the year 1910, he was almost fully a nocturnal being, sleeping during the day when others were up and about, rising at night while the rest of the world slept; he was an artist (publishing in literary magazines from the age of twenty-one),[31] an occupation known to pose many difficulties in terms of livelihood; he felt the stigma of Jewishness, although he was only half-Jewish, had been raised as a Catholic, and the French society of the time had become more relaxed regarding Jews who had something to offer, such as wealth, talent, or wit; he feared exclusion in love, and thus in his relations with women, he always chose women too old for him, too far above him socially, too far below him socially, that is, courtesans, or women already engaged or married—all relations with no possibility of a future; in his homosexual relations, he chose to fall in love only with the "employed secretary," a liaison that posed no threat to acceptance since it was based on material security; finally, he was excluded by his bourgeois background and his invalid lifestyle.[32]

But by far the most radical instance of Proust's sense of exclusion is based on the knowledge that at every moment of his life, in every personal relationship, he is living a lie, must live the lie, and can see only one possibility of freeing himself from the misery of living this lie. That lie is the truth of his homosexuality. And the one possibility of freedom is through art, yet that avenue is fraught with difficulty.[33] He cannot, like Gide, reveal himself unprotected to the world, since that would hurt not only himself, but his family as well, and particularly his mother. Proust was, as Painter points out, "a remorseful, Gide a triumphant invert; and by Gide, whose art was based on confession, the great opposing sexual tensions of *A la Recherche* were mistaken for a figment of duplicity."[34]

At issue here is the fact that Proust could not bring himself to accept his homosexuality and the place to which it relegated him in social life, and he surrendered to the cultural injunctions that found it a vice at once "unnatural, degrading, and shameful."[35] But the pain of this conflict, that between the desire to tell the truth, to live a single, rather than a double, life, to be what he was in the eyes of all, helped Proust to create the *Recherche* as surely as the irritation caused by a grain of sand in the belly of an oyster creates a pearl. The importance of homosexuality in this capacity in the *Recherche* is documented by Rivers:

> Proust's correspondence shows that he regarded the treatment of homosexuality in *A la recherche* as inseparable from—indeed, as undergirding—both the long-range structure and the principal aesthetic objectives of the novel.[36]

As such, homosexuality, or the Hidden Diaspora (all of those who hold the sexual preferences of this often maligned group, and who feel the need to hide membership from public view), may be understood as the central theme of the text. For what else is the Hidden Diaspora other than the comedy of social life? The closeted homosexual is not the only being in the social world with something to hide. Everyone in the *Recherche* seeks, if not to hide their true feelings from the eyes of the world, then to hide their true feelings from themselves. Though the necessity to hide may seem a harmless game, a frivolous social formality, in the *Recherche* the game is as serious and ugly as any battle of life and death. None of its characters wants to be caught naked and defenseless, their feelings publicly exposed, as is the Baron de Charlus during the last party he attends at the Verdurins. Though many may say the central themes of the *Recherche* are society, love, jealousy, friendship, time, memory, the imagination, and/or a host of other possible subjects, they are all connected to this basic and fundamental conflict which, for reasons that will be seen, forms the materials of the symbolic Roman church underlying the literary Gothic cathedral that Proust built in *A la recherche du temps perdu*.

"MARCEL"/MARCEL AND THE HIDDEN "I"

Longtemps, je me suis couché de bonne heure. Parfois, à peine ma bougie éteinte, mes yeux se fermaient si vite que je n'avais pas le temps de me dire: "Je m'endors." Et, une demi-heure après, la pensée qu'il était temps de chercher le sommeil m'éveillait; je voulais poser le volume que je croyais avoir encore dans les mains et souffler ma lumière; je n'avais pas cessé en dormant de faire des réflexions sur ce que je venais de lire, mais ces réflexions avaient pris un tour un peu particulier; il me semblait que j'étais moi-même ce dont parlait l'ouvrage: une église, un quatuor, la rivalité de François I et de Charles Quint. Cette croyance survivait pendant quelques secondes à mon réveil; elle ne choquait pas ma raison mais pesait comme des écailles sur mes yeux et les empéchait de se rendre compte que le bougeoir n'était plus allumé. Puis elle commençait à me devenir inintelligible, comme après la métempsycose les pensées d'une existence antérieure; le sujet du livre se détachait de moi, j'étais libre de m'y appliquer ou non; aussitôt je recouvrais la vue et j'étais bien étonné de trouver autour de moi une obscurité, douce et reposante pour mes yeux, mais peut-être plus encore pour mon esprit, à qui elle apparaissait comme une chose sans cause, incompréhensible, comme une chose vraiment obscure. Je me demandais quelle heure il pouvait être. . . . (I, 3)[37]

For a long time I used to go to bed early. Sometimes, when I had put my candle, my eyes would close so quickly that I had not even time to say to myself: 'I'm falling asleep.' And half an hour later the thought that I it was time to go to sleep would awaken me; I would make as if to put away the book which I imagined was still in my hands, and to blow out the light; I had gone on thinking, while I was asleep, about what I had just been reading, but these thoughts had taken a rather peculiar turn; it seemed to me that I myself was the immediate subject of my book: a church, a quartet, the rivalry between Francois I and Charles V. This impression would persist for some moments after I awoke; it did not offend my reason, but lay like scales upon my eyes and prevented them from registering the fact that the candle was no longer burning. Then it would begin to seeem unintelligible, as the thoughts of a former existence must be to a reincarnate spirit; the subject of my book would separate itself from me, leaving me free to apply myself to it or not; and at the same time my sight would return and I would be astonished to find myself in a state of darkness, pleasant and restful enough for my eyes, but even more, perhaps, for my mind, to which it appeared incomprehensible, without a cause, something dark indeed. I would ask myself what time it could be.

In this first passage of *A la recherche du temps perdu*, Proust sets up an opposition, sleep/awake, that serves to comment both on the nature of reality and on the way in which reality will be represented throughout the text. The narrator, who remains as yet unnamed, is portrayed in a strange state of consciousness: waking, he falls asleep so quickly, he does not realize that he is no longer awake. Sleeping, he tells himself that it is time to stop reading and go to sleep, and he awakens. Reality is topsy-turvy and completely unreliable—which state of consciousness is the true reality? Or is it that reality is real only when the consciousness is attuned to it, and whenever the consciousness is not attuned to it, that which was thought to be real fades into the background, takes on the character of unreality? Or is it that there are two separate but equal realities, the objective reality of waking life, and the fantastic, surreal reality of sleep, to which dreams, those distortions of waking reality, are perennial visitors?

The question of what constitutes the narrator's reality is then further complicated: the narrator is, between waking and sleeping, in the process of reading a book. In objective, or waking reality, the story with which the book is concerned remains a story contained within the book, as either a fictional account, if the subject of the book is imaginative, or an interpretation of a factual event, if it is historical. The narrator's waking reality while reading, then, is made up of what he perceives as the reality of the book, and in the background, what he perceives with less attention as the actual reality of his surroundings—he can imagine the appearance of the place in which he is reading, though he cannot see it, since his eyes are on his book. The reality of the book is also pierced by the intrusion into the narrator's consciousness of actual reality in the form of sounds or changes in light. But in waking life, while the narrator is reading, he is aware that he is reading, that the reality to which his consciousness is currently attuned is that of the book, and that there is another and actual reality surrounding him, of which he is still a part (though not fully present since his attention is concentrated on the book) in the character of someone who is reading a book.

In the above instance, however, the book that the narrator is reading serves as a bridge, the edge between two separate and seemingly different realities, that of waking and that of sleeping. In his waking reality, the narrator is aware that he is reading, and that his own reality is separate from that of the book. But in falling asleep unawares, it is as if another, a double of the unconscious narrator, rises up and continues to read while the actual narrator is sleeping. This double is a hidden reader, because he is a part of the actual narrator's dream life. But the difference between the reading of the actual narrator and the reading of the dream narrator is that in one, the story of the book remains separate from the narrator, within the book; in the other, the narrator himself becomes the subject of the book, and becomes also whatever that book is talking about: "une église, un quatuor, la rivalité de François I et de Charles Quint." But because the book is a part of actual reality, this alteration of its contents to include the narrator in its story fuses the two realities of waking and sleeping together in such a way that when the dream narrator moves to put the book down, the actual narrator comes immediately to the fore.

Here, an important link between the two realities is found: the concept of the imagination is silently interposed between them. The dream narrator moves to put down a book which the actual narrator *imagined* was yet in his hands. What constitutes actual reality for the dream narrator is thus an *imaginative* reality for the actual narrator. He, the actual narrator, is momentarily bewildered, long enough so that what had just happened in the reality of the dream narrator registers in his conscious mind an image whose seeming reality quickly fades far away, leaving him totally awake and suddenly alone in the darkness. His book becomes again just a book, a reality separate from his own.

Reality for the actual narrator suddenly becomes the darkness that surrounds him, which he describes as "une chose sans cause, incompréhensible, comme une chose vraiment obscure." His links with any other reality than his own, personal reality are thus understood to be formed through only two avenues: books, which either create a new world or re-create an actual one; and the imagination, which is not only linked to the actual narrator through the way in which he perceives the world around him, but is linked (and links the narrator as well) to the reality of books through the imaginations or imaginative perceptions of those who create them.

The narrator's question, "Je me demandais quelle heure il pouvait être . . ." raises another question about the nature of reality in the text, which further emphasizes the importance of the imagination within it by firmly establishing the place of chronological time, or objective reality, as secondary to the reality of the narrator's own perceptions. At this moment in the text, the narrator has no idea what time it is. He only knows that it is the middle of the night, that he is awake, and that the world seems very large and very dark. Without being able to locate himself within the framework of chronological time—that is, the time of seconds, minutes, hours, days, weeks, months, years—the narrator is, as it were, thrown into a sort of Heideggerian Being.[38] Thus, because time cannot be controlled by compartmentalizing it into an easily assimilated unit of existential possibility, by, for example, realizing that it is so many hours after midnight, and therefore so many hours before morning, that *this* morning is the day on which a particular event will take place, and that it will take place a week after another related event took place, the narrator finds himself within the enormity of Time, the time of eternity and of infinity. Within this idea of time, his consciousness becomes only a narrow and limited space of existence; and, without the markers represented by the chronological time created by man, that finite existence has nothing to cling to save its own imagination and its own perceptions. Through these, it creates another reality that is transposed on top of the reality that may be called actual or objective, as exemplified in the continuation of the passage quoted above:

> J'entendais le sifflement des trains qui, plus ou moins éloigné, comme le chant d'un oiseau dans une forêt, relevant les distances me décrivait l'étendue de la campagne déserte où le voyageur se

hâte vers la station prochaine; et le petit chemin qu'il suit va être gravé dans son souvenir par l'excitation qu'il doit à des lieux nouveaux, à des actes inaccoutumés, à la causerie récente et aux adieux sous la lampe étrangère qui le suivent encore dans le silence de la nuit, à la douceur prochaine du retour. (PI, 3–4)[39]

I could hear the whistling of trains, which, now nearer and now farther off, punctuating the distance like the note of a bird in a forest, showed me in perspective the deserted countryside through which a traveller is hurrying towards the nearby station; and the path he is taking will be engraved in his memory by the excitement induced by strange surroundings, by unaccustomed activities, by the conversation he has had and the farewells exchanged beneath an unfamiliar lamp, still echoing in his ears amid the silence of the night, by the imminent joy of going home.

In this passage, something that is a part of actual reality, the sound of the trains in the distance, creates an imaginative scene in the narrator's mind, and suddenly the reader is confronted with another reality, that of the traveler hurrying to the train station; though it is obvious that this scene takes place in the mind of the narrator, who is to say that it is not also taking place at the same moment in actual fact, exactly as the narrator has imagined it? The reader does not know, for the scene is described within the context of the narrator's reality, alone in his bed in the dark, and the reader can know only that which the narrator knows. And it is precisely this point that is made in this passage—the narrator, and anyone, for that matter, can only know what is immediately evident to his or her perception, or that which he or she can imagine.

From this vantage point, it may be understood that the role of the imagination in the *Recherche* becomes extremely important when it is applied to personal relationships, or to the impressions that one forms of others. This idea also touches on one of the most important themes of the *Recherche*—that of the impossibility of ever truly knowing another person. This theme is most commonly discussed in terms of the nature of jealousy in love, with regard to the relationship between Swann and Odette and/or that of the narrator and Albertine, but for the purposes of this argument, it applies to the theme of homosexuality. The fact that in the *Recherche*, homosexuality is a hidden characteristic of any human being who professes it, that it is never completely evident to the naked eye of the unsuspecting observer, makes use of the concept of imagination in a particular way. With the narrator's realization of the existence of homosexuality in Jupien and, more important, in the Baron de Charlus, it becomes obvious that the imagination plays a primary role not only in the way in which one conceives the identity of another human being, but the way in which the *sexual* identity of another human being is conceived:

Dès le début de cette scène une révolution, pour mes yeux dessil-
lés, s'était opérée en M. de Charlus, aussi complète, aussi immédi-
ate que s'il avait été touché par une baguette magique. Jusque-là,
parce que je n'avais pas compris, je n'avais pas vu. Le vice (on parle
ainsi pour la commodité du langage), le vice de chacun l'accompa-
gne à la façon de ce génie qui était invisible pour les hommes tant
qu'ils ignoraient sa présence. La bonté, la fourberie, le nom, les relations mondaines, ne se laissent pas découvrir, et on les porte
cachés. (PIII, 15)[40]

From the beginning of this scene my eyes had been opened by a
transformation in M. de Charlus as complete and as immediate as
if he had been touched by a magician's wand. Until then, because I
had not understood, I had not seen. Each man's vice (we use the
term for the sake of linguistic convenience) accompanies him
through life after the manner of the familiar genius who was invisible to men so long as they were unaware of his presence. Our
kindness, our treachery, our name, our social relations do not dis-
close themselves to the eye, we carry them hidden within us.

On viewing this scene between Jupien and M. de Charlus, the narrator suddenly becomes aware of many things concerning the Baron that had troubled
him without his being able to understand the reason why. His perception of
reality as it pertains to M. de Charlus has been drastically and irremediably
altered—he now sees, as it were, two individuals in the form of the Baron de
Charlus: the man, who is readily apparent to all, and the "woman" who is
hidden from view. This last is to be seen only by those who are like the Baron
himself, or by those whose deeper knowledge removes from their eyes the
veil placed over them by a culturally imposed concept of conventional sexuality, allowing them to see the Baron as he actually is. The movement of the
Baron in the *Recherche* is from that of a man who fits the culturally accepted
notion of masculine sexuality to his true reality, that of an effeminate homosexual leaning toward sadism—a movement that reveals the depth of the
fallacy of conventional notions of sexuality, and how much such notions
owe to the imagination.

But what is most important in terms of the narrator's new perception of
reality as it relates to the Baron de Charlus, however, is that the Baron also
forms the most exclusive part of what the narrator perceives as the magical
clan of the Guermantes. The very name of "Guermantes" causes him, in his
youthful ignorance, to imagine them as greater than they are, because he
thinks of them only as mythical images like that of "l'image de Geneviève de
Brabant, ancêtre de la famille de Guermantes, que la lanterne magique
promenait sur les rideaux de ma chambre ou faisait monter au plafond—

enfin toujours enveloppés du mystère des temps mérovingiens et baignant comme dans un coucher de soleil dans la lumière orangée qui émane de cette syllabe: 'antes.' ([t]he image of Geneviève de Brabant, ancestress of the Guermantes family, which the magic lantern sent wandering over the curtains of my room or flung aloft upon the ceiling—in short, invariably wrapped in the mystery of the Merovingian age and bathed, as in a sunset, in the amber light which glowed from the resounding syllable 'antes.') (PI, 169).[41] Having found, leveled in the existence of one being, the greatness of myth and the blot of vice, reveals to the narrator more clearly than ever before (and to the reader along with him), the possibility that people are not always as one may think they are, that initial perceptions of them are often distorted by one's imagination, and that the perceptions of the mind, or what one takes for reality, are often as unreliable as the reality of a dream.

    This realization of the role of the imagination in perceiving the external world becomes even more important when the relationship of the narrator to Proust, both as author and as Marcel *mondain*, is considered. As previously discussed, from very early in his life, Proust the man finds himself suffering the pangs of exclusion, for the many external causes already elaborated. But all of these causes are yet as one compared to the suffering of living the lie of homosexuality, which must be kept a painful and festering secret from all those around him whom he loves, and even from those from whom he would seek love, particularly in the form of friendship. This is the secret that follows Proust even into the social world, which is with him as he creates Marcel *mondain*, and which even the social acceptance won by Marcel *mondain* in the highest levels of society cannot erase. This situation has been fully elaborated above with regard to all but one question: How does Proust accomplish the one moment of authenticity in the *Recherche*, the moment when he can say "I" without seeming to, the moment when the double identity of his narrator becomes one?

    The transformation of the role of the imagination in the *Recherche* discussed above offers an initial approach to this problem. Proust the man perceives a social stigma with regard to himself. He desires to palliate the stigma by gaining social acceptance in the highest society of his world, the Faubourg St. Germain, the society which, subsisting on the mystique rendered by rigid exclusiveness, automatically excludes those not of their own, and would undeniably exclude one like himself—homosexual, half-Jewish and bourgeois. Such a desire must give to that which is desired a romantic aura of perfection that, if acceptance is attained, would wash away the shame of exclusion. But the emptiness of Marcel *mondain* is a testimony to the failure of this idea. Social acceptance for Proust is a sham because it is built on a lie, an image of himself that he projects for other people, the image of sexual conventionality. Behind the facade of Marcel *mondain*, Proust knows the truth about himself. Thus, he can see that the Marcel others think they know is in reality only a figment of their imaginations, someone who does not actually exist. This failure of Marcel *mondain* leads to the realization that *transcendance*, rather than social acceptance, is the key to the problem of authenticity in Proust's life and work, as Zenou elaborates:

> Exilé dans le monde factice de Sodome et Gomorrhe, prisonnier de son narcissisme, il ne s'ouvrira jamais à l'autre, au juif qui est en lui et qui est *sa promesse*. Refusant d'etre sauvé par Dieu, il se choisira lui-même comme Dieu, sanctifiant les mots qu'il écrira et n'acceptant qu'une rédemption: celle de l'art, ressuscitant les moments perdus et arrachant au flux du devenir les moments précieux, voués à l'oubli.[42]

> Exiled in the imaginary world of Sodom and Gomorrah, prisoner of his narcissism, he [Proust] will never open himself to the other, to the Jew who resides in him and who is his promise. Refusing to be saved by God, he will choose himself as God, sanctifying the words he will write and accepting one sole redemption: that of art, reviving lost moments and tearing from the flux of becoming precious moments, consecrated to oblivion. (My translation)

While Zenou here identifies that which Proust rejects in himself as a combination of his Jewishness and his homosexuality, it is, finally, the issue of homosexuality alone that becomes the primary representational problem of the *Recherche*. It is only through art that Proust can tell the truth, yet, in doing so, find true acceptance because art will permit him to transcend the society that would deny him for telling the truth. As such, the failure of Marcel *mondain* is clear, and from this failure, "Marcel," the fictional aspect of "Marcel"/Marcel,[43] and through him, the *Recherche*, are born.

In discussing "Marcel," however, it is necessary to return for a moment to Martin-Chauffier's essay regarding the relationships pertaining between Proust as man and author and his narrator. As already established in the prior discussion of this essay, the identity of "Marcel" is double, but it is not double in the manner described by Martin-Chauffier, as that of "Marcel" the narrator and that of "Marcel" the hero. The alter ego of "Marcel" the narrator is not "Marcel" the hero, but Proust himself, and this is evident not only in the fact that "Marcel" is a fictional creation of Marcel, the author, but through "Marcel's" strange relationship to homosexuality in the text, and through the fact that, while representing himself in the text as a heterosexual who is merely an uninvolved observer of sexual deviance, "Marcel" is himself sexually deviant, and is, thus, quite different from the image he projects. This becomes obvious when it is noted that "Marcel's" primary en-

counters with homosexuality in the *Recherche* are coupled with what becomes his own brand of sexual deviance: voyeurism.

However, what is important is not so much the fact that "Marcel" is a
voyeur, but what voyeurism offers to the novel in the way of form and structure—how, through it, the fictional "Marcel" relates to the author, Marcel.
Because "Marcel" is the only character in the text about whom it is never
asked if he is in reality who and what he purports to be, particularly in terms
of sexuality, an analysis of his voyeurism as an instance that he is not what
he says he is reasserts his status as an imaginative entity in whose heterosexual identity Marcel, the author has a stake, because that heterosexual identity is important to the structure of the novel. This is suggested in Joel
Rudinow's elaboration of the nature of voyeurism:

> The voyeur seeks a spectacle, the revelation of the object of his in-
> terest, that something or someone should be open to his inspection
> and contemplation; *but no reciprocal revelation or openness is con-
> ceded*, for the voyeur requires at the same time to remain hid-
> den. . . . this understanding [is] based on the voyeur's profoundly
> accurate perception that to treat something as voyeuristic spectacle
> is to ruin it for other, more fundamental human purposes: it cannot
> be touched, one cannot be touched by it . . . In general, one cannot
> enter into any relationship with it which is mutual, reciprocal, or
> symmetrical, in so far and so long as one treats it voyeuristically.[44]

In this way, voyeurism helps to establish the perspective needed to ensure
"Marcel's" personal distance from the subject of homosexuality in the text.
Not only is the attempt made to establish "Marcel" as a heterosexual, but he
is made also merely a spectator of physical instances of homosexuality. As
such, he can speak about the nature of homosexuality with the insight of a
homosexual, yet not risk the appellation, "homosexual." Or so it seems. The
fact that such distance is established through another form of sexual deviance
yet remains a clue to the reality of the double nature of "Marcel," that the
voice which speaks about homosexuality in the text is not that of "Marcel,"
but rather, that of Marcel, the author. This double nature becomes more clear
through an analysis of the way in which voyeurism functions in the text.

The hint of voyeurism in the *Recherche* begins very early on, with
"Marcel's" first sexual experiences alone in the room at the top of the house
in Combray:

> Hélas, c'était en vain que j'implorais le donjon de Roussainville,
> que je lui demandais de faire venir auprès de moi quelque enfant de
> son village, comme au seul confident que j'avais eu de mes premiers
> désirs, quand au haut de notre maison de Combray, dans le petit

cabinet sentant l'iris, je ne voyais que sa tour au milieu du carreau de la fenêtre entrouverte, pendant qu'avec les hésitations héroïques du voyageur qui entreprend une exploration ou du désespéré qui se suicide, défaillant, je me frayais en moi-même une route inconnue et que je croyais mortelle, jusqu'au moment où une trace naturelle comme celle d'un colimaçon s'ajoutait aux feuilles du cassis sauvage qui se penchaient jusqu'à moi. (PI, 156)[45]

Alas, it was in vain that I implored the castle-keep of Roussainville, that I begged it to send out to meet me some daughter of its village, appealing to it as to the sole confidant of my earliest desires when, at the top of our house in Combray, in the little room that smelt of orris-root, I could see nothing but its tower framed in the half-opened window as, with the heroic misgivings of a traveller setting out on a voyage of exploration or of a desperate wretch hesitating on the verge of self-destruction, faint with emotion, I explored, across the bounds of my own experience, an untrodden path which for all I knew was deadly—until the moment when a natural trail like that left by a snail smeared the leaves of the flowering currant that drooped around me.

Here, the young "Marcel" already shows the signs, which he continues to display throughout the novel, of an inability to create intimate personal relationships with others that leads to sexual disconnection and solitude. But what is interesting in this scene is that it takes place at the top of the house in a room where one would think the occupant would have total privacy, that the occupant would go to this room in order to *find* total privacy. Instead, what one finds is that the occupant is readily visible from the outside, by the castle-keep at Roussainville. In fact, the impression rendered by this scene is one of distance from the world, measured by the height of this room above the world of others, yet one of being part of the world as a spectator of all that goes on below. This instance of solitary, yet not completely private, sexual pleasure seems a variation of the sexual pleasure of homosexuals that "Marcel" describes later in the text, in which the fact that the homosexual has such preferences is openly visible, but may be seen only by those who have the capacity to see. "Marcel's" solitary pleasure in the room at the top of the house in Combray is openly visible, yet capable of being seen only by the castle-keep at Roussainville, whose tower places him on a level with that room.

This scene is, however, dominated by a window, and by all that a window represents: the possiblity of seeing and being seen, the division between inside and outside, the "bridge" and the "frontier" that separates "self" from "other," yet also serves to unite the two in a decidedly unorthodox way. The possibility of "Marcel's" being seen through the window, and his knowledge that it is possible to be seen, introduce a new dimension into the sexuality of "Marcel" that suggests a hidden confession of homosexuality on the part of the *Recherche*'s narrator in quite another, and far more complicated, form than that undertaken by Gide, whose "I" narrator was avowedly autobiographical. The confession of "Marcel" in this instance would seem rather a symbolic confession, the kind of confession that is understood as part of a guilty consciousness, like that experimented with by Dostoevsky in *Crime and Punishment.* In that text, the desire to confess drives the novel's hero, Raskolnikov, to take fantastic risks with the police concerning his guilty secret. He plays a kind of cat-and-mouse game with the authorities, sometimes even daring them to accuse him, plagued always by the question to confess or not to confess. "Marcel's" confession is not entirely of this nature, being nonverbal, but in his actions, in his voyeurism, in the significance of seeing and being seen in the *Recherche* and his own sexual deviance, the urge to confess may yet be discerned. This urge also suggests that "Marcel's" confession is undertaken not by "Marcel," the fictional narrator of the *Recherche*, but by Marcel, its author, expressing himself as a hidden, rather than an autobiographical, "I." To understand how this happens, however, it is necessary to burrow deeper into the nature of voyeurism in the text and what it represents.

Actual voyeurism on the part of the narrator begins in the *Recherche* with "Marcel's" viewing of the scene of sadism between Mlle Vinteuil and her friend in Mlle Vinteuil's home in Montjouvain:

> Étant allé jusqu'à la mare de Montjouvain où j'aimais revoir les reflets du toit de tuile, je m'étais étendu à l'ombre et endormi dans les buissons du talus qui domine la maison . . . Il faisait presque nuit quand je m'éveillai, je voulus me lever, mais je vis Mlle Vinteuil . . . qui probablement venait de rentrer, en face de moi, à quelques centimètres de moi, dans cette chambre où son père avait reçu le mien et dont elle avait fait son petit salon à elle. La fenêtre était entrouverte, la lampe était allumée, je voyais tous ses mouvements sans qu'elle me vit, mais en m'en allant j'aurais fait craquer les buissons, elle m'aurait entendu et elle aurait pu croire que je m'étais caché là pour l'épier. . . . Dans l'échancrure de son corsage de crêpe Mlle Vinteuil sentit que son amie piquait un baiser, elle poussa un petit cri, s'échappa, et elles se poursuivirent en sautant, faisant voleter leurs larges manches comme des ailes et gloussant et piaillant comme des oiseaux amoureux. Puis Mlle Vinteuil finit par tomber sur le canapé, recouverte par le corps de son amie. . . . (PI, 157–60)[46]

Having gone as far as the Montjouvain pond, where I enjoyed seeing again the reflection of the tiled roof of the hut, I had lain down
in the shade and fallen asleep among the bushes on the steep slope
overlooking the house . . . It was almost dark when I awoke, and I
was about to get up and go away, but I saw Mlle Vinteuil . . . who
had probably just come in, standing in front of me, and only a few
feet away, in that room in which her father had entertained mine,
and which she had now made into a little sitting-room for herself.
The window was partly open; the lamp was lighted; I could watch
her every movement without her being able to see me; but if I had
moved away I would have made a rustling sound among the bushes,
she would have heard me, and she might have thought that I had
been hiding there in order to spy upon her. . . . In the V-shaped
opening of her crepe bodice Mlle Vinteuil felt the sting of her
friend's sudden kiss; she gave a little scream and broke away; and
then they began to chase one another about the room, scrambling
over the furniture, their wide sleeves fluttering like wings, clucking
and squealing like a pair of amorous fowls. At last Mlle Vinteuil collapsed exhausted on the sofa, with her friend on top of her.

Here, "Marcel" is protrayed alone in a darkness that is not as complete as
the darkness of dead night, but which is yet dark enough so that he cannot
be seen from the inside. This time he is outside, rather than at home in his
bed. In the scene with which the *Recherche* opens, the darkness in which the
narrator is portrayed is, while overwhelming to him in its obscurity, secure
in that he knows it conceals the familiarity of his daily environment. He is
safe in his room, in the home of his parents, and the window to the outside
is in his mind, in his imagined scene of the traveler hurrying to the train station. The comfortable familiarity of his room implies the security of beginnings and of innocence, the protected cocoon of childhood, when the world
outside seems an untamable and uncontrollable yet distant force.

In the scene above, however, "Marcel," having journeyed away from his
parents (as in the natural movement of life), finds himself outside and some
distance away from the familiar surroundings of his home, and wakes to find
before him a real window through which a scene that does not need to be
imagined takes place. The division between "self" and "other" which was
only hinted at in the opening passage of the *Recherche* is here made concrete.
"Marcel," the innocent child, through his fear of being apprehended in the
act of trying to move away, becomes now the viewer of a scene far from innocent in its nature. It is important to note here, however, that his viewing
of this scene is not entirely voluntary. There is no conscious action involved
on the part of "Marcel," beyond his desire not to be taken for someone who

is trying to spy through Mlle Vinteuil's window. But the truth of the matter is that he does, in fact, watch, and this watching, or seeing from the outside, is represented as happening to "Marcel" immediately after his solitary pleasures in the room at the top of the house in Combray are related, the room in which it is he who can be seen from the outside. This introduces a relationship between seeing and being seen which, on a symbolic level, implies that only in the intimacy of his own solitude can "Marcel" be vulnerable and open to others, that is, "seen," whereas away from that solitude, in the outside world, he must remain safely concealed, that is, "not seen."

As he introduces the scene at Montjouvain, "Marcel" speaks of it as "une impression" an impression (my translation) (PI, 157)[47] whose full import would not become clear to him until much later. More important, however, is what "Marcel" does not say. As his first experience with sexual activity other than that in which he has engaged by himself, the scene through the window at Montjouvain must needs have a concerted effect on the young "Marcel." And it is this effect that is left out of the novel: what "Marcel" does not explore is the question of the impact of this scene on *himself*, in terms of his own sexuality, in terms of what he afterward thinks of sexuality in general and the sexuality of women in particular. The scene at Montjouvain is the only scene in which the activities of the votaries of Gomorrhe are made explicit. As a result, "Marcel" carries this scene in his imagination, so that much later, when he is involved in his relationship with Albertine, it is his *imagination* about what she could be doing with other women when she is away from him that plagues him and forces him to monitor her every move. Although his suspicions as to Albertine's true nature are mentioned long before (PII, 183),[48] the scene at Montjouvain is revived in his memory by her admission of having been friends with Mlle Vinteuil, and it is the thought of this that pushes him to take her prisoner in order to prevent her from further engaging in the activities in which he imagines she has already, and often, taken part:

> Vous vous rappelez que je vous ai parlé d'une amie plus âgée que moi qui m'a servi de mère, de soeur, avec qui j'ai passé à Trieste mes meilleures années . . . cette amie . . . est justement la meilleure amie de la fille de ce Vinteuil, et je connais presque autant la fille de Vinteuil. . . . A ces mots prononcés comme nous entrions en gare de Parville, si loin de Combray et de Montjouvain, si longtemps après la mort de Vinteuil, une image tenue en réserve pendant tant d'années que, même si j'avais pu deviner en l'emmagasinant jadis qu'elle avait un pouvoir nocif, j'eusse cru qu'à la longue elle l'avait entièrement perdu; conservée vivante au fond de moi . . . pour mon supplice, pour mon châtiment peut-être, qui sait? d'avoir laissé

mourir ma grand-mère; surgissant tout à coup du fond de la nuit où elle semblait à jamais ensevelie et frappant comme un Vengeur afin d'inaugurer pour moi une vie terrible, méritée et nouvelle, peut-être aussi pour faire éclater à mes yeux les funestes con-séquences que les actes mauvais engendrent indéfiniment, non pas seulement pour ceux qui les ont commis, mais pour ceux qui n'ont fait, qui n'ont cru, que contempler un spectacle curieux et diver-tissant, comme moi, hélas! en cette fin de journée lointaine à Montjouvain, caché derrière un buisson, ou (quand j'avais com-plaisamment écouté le récit des amours de Swann) j'avais dan-gereusement laissé s'élargir en moi la voie funeste et destinée à être douloureuse du Savoir. (PIII, 499–500)[49]

You remember my telling you about a friend, older than me, who had been a mother, a sister to me, with whom I spent the happiest years of my life, at Trieste . . . this friend . . . is the best friend of your Vinteuil's daughter, and I know Vinteuil's daughter almost as well as I know her . . .' At the sound of these words, uttered as we were entering the station of Parville, so far from Combray and Montjouvain, so long after the death of Vinteuil, an image stirred in my heart, an image which I had kept in reserve for so many years that even if I had been able to guess, when I stored it up long ago, that it had a noxious power, I should have supposed that in the course of time it had entirely lost it; preserved alive in the depths of my being . . . as a punishment, as a retribution (who knows?) for my having allowed my grandmother to die; perhaps rising up sud-denly from the dark depths in which it seemed forever buried, and striking like an Avenger, in order to inaugurate for me a new and terrible and only too well-merited existence, perhaps also to make dazzlingly clear to my eyes the fatal consequences which evil ac-tions eternally engender, not only for those who have committed them but for those who have done no more, or thought that they were doing no more, than look on at a curious and entertaining spectacle, as I, alas, had done on that afternoon long ago at Mon-tjouvain, concealed behind a bush where (as when I had compla-cently listened to the account of Swann's love affairs) I had perilously allowed to open up within me the fatal and inevitably painful road of Knowledge.

A review of this passage reveals several important revelations that have a bearing on the sexuality of "Marcel," and a profound effect on the way in which he later relates to women. First, the darkness, or as "Marcel" terms it, "la nuit," is no longer represented as outside himself, as it is in the opening passage of the *Recherche*. Soon after, in the scene in which he looks through the window at Montjouvain, "Marcel," outside of the protection of his childhood world, that is, the world of innocence and joy, finds himself in an environment where night is represented as only just falling. In the above scene, the darkness of night is now to be found inside him. This darkness is also much changed in character, no longer "incomprehensible" as in the beginning of the *Recherche*, nor something that is approaching, as in the scene at Montjouvain, but something heavy and opaque, which has served to hide within its heavy mass the evil which was a part of the actions of Mlle Vinteuil and her friend, and taking on, in so doing, a character of its own. What is important, however, is not simply that this darkness represents the sense of evil that is now awakened in "Marcel." The clue to the changed quality of this darkness may be found in "Marcel's" attempt to offer a reason for why this image would suddenly rise up within him: "pour mon supplice, pour mon châtiment peut-être, qui sait? d'avoir laissé mourir ma grand-mère . . ." "Marcel" thus perceives this darkness as being perhaps a punishment for his behavior toward his grandmother and her death, and it is in this revelation that the true nature of the darkness he perceives deep within himself is discovered. Though he did not mean to do it, "Marcel" participated in the "evil" of homosexuality by watching Mlle Vinteuil and her friend. As such, he destroyed, through his passive participation in the homosexual pleasure of the two young women, the "innocence" of partaking in a solitary pleasure while yearning for a woman (which implies a desire for heterosexual pleasure) in the room at the top of his parents' home in Combray. The character of the darkness in "Marcel" is thus that of *guilt*, rather than evil, since he perceives the remembered image of Mlle Vinteuil and her friend as something that wells up within him in order to punish him for having "laissé mourir ma grand-mère." The importance of this phrase is that "Marcel," through it, connects the guilt of homosexuality with the idea of having done wrong to his family. The significance of such a connection is that it subtly implies an authorial confession of guilt with regard to homosexuality that is safely hidden where it cannot be easily detected—in a reference to the homosexuality of Albertine.

As such, the outline of the narrator as "Marcel"/Marcel is dimly perceived, but is not fully apprehensible without going even deeper into the above passage. What does the mystery of Gomorrhe say about the misery of Sodom? If one takes note of the fact that the narrator perceives his having listened to the sad tale of the love between Swann and Odette as having unwittingly committed the same error as that which he committed at Montjouvain, it is immediately understood that, in the narrator's mind, this too is a form of voyeurism, though auditory, rather than visual. It becomes, however, visual in the narrator's attempt to imagine the sufferings of Swann, to "essayé de me mettre à la place de celui-ci" to try to put myself in his place (my translation). (PIII, 228).[50] Thus, through the narrator's remorse about his past actions (which can be linked to a sexual deviance of his own), and the relation of these actions to the theme of lesbianism in the novel, the mystery of Gomorrhe may be understood as integral to an understanding of the *Recherche*'s version of masculine homosexuality. Lesbianism, as the inverse of masculine homosexuality, serves as the repository of all of the feelings of remorse, insecurity, jealousy, isolation, uncertainty, fear, and suffering that, as described earlier in the novel, accompany the closeted masculine homosexual who actively seeks love. It is the suspicion that Albertine may be engaging in lesbian encounters without the narrator's knowledge that causes him to suffer as he does, not the intensity of his love for her.

In this way, the issue of homosexuality in, and its influence on, one of the two primary love relationships in the *Recherche* is highlighted. Yet it is highlighted in a discussion of Gomorrhe for two reasons—and the nature of these reasons again suggests a duplicity in "Marcel" that cannot be explained through a discussion of "Marcel" alone. The first is that if all of the aforementioned emotions that are centered around the issue of homosexuality are dealt with in a secondary but thematically related aspect of the novel, such as that of lesbianism, the narrator is then free to discuss masculine homosexuality with the distance required to portray it in objective detail. Such a position enables the narrator to address the subject without the tone of remorse that guilt would lend. But this, however, is once more a question of structure and form. Is this really a subject that would concern "Marcel," the narrator? Or is it rather the concern of Marcel, the author as narrator, the text's hidden "I"—who, camouflaged by "Marcel," may quite safely express feelings of remorse about homosexuality that would be dangerously compromising anywhere other than when describing "Marcel's" relationship with Albertine?

The second reason opens an avenue by which this question may be further explored. This reason is found in the narrator's allusion to having listened to the story of the love affair between Swann and Odette. Perceiving this action as possessing an evil that had been for him, in the innocence of childhood, like the apple in the Garden of Eden (giving him forbidden knowledge), "Marcel's" recollection of this affair serves to exacerbate his insecurity with regard to Albertine, which the scene at Montjouvain helped to solidify:

Parfois même, sans que j'eusse revu Albertine, sans que personne m'eût parlé d'elle, je retrouvais dans ma mémoire une pose d'Albertine auprès de Gisèle et qui m'avait paru innocente alors; elle suffisait maintenant pour détruire le calme que j'avais pu retrouver, je n'avais même plus besoin d'aller respirer au-dehors des germes dangereux, je m'étais . . . intoxiqué moi-même. Je pensais alors à tout ce que j'avais appris de l'amour de Swann pour Odette, de la façon dont Swann avait été joué toute sa vie. Au fond si je veux y penser l'hypothèse qui me fit peu à peu construire tout le caractère d'Albertine et interpréter douloureusement chaque moment d'une vie que je ne pouvais pas contrôler tout entière, ce fut le souvenir, l'idée fixe du caractère de Mme Swann, tel qu'on m'avait raconté qu'il était. Ces récits contribuèrent à faire que . . . mon imagination faisait le jeu de supposer qu'Albertine aurait pu, au lieu d'être une jeune fille bonne, avoir la même immoralité, la meme faculté de tromperie qu'une ancienne grue. (PIII, 199–200)[51]

Sometimes even without my having seen Albertine, without anyone having spoken to me about her, I would suddenly call to mind some memory of her with Gisele in a posture which had seemed to me innocent at the time but was enough now to destroy the peace of mind that I had managed to recover; I had no longer any need to go and breathe dangerous germs outside—I had . . . supplied my own toxin. I thought then of all that I had been told about Swann's love for Odette, of the way in which Swann had been tricked all his life. Indeed, when I come to think of it, the hypothesis that made me gradually build up the whole of Albertine's character and give a painful interpretation to every moment of a life that I could not control in its entirety, was the memory, the rooted idea of Mme Swann's character, as it had been described to me. These accounts contributed towards the fact that . . . my imagination played with the idea that Albertine might, instead of being the good girl that she was, have had the same immorality, the same capacity for deceit as a former prostitute.

Though the narrator questions the validity of his comparison between Albertine and Odette due to differences in their backgrounds (PIII, 226–28),[52] the fact that he compares them at all raises an interesting issue with regard to the present discussion. It is, as such, revealed that the structure of the *Recherche* is built on the relation between two intensely painful love relationships, neither of which are gratifying to the participants, both of which end in emptiness and disillusionment. Both relationships are created on the basis of an imagined idea with which the perpetrator falls in love, rather than the person about whom the idea is conceived. Swann falls in love with Odette because she reminds him of Botticelli's *Zipporah* (PI, 220).[53] The narrator of the *Recherche* falls in love with Albertine because she, in her elusiveness (PIII, 193)[54] creates the empty space into which his imagination could fall, sparked by Professor Cottard's suggestions that a sexual liaison between Albertine and Andrée could exist (PIII, 193),[55] and fed by the memory of what he had heard concerning the love life of Swann:

> Sans doute j'avais été depuis longtemps, par la puissance qu'exerçait sur mon imagination et ma faculté d'être ému l'exemple de Swann, préparé à croire vrai ce que je craignais au lieu de ce que j'aurais souhaité. (PIII, 228)[56]

> Certainly, I had been for a long time by the power exercised by my imagination and my ability to be touched by the example of Swann, prepared to believe what I feared rather than what I would have wished. (My translation)

It is from this time, when the narrator's imagination takes over with regard to his relationship with Albertine, when she no longer seems the girl he knew because she has been distorted by his imagination (PIII, 198),[57] that he begins to fancy himself in love with her. But the fact that the narrator identifies so strongly with Swann and the problems of his love life, as evidenced by the above quotation, lead yet again to the possibility that the concerns addressed are not only those of "Marcel," but of some greater force underlying "Marcel's" actions and motivations; and, through this concern, a clear linkage between lesbianism in the *Recherche* and the affair of Swann and Odette may be discerned. As such, a brief analysis of the way in which several objective aspects of this affair relate to the narrator is illuminating.

It must first be remembered that Swann, as a Jew who moves in the society of the Faubourg–St. Germain, has accomplished the singular feat of obtaining social acceptance in spite of the possession of a certain quality—Jewishness—that would ordinarily gain him rejection in that social world. As such, he represents the apogee of desire in the text, as holder of the most sought-after social position to be attained. He is thus part of the romantic reality that subjective desire imagines in the text, since almost everyone is trying to move into the social circles that are one or more levels above them. But the imagination, which plays such a crucial role in the *Recherche* because it is the reason why snobbism, the novel's primary motivating force, can exist as such, is also Swann's downfall. It is because of his imagination that he falls in love with Odette, and as a result of this liaison, begins the long descent down the social mountain slope that he had climbed, at the top of which was the Faubourg–St. Germain. Thus, the romantic reality created in the *Recherche* by the imagination is understood to be tarnished, so that three realities may be seen to operate simultaneously in the text: the actual reality of dinners and parties and conversation, an imagined reality of being part of the dinners and parties and conversation in the circles from which one is excluded, and the reality of the imagined reality, which is discovered to be far uglier than one could ever have imagined. For Swann, the actual reality of the imagined reality is that he is married to Odette yet no longer loves her, so that the social stigma of having married a former prostitute is not even mitigated for him by the joys of connubial bliss.

As such, Swann lives a double life—one in which he attempts to reconstruct a social world on the level of his wife, and the other, his old social life, in which he makes an appearance from time to time, alone. This double life has been referred to earlier in this chapter as a "paradigm of acceptance-exclusion." The fact that the relationship between Swann and Odette may be viewed as a paradigm becomes quite interesting in view of its thematic connection, through lesbianism, to the idea of homosexuality. On the one hand, through the comparisons that are made between Albertine and Odette, the relationship of Swann and Odette is linked to lesbianism. On the other, through comparisons that are made between the narrator and Swann, it is linked to masculine homosexuality. When viewed in this way, the marriage between Swann and Odette reveals all that the narrator "Marcel" does not say with regard to masculine homosexuality, lending an entirely new perspective to any reading of the first part of *Sodome et Gomorrhe* (PIII, 1–33).[58] What does this "paradigm of acceptance-exclusion" imply other than the success of Marcel *mondain* (Swann) and the shame of hidden homosexuality (Odette), ineradicable because of necessity forever concealed? The fact that Swann and Odette are married yet socially separate is representative of the existential division required in any individual who feels the necessity to hide a homosexual nature. Such division is to be found everywhere in the *Recherche*, as Poulet elaborates:

> In Proust . . . everything that lives, lives closed up in itself, and at the same time excluded from everything that is not itself. And this rigorous inclusion-exclusion, which splits existence in two, like a wall of which it is impossible to perceive at one and the same time the internal face and the external face, has for a result that on the one hand each being is exterior to all others, and nevertheless is enclosed within itself, without the possibility of communicating with the outside.[59]

But there is one moment in the *Recherche* where this splitting of existence, this dichotomy between internal and external, does not take place. In the first section of *Sodome et Gomorrhe*, the narrator, "Marcel," is portrayed as watching the Duchesse de Guermantes's strange plant from the open ground-floor window (PIII, 3).[60] Before this window, he is again made the involuntary witness to a scene of sexual deviation such as that at Montjouvain, yet this time there are a number of important differences. The first is that the scene that now takes place before "Marcel's" eyes is one of masculine homosexuality, rather than lesbianism. It is initiated outside, in broad daylight, while "Marcel" remains hidden, watching, in the shadow of his home. The most important difference, however, is in "Marcel's" subsequent actions. From the moment the Baron de Charlus, who has come at an unusual hour to call on Mme de Villeparisis, begins his trek away from the home of that lady, "Marcel" is actively engaged in the voyeuristic activity of viewing him with the conscious awareness that it is without the other's knowledge. Although the scene is not yet explicitly sexual, "Marcel's" action is voyeuristic in that he is aware that the Baron would not like to be watched, and is aware also that he is thus invading the Baron's privacy. This time, though the narrator makes as if to move, as in the scene at Montjouvain, he does not want to go *away*; he is interested in further concealing himself, that he may continue to watch the Baron unperceived: "J'allais me déranger de nouveau pour qui'il ne pût m'apercevoir; je n'en eus ni le temps, ni le besoin" I was going to move again so that he would not be able to see me; I had neither the time nor the need of it. (My translation) (PIII, 6).[61] His statement "je n'en eus . . . le temps" implies that though he wants to give the impression that his viewing of the subsequent scene is again involuntary, this impression is overpowered by his prior motivation, which was to watch the Baron alone.

Both the above scene and the scene at Montjouvain take place in close proximity to wherever the narrator happens to be at that moment. However, at this point, "Marcel" does something unprecedented and aggressive, something that, when viewed in terms of the above discussion, leaves no room for doubt regarding the nature of his double identity as consisting of both fictional and authorial aspects. After it becomes clear that the encounter between the Baron de Charlus and Jupien is of a homosexual nature, the two men enter Jupien's shop and the narrator is suddenly excluded (PIII, 9).[62] Unable to follow their conversation further, "Marcel" finds himself "fort ennuyé," (greatly annoyed) (PIII, 9)[63] and makes a *conscious decision* to spy on them. He remembers a place from which he can be privy to everything that takes place in Jupien's shop, to explain which I will quote a rather long passage from the text:

J'avisai alors la boutique à louer séparée seulement de celle de Jupien par une cloison extrêmement mince. Je n'avais pour m'y rendre qu'à remonter à notre appartement, aller à la cuisine, descendre l'escalier de service jusqu'aux caves, les suivre intérieurement pendant toute la largeur de la cour, et arrivé à l'endroit du sous-sol . . . monter les quelques marches qui accédaient à l'intérieur de la boutique. Ainsi toute ma route se ferait a couvert, je ne serais vu de personne. C'était le moyen le plus prudent. Ce ne fut pas celui que j'adoptai, mais longeant les murs, je contournai à l'air libre la cour en tâchant de ne pas être vu. Si je ne le fus pas, je pense que je le dois plus au hasard qu'à ma sagesse. Et au fait que j'aie pris un parti si imprudent, quand le cheminement dans la cave était si sûr, je vois trois raisons possibles, a supposer qu'il y en ait une. Mon impatience d'abord. Puis peut-être un obscur ressouvenir de la scène de Montjouvain, caché devant la fenêtre de Mlle Vinteuil. . . . Enfin j'ose à peine . . . avouer le troisième raison, qui fut, je crois bien, inconsciemment déterminante. Depuis que pour suivre . . . les principes militaires de Saint-Loup, j'avais suivi avec grand détail la guerre des Boers, j'avais été conduit à relire d'anciens récits d'explorations, de voyages. . . . Pensant aux Boers qui, ayant en face d'eux des armées anglaises, ne craignaient pas de s'exposer au moment où il fallait traverser, avant de retrouver un fourré, des parties de rase campagne: "Il ferait beau voir, pensai-je, que je fusse plus pusillanime, quand le théatre d'opérations est simplement notre propre cour, et quand, moi qui viens d'avoir plusieurs duels sans aucune crainte, à cause de l'affaire Dreyfus, le seul fer que j'aie à redouter est celui du regard des voisins qui ont autre chose à faire qu'à regarder dans la cour. (PIII, 9–10)[64]

I then bethought myself of the vacant shop, separated from Jupien's only by an extremely thin partition. In order to get to it, I had merely to go up to our flat, pass through the kitchen, go down by the service stairs to the cellars, make my way through them across the breadth of the courtyard above, and on arriving at the place in the basement . . . climb the flight of steps which led to the interior of the shop. Thus the whole of my journey would be made under cover, and I should not be seen by anyone. This was the most prudent method. It was not the one that I adopted; instead, keeping close to the walls, I edged my way round the courtyard in the open, trying not to let myself be seen. If I was not, I owe it more, I am sure, to chance than to my own sagacity. And for the fact that I took so imprudent a course, when the way through the cellar was so safe, I can see three possible reasons, assuming that I had any reason at all. First of all, my impatience. Secondly, perhaps, a dim memory of the scene at Montjouvain, when I crouched concealed outside Mlle Vinteuil's window. . . . I hardly dare confess to the third and final reason, but I suspect that it was unconsciously decisive. Ever since, in order to follow . . . the military principles enunciated by Saint-Loup, I had been following in close detail the course of the Boer War, I had been led from that to re-read old accounts of travel and exploration. . . . Thinking of the Boers who, with British armies facing them, were not afraid to expose them-

selves at the moment when they had to cross a tract of open country in order to reach cover, "It would be a fine thing," I thought to
myself, "if I were to show less courage when the theatre of operations is simply our own courtyard, and when the only steel that I,
who fought more than one duel fearlessly at the time of the Dreyfus case, have to fear is that of the eyes of the neighbours who have
other things to do besides looking into the courtyard.

It is interesting to note that in this passage "Marcel," on making the decision
to spy on the Baron and Jupien, immediately realizes that there are two ways
to go about positioning himself so that he may do so. After describing a
fairly complicated way of getting to the vacant shop next to that of Jupien's
by traversing the house, he decides to do so by "longeant les murs," or edging along the walls outside. At this moment in the text, reading the edge, or
reading beyond conventional articulations of textual significance to discover
the silent and/or silenced cultural locations deep within, is given physical
form. "Marcel" edging along the walls outside, fully exposed in his guilty
occupation, *is* the edge beyond which, through which, the text's silent cultural significations are apprehended. In this scene, the issue of seeing and
being seen applies not only to what "Marcel" is about to do in watching the
two homosexuals, but to "Marcel" himself, and what he himself is actually
doing. "Marcel," on his way to spy on the Baron and Jupien, fears that others will see him as he attempts to do so. But why should "Marcel" fear the
eyes of others when he is in his own courtyard? If it is true that the neighbors
"ont autre chose à faire qu'a regarder dans la cour," why would they waste
time watching someone walking in his own courtyard? Even if any of the
neighbors had seen what had taken place between Jupien and M. de Charlus, how would they connect "Marcel's" being in the courtyard to his desire
to continue spying on the two men? As such, "Marcel" makes evident his
own fear of being seen, and the fact that this fear is connected to an act of
conscious voyeurism with regard to a scene of homosexuality lays open the
presence of a frightened and nervous Marcel, a hidden "I" camouflaged by
the fictional narrator, "Marcel."

This moment, in which "Marcel" risks being seen by all, creates the
possibility for the voice of "Marcel" to collapse into the voice of Marcel, so
that fictional and authorial narrator may, for a brief instant, seem one and
the same. One clue to this occurrence is the fact that "Marcel" gives reasons
for his actions, citing his own impatience and also the scene at Montjouvain.
But by far the most important reason is the third, which he is almost afraid
to confess. First, his perception of this final reason *as a confession* colors the
whole episode in a way that points subtly, yet undeniably, to the hidden and
crouching author, Marcel, concealed behind the "cloison" of "Marcel."

Why should he represent this reason for his actions in particular as a confession? Placing in military terms his desire to follow the Baron and Jupien in an unconcealed, rather than concealed, manner, implies that the risk he is taking in doing so is greater *in his imagination* than it is in reality. Emphasizing this risk, therefore, dramatizes not only the idea of confession, but the importance of the action as well. Furthermore, the fact that "Marcel" compares the eyes of his neighbors to the steel of a weapon in a duel implies that he views public knowledge of his actions as being the same sort of threat to his existence as a sword in the hands of an opponent. He then describes being seen by these neighbors in such a way that he minimizes the importance of their ability to see him. All of these things reveal that within the narrator, who may now be understood to be constituted as "Marcel"/Marcel, the partition, or edge, between author and fictional narrator has been, though cautiously, removed, and the two voices have collapsed into one.

A few pages later, the actual confession comes. It is a very long passage, too long to be quoted here—pages 16–19 in Part III of the French version, and pages 638–40 in Volume II of the English version. But what is distinctive about this passage, and of the utmost importance with regard to the present discussion, is that it is composed of one single sentence. In this one sentence, however, is expressed all of the fear, self-hatred, self-loathing, shame, and alienation engendered for the narrator by the fact of homosexuality—all of the violent emotions concerning masculine homosexuality that the reader will not find expressed with such intensity at any other point in the entire text. That this is done in one long sentence represents not only the force of these emotions, but the desperation caused by the necessity to withhold them from public view. As such, their single-sentence form lends them an intensity that indicates, with clear certainty, that the collapse of the narrator "Marcel"/Marcel into one voice reveals the existence of a hidden "I" that has not heretofore made its appearance in such sure terms.

The fact that in this passage, the reader is abruptly thrown into another, and previously unsuspected, world also points to the existence of this hidden "I". This is quickly understood in that the tone of the text suddenly changes from that of an ironic description of M. de Charlus to that of a coldly impassioned exposé of reality from the homosexual point of view. Who is speaking here? Can it really be "Marcel," the fictional narrator, who to this point has had, supposedly, only two experiences with homosexuality? How does he know all that this voice seems to know? That "Marcel," an avowed heterosexual, having been privy to only two incidents of homosexuality in which he did not even physically participate, could understand the homosexual's plight so well is unlikely. In this case, the reader's suspension of disbelief is willing only if "Marcel" makes clear that this is how he *imagines* life must be for the homosexual.

But why is the imagination, which is so important at all other moments in the *Recherche*, suddenly left out here? With "Marcel's" revelation concerning M. de Charlus, that he "appartenait à la race de ces êtres moins contradictoires qu'ils n'en ont l'air, dont l'idéal est viril, justement parce que leur tempérament est féminin, et qui sont dans la vie pareils, en apparence seulement, aux autres hommes" belonged to that race of beings, less paradoxical than they appear, whose ideal is manly precisely because their temperament is feminine, and who in ordinary life resemble other men in appearance only (PIII, 16),[65] the operations of the imagination to this point in the text are suddenly thrown into a tailspin. "Marcel" sees that the Baron is not only not what "Marcel" thought he was—he is not even what he himself purports to be. It is as if reality has been caught with its clothes off: the figurative clothes of the imagination. All conventional reality in the *Recherche* is thus shown to be imaginative, and all imaginative reality, as such, a farce. Yet though reality is constantly put into question throughout the majority of the novel, it is not questioned here. In this one-sentence passage of nearly two pages, reality is neither the world of conventional perception, nor that created by the romantic imagining of subjective desire. It is instead the reality of transcendence, the truth in which both conventional and imagined worlds dissolve. In the absence of the imaginative link, one can no longer look to "Marcel" as the sole origin of this passage, since he, too, is only a product of the imagination. One must look, rather, to another source for its generation, and that source can only be Marcel, the author as narrator, in the process of revealing the hidden "I."

In the chapter to follow, these same issues, of silence and voice, cultural politics and cultural spaces, and the edge beyond which cultural silences may be read to reveal silenced cultural voices, are taken up once again—this time in the analysis of the institutionalization of James Joyce's work both in the university and within Joyce studies, the institutionalization in the university of Joyce studies itself, and the impact of these on our understanding of the role of Joyce's work in the exploration of new conceptions of cultural possibility in literary modernism and modernity here begun.

CHAPTER 4

Stephen Dedalus and the "Swoon of Sin"

A YOUNG SCHOLAR "JOYCED," OR THE CULTURAL POLITICS OF INSTITUTIONALIZATION

It could be viewed by some as rather precious that a critical argument purporting to interpret an aspect of *A Portrait of the Artist as a Young Man* should begin with a discussion of the scholar-critic in the act of doing so, as if describing a self-reflexive similarity between the activity of interpretation and the processes of the novel itself. After all, if the text is about Stephen Dedalus, one might ask, Why not get on with it?

The answer to this question has to do with one's relationship to Joyce, the writer. For those who come to the subject with some knowledge not only of the text in question, but of Joyce's work in general and of the critical terrain in which it is ensconced, such a beginning is not something at which one would immediately look askance. In fact, to the more discerning of these, a queer dichotomy between the title and the subtitle of the present chapter may even be recognized. This dichotomy, one in which the word "institutionalization" seems to stand out like the neon sign of your favorite hotel restaurant, is in fact the representation in miniature of the textual dichotomy experienced by the contemporary scholar-critic on the verge or in the act of writing about Joyce. This is because, as the critical endeavor with regard to Joyce now stands, "writing about Joyce" is not just to write about Joyce himself or any one or all of his texts, but to write about "writing about Joyce." The extant text is an obvious example of this activity, since it has declared itself as such, but there are other aspects of writing about "writing about Joyce" that are not so self-evident as that.

What is at issue for the contemporary critic whose interest in Joyce leads him or her toward the task of exploring and interpreting the fascinating and prismatic subtlety of Joyce's prose is not just the confrontation with the work of genius itself, as it has been traditionally described—which is, already, a demanding undertaking just in terms of sheer mass. The difficulties of coping[1] with this mass are also increased through the necessity to address the rigidly defined categories of thought by which it is surrounded. One such category is the idea that Joyce's prose forms, in its different parts, one whole contained and informed by one mysterious, overarching design, something that has long been a standard assumption in Joyce criticism, and that relates in very important ways to the notion of the "Proustian" universe discussed in chapter 3.[2] While a working knowledge of Joyce's corpus enables the critic to understand the myriad ways in which this may be true, it also does not do much to bring the scholar-critic closer to writing about Joyce because it forms an aspect of "writing about Joyce." Through the creation of a context within which Joyce's work is to be viewed, the idea that Joyce's prose forms one gigantic whole opens up a *category* of discussion with regard to his work. This category is not, however, to be found in the work itself, but is codified in the critical text, or the cultural space surrounding Joyce's novels, in which it is advanced as an idea. As such, while it is deeply concerned with Joyce's work, it is yet largely external to that work.[3] Once codified in the critical framework, however, such a category, if it draws adherents (which in this case, it did) then loses its identity in the massive "text" of that which has been written about Joyce. In this sense, then, the cultural space (created by the critical "text") surrounding Joyce's work is very different from that concerning Proust's *Recherche*. At the time it was conceived, this category was developed as a way of approaching some of the interpretive difficulties specific to Joyce's prose. It has by now become such a critical commonplace that not only is it no longer even a subject of debate—it is not noticed as a subject at all. This is evidenced by the proliferation of books on Joyce that deal with his corpus from *Chamber Music* through *Finnegans Wake*, showing how each text elaborates the one that came before, and develops into the next. The categories of reading and interpretation established, variety in such reading and interpretation is then focused on different views of the way in which this sequential development is accomplished. While such approaches to the development of Joyce's corpus represent a complex multitude of critical opinions, the essential form of the work that concentrates on this subject often remains the same: an introductory chapter, followed by one chapter each on each of the works in chronological succession, ending with a concluding chapter summing up the author's conclusions on the matter.

In this way, it may be understood how the idea that Joyce's corpus constitutes one whole dominated by one overarching design could become writing about "writing about Joyce," rather than writing about Joyce. The establishment of such an approach in critical form through repetition and agreement in the work of many different critics serves to institutionalize and legitimate an interpretive category which, because it is not essentially challengeable (its validity being "proven" by Joyce's work), also begins to dictate the boundaries within which subsequent critics may begin the act of interpretation, if they accept that a part of the critical task is to engage with other arguments that touch on their ideas. Reading is thus both influenced and contained by what has already been read, and how such reading has been done. This is, however, but one of many examples of the way in which "writing about Joyce," in the form of critical categories that exist as givens, has infiltrated and become part of the idea of writing about Joyce.

This critical situation is certainly due to the unconventional form of Joyce's work, but perhaps it is also partially a result of the way in which Joyce was received, from the beginning of his career, in the English-speaking community. From his first attempts to publish *Dubliners*, Joyce encountered a myriad of problems in the English-speaking community which at that time, since he was relatively unknown, consisted for him only of Ireland and Great Britain.[4] Seeking a wider, less provincial audience than were, in his view, the Irish, Joyce thought this could be more easily attained through having his book brought out by an English, rather than an Irish publisher. Although he began his search with the English publisher Grant Richards, who accepted *Dubliners* for publication in 1906, Joyce later encountered an obstacle in the form of English law, which stated that the printer who set objectionable material into print was as guilty as the publisher who brought it out, and equally subject to prosecution. When the printer who was to set *Dubliners* for Grant Richards objected to certain passages in the text and refused to do so, plans for publication were stalled as Richards and Joyce became embroiled in arguments over the content of his work.

A year later, Richards flatly refused to publish *Dubliners*, and the text was then rejected in turn by the English publishers Elkin Mathews, Hutchinson & Co., Alston Rivers, and Edward Arnold. In 1909, Joyce sent it at last to the Irish publisher Maunsel & Co. and its managing director, George Roberts, signed a contract with him for publication. A year later, Roberts too expressed objections to the content of the stories. Although Joyce made changes, *Dubliners* was still languishing in the publisher's office in 1911, and it was not until 1912 that Roberts finally refused to publish it. After this, Joyce offered it to *The English Review* and then to Mills & Boon, and each of these also rejected it. It was not until he received an unexpected letter from Ezra Pound that Joyce had some hope of ever publishing *Dubliners*. Pound liked the stories, and after a few of them were published in *The Egoist*, Joyce felt he had the leverage to inquire again about publication in book form with Grant Richards, who in 1914 finally agreed to publish. Joyce had spent nine years in the attempt.

Also in this year, *The Egoist* began to publish *A Portrait of the Artist as a Young Man* in serial form. However, when Joyce tried to have it published in book form with Grant Richards, the same troubles began. Richards rejected it in 1915, and after that, it was submitted to Duckworth, whose reader rejected it. T. Werner Laurie, when approached, refused to publish it without changes. Harriet Shaw Weaver, Joyce's patroness, suggested that if no publisher were to be found, and if her editorial board would agree, that *The Egoist* would try to publish it. While this seemed the answer to Joyce's worries, it was also met with a seemingly insurmountable difficulty: seven printers in succession being approached with the task, all refused in light of the recent prosecution of D. H. Lawrence's *The Rainbow*. It was not until 1916 that the American publisher B. W. Huebsch agreed to publish *A Portrait*, bringing out at the same time an American edition of *Dubliners*.

Joyce's publishing difficulties were no less acute with *Ulysses*, and were in some ways worse than they had been with his earlier work. In January 1918, the earlier chapters of *Ulysses* were polished enough to warrant publishing, and Joyce decided to try doing so in serial form, as he had done with *A Portrait of the Artist as a Young Man*. The first three chapters were duly read by Ezra Pound, who arranged to begin publication in the American journal *Little Review*, in March, 1918. Publishing *Ulysses* in England, however, was a different matter. Harriet Shaw Weaver tried to help Joyce with this, but making the rounds of the wary printers, she was again unsuccessful. While the idea of a Paris printing remained interesting, Joyce felt that an American edition was a more promising endeavor, since B. W. Huebsch had published *Dubliners* and *A Portrait* in 1916, *Exiles* and *Chamber Music* in 1918, and was interested in publishing *Ulysses*.

But the possibility of an American edition was just as risky legally in America for those who would be involved in producing the book as it was for those who would be involved in doing so in England. In fact, it was slightly more so, since in 1919–1920, the United States Post Office had confiscated and burned several numbers of the *Little Review*, which had contained episodes from *Ulysses*. In view of this action, any publisher who dared set the book in print risked being prosecuted for obscenity.

This is indeed what happened to the *Little Review* in the fall of 1920. After a less than notorious trial, the publishers were convicted of publishing obscenity, fined, and the publication of *Ulysses* ordered discontinued. As a result of this conviction, B. W. Huebsch, with some reluctance, announced that publication would not be possible without some changes in the text. Joyce's refusal to make any changes forced the publisher to reject the manuscript entirely. It was in this desperate situation that Sylvia Beach of Shakespeare & Co. asked for the publication rights, which Joyce immediately granted. *Ulysses* was finally published in Paris in February of 1922. The

American edition, published by Random House, was not available until 1934, and the English edition in England did not follow until 1936.[5]

An analysis of this publishing history, in revealing a certain cultural politics at work in the fact that Joyce's artistic reception was far from warm, also reveals the existence of an attitude toward his work that, as can be seen by the number of rejections it received, has marked it from the very beginning.[6] The fear of so many printers to set it, and of so many publishers to publish it, lent to Joyce's work an aura of taboo that it was hard put to shake off. This aura of taboo was intensified in America with the trial of the publishers of *Little Review*, their subsequent conviction on charges of obscenity, and the discontinuation of publication of *Ulysses*.

This situation might account in part for the slowness with which Joyce's work was initially accepted by the American English-speaking academic community, why he never became as popular in England as he subsequently did in America, and why only certain avenues of interpretation were initially established in reading his work. But one thing the aura of taboo surrounding Joyce's work did was to make of him a Figure, one of whom it could be said, "Objective reportage has done more than subjective adulation to expand the enigmatic image of Joyce, the Legend."[7] This cultural idea or image of Joyce himself was instrumental in the development of the idea of "writing about Joyce." Joyce's image did much to put off the timid critic, as well as the timid reader, and "writing about Joyce" became a useful means to make him more accessible to those who wished simply to understand his work, as well as to those who desired to undertake the huge task of reading and interpretation with regard to his texts. It also had much to do with making Joyce the sole property of academe, his texts being deemed too difficult for the ordinary reader to understand without the professional help offered, sanctioned, and thereby legitimized by the university. The university, then, was largely the only place where the knowledges that would make Joyce's work intelligible to the general population could be produced, in the form of critical interpretations. To a large degree, due to the difficulty of his prose, Joyce thus became the modernist author *par excellence* of the New Critical scholar-critic, and the institutionalization of his work in the university, slow in coming, took off with seemingly lightning speed once the New Criticism itself was established there.[8] Here as well, the relationship between Joyce and institutionalization must be understood as doubly complex: on the one hand, the entry of his work into the university marks its initial institutional acceptance; on the other hand, the institutionalization of the critical-cultural text surrounding his work marks yet another instance of such institutional acceptance.

The first American critical work devoted entirely to Joyce, Harry Levin's *James Joyce: A Critical Introduction*,[9] was only published at the time of Joyce's death (1941), and three years after the publication of his final work, *Finnegans Wake*, in 1938. Its object was to clarify Joyce's creative endeavors by serving as an aid to overcoming "the obstacles that sometimes discourage the reader of Joyce."[10] There was next to nothing else until six years later, with the publication of Richard Kain's *Fabulous Voyager*[11] in 1947, which concentrated primarily on *Ulysses* and inaugurated the flood of Joyce criticism that began in the decade 1950–1960.[12]

During the decade from 1960–1970, however, a major change took place in the community of Joyce scholar-critics that affected not only the critical framework surrounding Joyce's work at that time, but all such critical acts to come as well, by creating a forum that, as time passed, was instrumental in the production of the idea of what it *means* to write about Joyce, the problem with which the present discussion is concerned. This monumental change was effected in 1966 by Fritz Senn and Thomas Staley, who came up with the idea of organizing a meeting to provide an opportunity for scholar-critics from America and Europe to share their work on James Joyce.[13] These two scholar-critics, with the help of a third, the late Bernard Benstock, put together what came to be called the First International James Joyce Symposium, held in June 1967, and the process of critical institutionalization suggested at the opening of this chapter was begun. While this first meeting was relatively small, attracting approximately seventy-five paid registrants, it had a very important result: this was the creation of the James Joyce Foundation, whose purpose was to aid in the furtherance of contacts among the international community of Joyce scholar-critics, critics, students, and readers.[14] From this modest beginning, however, the Symposia quickly grew in size and importance until the Ninth International James Joyce Symposium in Frankfurt-am-Main recorded upward of four hundred registrants.[15]

As such, the word "institutionalization" in the subtitle of the present chapter reveals the existence of yet another, and larger, "text" than that constituting the creative works of Joyce, a text with which the critic who desires to write about Joyce must also, necessarily, be concerned. This "text" is the cultural space formed from the combined efforts of all who have written about Joyce from the beginning, and all who continue to write about him to the present. Of course, all scholar-critics must grapple with the critical-cultural spaces surrounding the authors in whom they are interested, but the peculiar quality of the cultural space surrounding the work of James Joyce is that, as aforementioned, it often seems to authorize the reading, interpretation, and discussion of only certain issues with regard to each of his texts, and that it is so massive as to represent layers on layers of material specifically related to these authorized avenues of interpretation. It has become so dense and so widespread that it produces books like that of Janet Egleson Dunleavy, *Reviewing Classics of Joyce Criticism*,[16] in which the texts that constitute the canon of Joyce criticism are discussed and, in this way, rein-corporated into the massive "text" of critical work on Joyce of which they are already the foundation. This critical body of writing also shows no signs of abating, but only of growing ever more vast. A quick survey of the number of dissertations on Joyce produced in English in the United States, Canada, and the Netherlands underwrites this assumption: the 1940s saw a total of three dissertations completed on Joyce; the 1950s, a total of nine-teen; the 1960s, sixty-four; the 1970s, one hundred seventy-six. Though only sixty-four more dissertations on Joyce were produced in the five-year period between 1980–1984, when the total number of Joyce dissertations produced in English for the period 1942–1984 is compared to the over forty dissertations on John Steinbeck and the over eighty on Ernest Hemingway for the same period, it becomes obvious that critical production in Joyce cir-cles remains at a premium.[17] One glance at the amazing range of materials written on Joyce from the late 1980s to the present, as listed in such Web databases as the MLA International Bibliography, suggests that the steady stream of production in this area even now has yet to slow. Gottlieb Gaiser has pointed out further evidence of this in describing Robert Deming's 1977 *Bibliography of James Joyce Studies* as having listed 5,885 entries, while the 1964 edition of the same bibliography listed only 1,434.[18] Thus, the late Bernard Benstock's sizing up of the critical situation in Joyce studies in an ar-ticle written before the First International James Joyce Symposium was, in a sense, a portent of what was to come in later years: "Joyce, the man, the work and reputation, has now evolved into Joyce, the Industry."[19]

The idea of the Joyce "industry" gains more weight when one considers the fact that the name of Joyce (most likely instigated by Joyce's linguistic ex-perimentation in *Finnegans Wake*) has become an adjective, a noun, a verb, and is often substituted as a portion of a word, such as the word "synjo-sium," in the title of an article quoted later on in this chapter. The use of the name Joyce as a part of speech has even gained the credibility of academic acceptance, as Gaiser explains:

> Traces of ritual [Bloomsday, walking tours in Bloom's footsteps] may reveal a certain resemblance of Joyce criticism to a fan-club, but they also indicate a strong in-group consciousness that has even found its way into language. "Joycean," as most Joyce spe-cialists choose to call themselves, was not listed in the 1961 edition of the *Oxford English Dictionary* (comprising English vocabulary up to 1933), but has now been entered in the current *Supplement*, both as an adjective ("of, pertaining to, or characteristic of the Irish writer James Joyce (1882–1941), or his work") and as a noun to label an "admirer or follower of Joyce."[20]

With such credibility also comes license, and the license of word play is something found not only at the heart of Joyce's work, but in much of the critical work surrounding it as well. The license of word play reinforces the idea of "writing about Joyce," since the subject itself is self-reflexively, yet quite legitimately, encoded in language and provides an endless source of discussion, as Senn elaborates:

> The platitudinous payoff of all this, predictably, is that in identifying we are *doing* something. All the meanings we concede, knowingly or not, to the term "Joyce" imply some kind of activity. At one extreme the word does duty for a life lived in various cities in the course of almost sixty years; at the other possible ends of the scales it suggests writing, thinking, creating, developing, intending—you name it, and you name it appropriately by verbs. Such verbs also become our panels and lectures and animated disputes. Aware of such dynamisms, some of us have quite independently— when this could still be done with impunity and even self-respect— coined the verb REJOYCE or REJOYCING.[21]

Such a relationship to language on the part of the author requires a self-consciousness and awareness of its critical implications that demands examination. It is almost as if Joyce and the language which surrounds his work, the language within which his work must be interpreted, cannot be separated— as if he not only wrote in that language, but rather, somehow *was* that language. A more than cursory glance at the critical implications of such a relationship allows for the understanding that it was not Joyce himself who created this situation with regard to himself and language, but rather, those who study and interpret his work who did so. The idea of the name "Joyce" as a part of speech institutes a form of writing about "writing about Joyce" that is practically impossible to escape when writing about Joyce, and it must be used with a kind of romantic irony that allows for the realization that there is indeed a difference between writing about Joyce and writing about "writing about Joyce." The nature of the milieu, that is, Joyce studies, as it now stands requires the adaptation to a certain set of norms that have been codified in the shared values of the international community of Joyce scholar-critics. This codification occurred through the process of Joyce's transformation from rebel outsider to avant-garde insider to entrenchment in the canon of twentieth-century literature to semiotic infiltration of the English language.[22]

But the very necessity of adaptation also requires a rigorous questioning of this need to do so. What exactly does it mean for the contemporary critic and scholar of Joyce to be faced with the Joyce Industry, a massive cultural space that not only dictates how Joyce's texts should be understood, but also in many ways determines which representations seeking to do so are to be authorized at all? In other words, how does such a scholar-critic confront a critical "text" that offers already formed the avenues that must be taken in the critical act with regard to Joyce's oeuvre? Such questions lie at the heart of relatively recent reevaluations of the Joyce Industry that look at the way in which it is currently characterized through examining the view of Joyce critics and criticism offered by the International Symposia:

> Three distinct approaches have previously been apparent to many who have attended these Symposia and the many other Joyce con- ferences and seminars that have proliferated across the world dur- ing the 1970s and 1980s. "Venerating" Joyce has long been in evidence, and can still be noticed on occasion: it has made Joyce an insurmountable obstacle, a totem for adulation, which if it has not actually impeded interpretation has at least set the first and form- ing condition, that Joyce was a genius and in such full control of his material and techniques that his intentions could only be sur- mised. Veneration has met with skepticism by the younger genera- tion of Joyceans, some of whom have even avoided the name Joycean for fear that it implies unquestioning adulation. In addi- tion, recent theoretical assumptions that all authors lack the au- thority that resides either in the text or with the reader have made veneration—even of Joyce—uncomfortable. Nonetheless, all of those who approach the Joyce texts find themselves having to con- tend with the redoubtable *presence* of James Joyce.[23]

In this passage, the problem of "writing about Joyce" is identified as being the result of Joyce "veneration" on the part of his admirers—a situation which, it is recognized, *could* be at odds with the act of interpretation, and which does indeed codify the terms on which such interpretation must be based. It is in- teresting to note, however, that this situation is referred to in terms of a *gener- ational* acclimatization; that while those who read and wrote about Joyce at or near the time of his inception into the academy tend to revere his artistic ac- complishment often to the detriment of interpretation, those who perform the same acts with regard to Joyce at a time when his position in the academy is not only secure but unshakeable approach his work from a more skeptical po- sition. This skepticism entails a certain intrepidity before the often offputting height of Joyce's achievement, and a desire to approach his work with ques- tions that force it to justify the position that "veneration" has accorded it. Younger generations can neither remember when Joyce was not a part of the canon of twentieth-century literature, nor can they remember a time when Euro-American modernism, and Joyce's influence over it, were not a potent force in that literature. Thus, for such new generations the relative greatness of

Joyce's technical innovation does not have the same punch that it might have had for a generation that had never before seen its like. This reveals even more clearly how the politics of cultural space is operative in relation to the university, because here the existence of an institutionalized cultural space that codifies Joyce's novels places a younger generation of Joyce scholar-critics in the position not so much of having to deal with the "presence" of James Joyce, but of having to cope with the presence of the critical text surrounding his work, or "writing about Joyce."

Because new generations of Joyce scholar-critics necessarily find themselves in the process of defining an interpretive project in many ways very different from the character of that defined by those who came before, the relationship between the old and the young in Joyce criticism comes to seem like that of the common generational gap—and the conflict between the different styles and approaches to interpreting Joyce characterized by this gap produces a change in the cultural space surrounding Joyce's work that parallels the introspective changes brought about by generational conflicts in other milieux:

> The Joyce "industry" is caught in a moment of self-evaluation, a heliotropic turn to questioning the contexts in which we have for so long situated Joyce's texts, with a backward glance reflected in both irony and nostalgia at a time when our mutual goal was easily defined but difficult to reach: that is, to "master" the Joycean *oeuvre*.[24]

This generational gap in many ways also reflects how the politics of cultural space is operative in the field of Joyce criticism. As seen in chapter 2, the politics of cultural space is complicated in analyses of literary modernism and modernity by the relation between the two narratives of Euro-American modernism and the pressure exerted on these by the polarized debate on canon revision and culture studies (which would also emphasize Euro-American modernism's legacy of exclusion). In response to such influences, the burgeoning field of Irish studies developed apace through the 1990s, separating Joyce's work from the national literary canon of England, and emphasizing his Irishness and its role in his work instead. Along with this concomitant emphasis on Joyce's status as an Irish citizen came the analysis of the socio-historico-political effects of imperialism on his work and the subjects it takes up.[25] Thus, the politics of cultural space in Joyce studies is also revealed in the type and nature of the critical work undertaken by the scholar-critics working in this field. Here, the edge between old and new articulations of Joyce's work forms both the "frontier" and the "bridge" by which it may be understood,[26] and the point at which its silent (and silenced) cultural articulations may be brought to the fore.

When dealing with Joyce's second novel, *A Portrait of the Artist as a Young Man*, the problem of writing about "writing about Joyce" becomes even more complex. Although Grant Richards had published *Dubliners* in England in 1914 and the publisher B. W. Huebsch had published both this text and *Dubliners* in America in 1916, these early works did not establish Joyce as a world figure. The text that did so was *Ulysses*, and as such it is only natural that when the critical response to Joyce began in America, it should have concentrated on that work. A 1962 Ph.D. dissertation asserts that up to that year, the attention that *A Portrait* received from critics to that time had been primarily in terms of what it could offer to the interpretation of Joyce's later works,[27] something that has been a recurrent theme in criticism of *A Portrait*. Thus the dilemma of writing about "writing about Joyce" is, with regard to this text, twofold: on the one hand, there are the established interpretive categories, such as autobiography, aesthetic theory, structure, symbol, motif, language, the sermons, epiphany, and stream-of-consciousness; on the other hand, there is, again, the obvious value of *A Portrait* in a discussion that concentrates on the idea that Joyce's work forms one whole informed by one mysterious, overarching design. These categories, along with the critical emphasis on *Ulysses* that was there from the beginning, place *A Portrait* in somewhat of an ignominious position with regard to Joyce's later works. Because it is not, in artistic achievement, as experimental as either *Ulysses* or *Finnegans Wake*, it is often thought not as interesting, complex, or valuable. The respect accorded the last two works as a result of their experimental daring overshadows *A Portrait* to the extent that it is left decidedly in the background.

The fact that the respect garnered by Joyce's two final works also generates the most critical attention concentrates the "text" of the Joyce Industry on these two novels as well—and it is an attention that has recently even increased, as Beja elaborates:

> A discernible change in Joyce studies . . . is not only the concentration on *Ulysses* and *Finnegans Wake*, but especially the concern with that latter text. What some have suspected for a long time has now become a widely accepted view: that ignoring the *Wake* when coping with Joyce seriously limits the range of Joycean perspectives . . . Perhaps the suspension of the awe with which Joyce has too often been surrounded, the veneration of genius that kept the *Wake* as a sacred book to be honored but not approached, as well as the suspension of the notion that it is a text that must be mastered and rendered up to explication, have opened *Finnegans Wake* for new considerations.[28]

The idea which Beja advances here, that "ignoring the Wake when coping with Joyce seriously limits the range of Joycean perspectives," reflects a new instance of writing about "writing about Joyce" that offers another category of interpretation in Joyce studies that codifies the critical "text" into a particular area of concern. While the richly figurative diversity and complexity of Finnegans Wake cannot be denied and may assuredly be recognized as useful in identifying "Joycean perspectives," the idea that ignoring this text places limitations on the possibility of interpretation cannot help but ensure that in order to gain the respect of the international community of Joyce scholar-critics, many of these will search for the way in which their work connects to Finnegans Wake, rather than simply following the particular path of interpretation they have chosen in order to see where it leads them.

As a part of the critical "text" surrounding Joyce's work, this idea also places a certain amount of pressure on the critical essay whose purpose is to interpret A Portrait or any of Joyce's works in isolation. This is because it places an added constraint on the idea that any one of Joyce's works can stand alone, thus suggesting that the act of interpretation be a task in which each text must be confronted in the effort to interpret any one of them. In the early 1980s, this shift in mainstream Joyce criticism already had the effect of fewer publications on A Portrait of the Artist as a Young Man. In one article, for example, Thomas Staley has noted that "less attention [has been] paid to Joyce's earlier fiction in the past years [1976–1981] than during any comparable five-year period for the last fifteen years, at least in so far as extended studies are concerned."[29]

Yet in spite of all of this, the importance of A Portrait in establishing Joyce's artistic point of view in such a way that those later accomplishments could be accomplished should not be denied. It is only through this text that Joyce, by a silent, subtle interweaving of objective and fictional, religious and secular realities, accomplished the linguistic explosion that resulted in Finnegans Wake. The problems that language poses in A Portrait are, then, not so much the key to understanding the linguistic exigencies of Ulysses or Finnegans Wake, but, rather, their raison d'être. And it is in this way that A Portrait is also revealed as a hidden, silent (and silenced) peak in Joyce's career as a novelist.

Such a reading of this novel inevitably posits a drastic revision of the critical "text" of Joyce studies, which would, as Beja identifies above, place this novel in a subordinate position to both Ulysses and Finnegans Wake. But if A Portrait or any one of Joyce's works is or are to be read within new and reevaluative contexts, then the questions it and/or they themselves demand must be addressed. In A Portrait, the most obvious of these questions, because they focus on the nature of language as a communicative tool and its power to produce meanings and create worlds, demand that other, more probing questions into the very nature of the critical and interpretive act be asked as well. In asking such questions, the scholar-critic is bound to come into conflict with accepted ways of understanding the text, as Joseph Buttigieg illuminates:

> The . . . circle of interpretation can be broken only by inaugurating a new beginning in the study of *A Portrait*. . . . Any true beginning demystifies the authoritativeness of the received tradition; that is it makes the scholar "controvert the dynastic role thrust upon him by history or habit." No authentically new interpretation of a text can take place unless some space is cleared for it first. To obtain that space one must confront the past critically; . . . one must revise the inherited versions of history. Beginning anew with *A Portrait* then, means liberating it from the boundaries within which . . . literary interpretation . . . [has] confined it.[30]

The "boundaries" of which Buttigieg writes are those inscribed by the development of the categories of thought that envelop Joyce's work and are codified in the literary criticism that surrounds it. As such, any attempt to read *A Portrait* or any other of Joyce's novels in a manner that does not reinforce these accepted categories cannot avoid the necessity of doing a certain violence to the critical "text" that upholds them.

In 1966, on the crest of the critical wave that gave birth to the International James Joyce Symposia and the James Joyce Foundation, Arnold Goldman wrote something that still seems applicable today:

> Only through an understanding of the ways in which conflicting responses can be related does it seem to me possible to make sense out of the criticism of Joyce to date; and only in this manner can the varieties of critical opinion hope to appear functions of Joyce's work itself.[31]

Even in 1966, before it was further institutionalized as a result of the changes brought about by that decade in Joyce studies, Goldman had recognized something that was occurring in Joyce criticism, and that has only been exacerbated by the passage of time: a proliferation of responses to Joyce's work that can become so abstract and so categorical as to leave the actual text behind. But while he recognizes the problem, his solution is only partially helpful. Although he asserts the idea that the scholar-critic must first understand the nature of the institution in which Joyce studies are ensconced, what Goldman's idea does not encompass is the necessary act of violence—that this same scholar-critic must first immerse him- or herself in, then jump out of, the institutionalized cultural space, in order to retrieve Joyce's text itself—that, in other words, to find him- or herself poised for the new act of interpretation, he or she must, inevitably, first be "joyced."[32]

RETROSPECTIVE: STEPHEN DEDALUS
AND THE "SWOON OF SIN"

If by reiteration of the original title of this chapter one gleans the impression simply that we have returned to the place from which it should have started to begin with, there has been no real consideration of its opening word. *The Oxford English Dictionary* cites the earliest usage of the word "retrospective" as having been in 1664, with the meaning "directed to, contemplative of, past time." However, a look at the root of this word, "retrospect," lends an interesting nuance to the meaning of "retrospective," which is also of some value to the present discussion. The earliest use of the word "retrospect" is listed as having been in 1602, meaning "a regard of or reference *to* some fact, authority or precedent," or "application to past time." A new meaning is listed from 1675, as "a backward look or view." By the end of the seventeenth century, the word "retrospect" was used to designate the idea of "a view or survey of past time, *esp.* with reference to one's own life or experiences." Also at this time, it referred to "a survey or review of some past course of events, acts, etc.; *esp.* a comprehensive or summary view of what has been done or has taken place in a particular sphere or line of things." Further, it designated the ideas "to indulge in retrospection" and "to look or refer back *to*, to reflect *on*." In the early eighteenth century, this word was used to denote the activity "to consider, regard, or think on (some person or thing) retrospectively."[33]

The American Heritage Dictionary[34] describes the word "retrospective" as both an adjective and a noun, meaning "looking back on, contemplating, or directed to the past," "looking or directed backward," "applying to or influencing the past," or "of or pertaining to a show exhibiting the work of an artist or school over a period of years." From all of these definitions, it becomes clear that the idea of an interpretation of *A Portrait of the Artist as a Young Man* in the context of retrospection suggests a number of implications that could take such a discussion in several directions. Those meanings accorded to the root word "retrospect," however, offer the clearest picture of the use of "retrospective" intended here. If "retrospective" is viewed as the idea of "looking backward with regard to a fact, authority or precedent, to look or refer back *to*, to reflect *on*," or, finally, "to consider, regard, or think on (some person or thing) retrospectively," then it has been accorded the proper meaning of its usage in this instance. As such, the reiteration of this essay's title implies a self-reflexive gesture toward the questions introduced and contextualized in the first section of this chapter: What exactly does it mean for the contemporary critic and scholar of Joyce to be faced with the Joyce Industry? How does such a critic confront a critical "text" that offers already formed the avenues that must be taken in the critical and interpretive act with regard to Joyce's oeuvre?

The response to these questions is posited both as an answer and as the inauguration of a moment of critical reevaluation such as that described above by Beja, because it is a question itself: What does it mean to consider the idea of an essay entitled "Stephen Dedalus and the 'Swoon of Sin'" within the context of the critical "text" of Joyce studies, and what does it mean to consider the same idea within the context of the foregoing section on the institutionalization of that critical "text?" While the section on institutionalization still constitutes a text outside the fictional text created by Joyce, it offers yet a possibility of contextualization that nullifies the critically created hegemony of Joyce's later works and takes *A Portrait* further away from the critical "text," bringing it closer to the scholar-critic him- or herself, so that a more isolated, yet "joyced," interpretation may be effected. As such, a direct look at the novel offers the terms by which it is possible to read and interpret it.

In its method of narration, *A Portrait* introduces an exploration into the nature of language and its effect on the individual that cannot be ignored. But even a cursory examination of *A Portrait* reveals that a discussion of the character of Stephen without a concomitant discussion of the way in which Joyce as objective author and Stephen as fictional hero are related (or which aspects of Stephen's life and personality are autobiographical in origin) offers only part of the picture, and this is even more so when undertaking a discussion of the importance of language in this text.

Just as we have seen in the case of Proust in Chapter 3, critics old and new have expressed varying opinions with regard to the question of autobiography in Joyce's work.[35] Joyce's own self-criticism, his idea that he lacked imagination and could not simply create material,[36] would seem to underwrite the idea that his work is autobiographical. The question here is not, however, whether or not Joyce's work is autobiographical, but rather the way in which a knowledge of certain aspects of Joyce's biography serves to illuminate the function and importance of language in *A Portrait*, and, as such, in Joyce's work as a general rule. Such an analysis of *A Portrait* is not so much, again, to be viewed as a *key* to understanding Joyce's later work, but as the *necessary condition* for the creation of that work. It is only through a knowledge of the role of language in Joyce's life that an appropriate understanding of its role in *A Portrait* may be achieved, and a clearer understanding of Joyce's development as an author ascertained.

In describing the purpose of his classic biography on Joyce, Richard Ellmann (as did Painter with regard to Proust) offers the foundation for an understanding of the relationship between life and art, and as such, the relationship between self and language, in Joyce's writing:

> This book enters Joyce's life to reflect his complex, incessant joining of event and composition. The life of an artist, but particularly

that of Joyce, differs from the lives of other persons in that its events are becoming artistic sources even as they command his present attention. Instead of allowing each day, pushed back by the next, to lapse into imprecise memory, he shapes again the experiences which have shaped him.[37]

From this, it is clear that for Joyce, language is the given, the raw material by which he apprehends his world and which, like clay, is molded again by him into new forms of awareness. In the case of *A Portrait*, however, the "joining of event and composition" can be most clearly illuminated when understood in relation to the most significant historical event in the Ireland of Joyce's time: the fall of Charles Stuart Parnell in 1891. A brief synopsis of the cultural situation in Ireland after Parnell's demise will make clear the significance of this event in terms of Joyce's relationship to language. Through it, we will also see how the politics of cultural space, as it relates to Joyce's novels, encompasses the actual political world of his time—something that has been until only recently largely neglected in the traditional Euro-American critical "text," which has read his work primarily as one of the most important foundations of Euro-American modernism.

The fall of Parnell and the defeat of the second Home Rule Bill by the House of Lords in 1893 represented the ultimate failure of Ireland's attempt to acquire, by constitutional means, the right to Home Rule from Victorian England. With the death of the nation's hopes that Home Rule might become a political reality, Ireland's artists, such as Yeats, Hyde, and Lady Gregory, were at last freed of political injunctions against the attempt to rejuvenate Irish culture through literary activity, and they began what came to be called the Irish Literary Revival. Seven centuries of colonization had left the Irish people clinging to a glorious past in fear and dread of the promise of an ignoble and inglorious future. In the wake of the nation's political failure, the glorification of this past became even more pronounced, with the foundation and development not only of the Irish Literary Revival, but also of such organizations as the Gaelic League and the Gaelic Athletic Association. While the Gaelic League concentrated on the rejuvenation of Irish identity, the Gaelic Athletic Association focused on the eradication in Ireland of non-Irish games, such as cricket and association football.

As such, it may be easily understood that in Ireland, the national way of life, which encompasses the sum total of the shared ideas of a collective about its cultural heritage, is only with difficulty separated from its political beliefs and practices. As a colonized country, the idea in Ireland of an indigenous culture *itself* is political, since such an idea is of necessity at odds with the colonizing culture. In this way, the place and influence of culture became a major factor in the Irish revolution, because it involved a clash between the Irish Literary Revival, which desired to inculcate nationalistic and aesthetic values in mainstream Irish society, the minority Protestant culture, which had its own shared ideas of the way life should be lived in Ireland, and the Roman Catholic majority's insistence on the interpretation of the Irish way of life in traditional Roman Catholic terms.[38] The ascendancy of the Roman Catholic interpretation over all other possible interpretations of Irish life was quickly established through agreement of the Catholic majority:

> The Gaelic League's search for an Irish identity was one that soon found itself accommodated to the making of the twentieth-century Roman Catholic nation. D. P. Moran was a key figure in reinterpreting the Gaelic movement to the coming times. He did so by insisting that the future lay not with ignorant peasants, but with the urban, Gaelic-language-equipped middle classes. He believed that a nation could only survive in the modern age if its best, fittest elements came to the top. The industrial revolution in England had opened her society to free competition, and the best and most capable part of her nation had risen only, however, to suffer from the creation of a subculture of profit-makers and unearned-income gatherers who then stifled all originality. The Great Famine had also sifted Irish society, but had sent the most able abroad. Now was the time for the nation to develop self-reliance, initiative, and an essential part of this process was the welding of the nation's culture, Gaelic, to its religion, Roman Catholicism. "When we look out on Ireland we see that those who believe or may be immediately induced to believe, in Ireland as a nation are, as a matter of fact, Catholic." "In the main non-Catholic Ireland looks upon itself as British and as Anglo-Irish." The Irish nation was *de facto* Catholic, and Protestants must accept the ideals of the majority. Absorption was the only way forward, or . . . partition, leaving the "Orangemen and their friends in their north-east corner."[39]

For Joyce, the political situation in Ireland after the fall of Parnell represented an exercise in futility, at least in terms of trying to attain Home Rule through English parliamentary democracy. This situation, in Joyce's view, led to a frustrating paralysis in Irish politics, which he documented in his short story "Ivy Day in the Committee Room."[40] His sense of the pointlessness of working for Home Rule through political avenues carried over into his understanding of the Irish Literary Revival and the Gaelic Movement— he was against the literary glorification of Ireland's past, just as he was against the battle between Protestant and Catholic Ireland, and for the same reason: both efforts preserved a status quo from which, for him, only a continued social, cultural, and political, but above all, silent, paralysis might be derived.[41] Joyce expresses his dissatisfaction with the cultural and political state of Ireland at this time in two letters to Nora Barnacle, in which he describes his opposition to the social forces by which Ireland was torn, as well as those whose combined purpose was to produce what were thought of as good Irish citizens and from which he himself inevitably felt pressured. These letters, written near the time of the couple's departure from Ireland into exile, reflect Joyce's increasing frustration with a world of ideas in which he was becoming increasingly aware that he could not and would never be able to assimilate himself. The first letter, written August 29, 1904, advances an attitude which, in its rejection of Catholicism and its emphasis on the traditional family unit, is one of the shaping influences of *A Portrait of the Artist as a Young Man*. In it, Joyce eschews all connection with the social mores with he was raised and which formed the backbone of his milieu, and expresses the aversion for conventional domesticity that caused him not to actually marry Nora until much later in their lives. He also disavows the Catholic church, establishes his position toward it and early twentieth-century Irish society as one of unequivocal rebellion, and describes himself as somewhat of an outcast as a result of his refusal to comply with social expectation.[42] Joyce's disgust with the social situation in Ireland as expressed in this letter is further exemplified in an excerpt from a second letter written to Nora Barnacle on September 16, 1904, in which he describes his view of Irish life. In this letter, Joyce expresses not only the difficulty of the war he has decided to wage on society, but his increasing alienation as a result of it. As his sense of alienation intensified, so also did his unhappiness with the reality of early twentieth-century Irish society. This dissatisfaction was also a discontent that had its origins in Joyce's ability to perceive what were for him the colonizing pressures on that society of both British imperialism and Roman Catholicism.[43]

As can be extrapolated from the position Joyce takes in these two letters, his relation to the social, cultural and political realities of early twentieth-century Ireland was very complex. Disillusioned by the disintegration of the Irish parliamentary party in the wake of Parnell's demise, Joyce had turned against Irish politics as the road to Home Rule.[44] Disaffected by the subsequent cultural push toward revival in the form of new directions in literature, as well as D. P. Moran's version of the Gaelic Movement (which valorized Irish Catholics and their ideology at the expense of Irish Protestants and theirs), Joyce also rejected these cultural aims in the interests of the nation as a whole and of individual freedom. Disheartened by the excesses of his drunken and irresponsible father and the ever-increasing poverty and deprivation of his childhood world, he rejected the Catholic ideal of home and family in favor of a life lived on the edge, clinging to the fringes of social participation in Ireland and, finally, exile.

For Joyce, writing itself became both the reason for and the result of his physical exile, by which he sought to escape the rigid confines established by the Irish realities that he had rejected. But Joyce's physical exile constitutes only one aspect of the idea of exile with regard to his disassociation with Ireland. When the idea of exile is considered in relation to his writing, it is revealed as infinitely more complex than simply the fact of presence or absence in a particular place. Writing becomes the artistic, and exile the social, representation of the rebellion against all that Joyce eschewed in Ireland, what were from his perspective its paralyzed and impotent politics, its musty morality and its stagnant worship of its past. Because he aimed in *A Portrait of the Artist as a Young Man* to bring into existence an idea of Ireland that did not yet exist, he could only achieve this goal by *causing* it to come from that silence into existence—that is, by writing the novel.

In the pursuit of his conception of the artist and art, Joyce, through the character of Stephen Dedalus, presented himself in miniature with the complicated cultural problems of late-nineteenth-century Irish society as a whole. The difficulty of creating in literature this something that did not yet exist but which was believed to exist was, first and foremost, a problem of language. The literary embodiment of this as yet silent, uncreated idea meant the creation of a literary form in the *English* language. But this literary form had to be entirely new, because English literature did not speak to the experience of Ireland, and offered no imitable models. This new literary form had therefore to be one that could be readily differentiated from the formal categories offered by English literature, but which would also be able to accomplish this in the silent shadow of the colonizer's language.[45]

In Joyce's view, the only way to revive the Irish national identity was to force the English language, the language of the colonizer, to mean with an *Irish* significance. For him, what was wrong with Ireland was not the political failure of Home Rule, but rather the nation's immersion, as a result of colonialism, in a foreign language deaf to the daily reality of Irish experience, and its entrapment in its own cultural ideologies also formed in that language and rigidly imposed. Thus it is language itself, in its power to confer meaning, to convey culture, to be the representative of the history of a nation, to represent—and to create—ideas by which individuals may be bound, against which Joyce rebels, because it is in the use of language that colonialism (in this case that of the British) concentrates its power. Wa Thiong'o elaborates this dilemma in analyzing the cultural effects of colonization:

The real aim of colonialism was to control the people's wealth: what they produced, how they produced it, and how it was distributed; to control, in other words, the entire realm of the language of real life. Colonialism imposed its control of the social production of wealth through military conquest and subsequent political dictatorship. But its most important area of domination was the mental universe of the colonised, the control, through culture, of how people perceived themselves and their relationship to the world. Economic and political control can never be complete or effective without mental control. To control a people's culture is to control their tools of self-definition in relationship to others. For colonialism this involved two aspects of the same process: the destruction or the deliberate undervaluing of a people's culture, their art, dances, religions, history, geography, education, orature and literature, and the conscious elevation of the language of the coloniser. The domination of a people's language by the languages of the colonising nations was crucial to the domination of the mental universe of the colonised.[46]

In turn-of-the-century Ireland, this domination was not just the result of the use of the English language, but also of the uses to which this language was put. With the accommodation of the search for Irish identity instituted by the Gaelic Movement to the making of a twentieth-century Roman Catholic Ireland,[47] the oppression of Irish national pride effected by the necessity to use a foreign language was augmented by the oppression of a religious idea that would exclude and/or oppress an equally Irish segment of the population who were Protestant and/or of foreign extraction, a group which, as Joyce made pains to point out in his 1907 essay, "Ireland, Island of Saints and Sages," had also included Ireland's national hero, Charles Stuart Parnell.[48] In this same essay, Joyce himself establishes the link between the cultural oppression of the British colonizer and the Roman Catholic Church:

> Un conquistatore non può essere dilettante e l'inglese no fece altro in Irlanda durante tanti secoli di quello che fà oggi il belga nello Stato Libero del Congo . . . Seminò la discordia fra le varie razze, coll'introduzione di un nuovo sistema agrario ridusse il potere dei capi nativi e diede grandi fondi ai suoi soldati, perseguitò la chiesa romana quando esta era ribelle e smise quando essa pure diventò uno strumento efficace die soggiogazione.[49]

> A conqueror cannot be casual, and for so many centuries the Englishman has done in Ireland only what the Belgian is doing today in the Congo Free State . . . she enkindled its factions and took over its treasury. By the introduction of a new system of agriculture, she reduced the power of the native leaders and gave great estates to her soldiers. She persecuted the Roman church when it was rebellious and stopped when it became an effective instrument of subjugation.

This linking of British persecution and Catholic domination produces a peculiar two-edged form of oppression that is doubly difficult to escape. From Joyce's perspective, on the one hand, there is the cultural imperative of a colonizing influence that demands the use also of a language foreign to Irish identity, thus dividing the Irish from their own culture and history. On the other hand, there is a spiritual domination also effected in the language of the colonizer, that of the Roman Catholic Church. In presenting itself as the means by which Ireland's deepest desire, that of a coherent national identity, is to be achieved, Roman Catholicism served to divide Irish society into violent factions—a division that also served the controlling interests of the British colonizer.

Joyce's understanding of this cultural situation of double oppression forces him to a realization of what was for him the subsequent uselessness of an Irish Literary Revival (which was concentrated on a past now too far away) in counteracting the cultural effects in Ireland of political failure, observing that "Ma, nell'attesa di tale risorgimento confesso che non vedo che cosa giova il fulminare contro la tirannide inglese mentre la tirannide romana occupa il palazzo dell'anima"[50] "in anticipation of such a revival, I confess that I do not see what good it does to fulminate against the English tyranny while the Roman tyranny occupies the palace of the soul." When cultural oppression in late nineteenth-century, early twentieth-century Ireland is understood in terms of this situation, the importance of language in *A Portrait of the Artist as a Young Man* becomes very clear. Through this it also becomes evident that it is because of the importance of language in *A Portrait*, and the nature of that importance, that this novel is central to and crucial in the creation of Joyce's later works.

In *Dubliners*, and even more so in *A Portrait of the Artist as a Young Man*, the effort to throw off the yoke of the colonizer makes of the act of writing a political and violent gesture, an act of stark civil disobedience. In this way, Joyce's attitude toward language is also revealed, so that its role in *A Portrait of the Artist as a Young Man* begins to be clearly recognizable.[51] It is also in the sense of civil disobedience that Stephen's *non serviam*[52] may be most clearly understood. Viewed as such, it becomes the credo for Joyce's personal and artistic life, as well as the basis for Stephen's artistic development. When Stephen's *non serviam* is understood as an artistic credo, and not simply as a refusal to take part in the social life of the Irish collective, it transcends the ideas expressed by Stephen in his explanation of his aesthetic theories to include all aspects of his life as a fictional hero, as well as Joyce's life as objective author. In this way, Stephen's *non serviam* becomes not only the most pertinent arbiter between the reality of Joyce, the author and that of Stephen the fictional hero, but the bridge by which these two realities may be distinguished—and the edge beyond which Joyce's silent and (traditionally) silenced literary rebellion may be discovered. It is also the means by which *A Portrait of the Artist as a Young Man* may be definitely classified as primarily fictional, rather than autobiographical.

In Joyce's actual life, the *non serviam* means the refusal to take part in the Irish Literary Revival or in the Gaelic Movement, the refusal to submit to the sacrament of marriage, the refusal to live in Ireland, the refusal to submit to English authority. For Stephen, however, the *non serviam* means something else. It means the refusal to serve nation, church, or state, but it also means the refusal to *be* what he is expected, by nation, church, or state, to be. Joyce's representation of this in *A Portrait* is the fictionalization of what has to take place in the subjective consciousness of the individual before he or she can even begin to live, as did Joyce, the idea of *non serviam*:

> [The] spirit of quarrelsome comradeship which he had observed lately . . . had not seduced Stephen from his habits of quiet obedience. He mistrusted the turbulence and doubted the sincerity of such comradeship which seemed to him a sorry anticipation of manhood. The question of honour here raised was, like all such questions, trivial to him. While his mind had been pursuing its intangible phantoms and turning in irresolution from such pursuit he had heard about him the constant voices of his father and his masters, urging him to be a gentleman above all things and urging him to be a good catholic above all things. These voices had now come to be hollow-sounding in his ears. When the gymnasium had been opened he had heard another voice urging him to be strong and manly and healthy and when the movement towards national revival had begun to be felt in the college, yet another voice had bidden him be true to his country and help to raise up her fallen language and tradition. In the profane world, as he foresaw, a worldly voice would bid him raise up his father's fallen state by his labours and, meanwhile, the voice of his school comrades urged him to be a decent fellow, to shield others from blame or to beg them off and to do his best to get free days for the school. And it was the din of all these hollowsounding voices that made him halt irresolutely in the pursuit of phantoms. He gave them ear only for a time but he was happy only when he was far from them, beyond their call alone or in the company of phantasmal comrades.[53]

In this passage, the necessity to be what others want him to be is represented as a conglomeration of voices speaking the expectations of different facets of the society in which Stephen lives. The fact that Stephen hears and understands these voices, however, gives rise to an understanding of the way in which language can operate to oppress the individual. There are so many voices and so many expectations that Stephen experiences them as a "din" to which he cannot give full attention, because he is already, though in an elementary way, in that strangely silent, isolated, exilic world that forms his sole reality by the novel's end. As such, the reality of the social world, the world of the Irish collective, is represented as existing in language, while Stephen is privy to another world, one inhabited by "phantasmal comrades," in which silence is paramount, and language has no place.[54] In this world, Stephen can be whatever he chooses to be, since there is no pressure exerted there by the external world of cultural ideas and injunctions that would demand of him to be one thing or another. This division of reality into one that is objective and external and another that is subjective and internal identifies the central dichotomy of the novel, into which the problem of language falls. From the very first page of *A Portrait*, the reader is given an understanding of the way in which language operates between "self" and "other"—creating contexts, identifying objects, determining identity:

> Once upon a time and a very good time it was there was a moocow coming down along the road and this moocow that was coming down along the road met a nicens little boy named baby tuckoo . . .
> His father told him that story: his father looked at him through a glass: he had a hairy face.
> He was baby tuckoo . . .[55]

This passage, which begins in the form of a fairy tale, blends into a description of objective reality and ends with a merging of subjective identity into the unreality of the fairy tale. As such, it sets the stage for a conflict between objective and fictional reality on which is inscribed the conflict between religious and secular reality that becomes the catalyst, through exile, for Stephen's artistic development. Both instances of conflict, that between objective and fictional reality and that between religious and secular reality, find their locus in the character of Stephen Dedalus, and are thus understood through the development of his relationship to language, which parallels his growth as an artist. Further, his growth may be understood to take place in relation to exile. The greater the rupture between himself and both secular and spiritual aspects of his society, the greater Stephen's capacity for artistic conceptualization.

Stephen's relationship to reality may thus be characterized by his relationship to language at any given moment in the text. The centrality of *A Portrait* in Joyce's corpus becomes clear in its handling of these different realities with regard to language and its various roles in Stephen's manner of perceiving the world around him. How does one determine what is "self" and what is "other?" What is the difference between objective and subjective reality, between the imagination and the world as-is? How can the boundaries between the real and the ideal be drawn, and how does this relate to the idea of religious and secular reality in the text? Such questions describe what is going on at the beginning of *A Portrait*, but by emphasizing the importance of language in the novel, they also bring to the fore its central problem: How does one (can one?) escape the "prisonhouse of language?" For even as one escapes the bonds of nationality through physical exile, the bonds of culture, tightly sewn through language, yet remain.

The problem of the real in this text becomes, then, a problem of self-understanding and, as such, of self-representation. The young Stephen is, in fact, trapped, from the very beginning of the novel, in the contexts within which language would inscribe him. Language is a self-contained system that exists outside himself. Before his relationship to language is established (when he is yet a baby at the novel's opening) Stephen exists as an extra-cultural "space" that he does not at first even know as himself, because he has not yet acquired the means (through language) to identify it. Language is the means by which he begins to *be*, the means by which his silent existence is objectified in the external world. His approximation of himself with "baby tuckoo" allows him some idea of himself as a separate entity from those whom he sees around him, that is, his mother and his father, but there are problems with this approximation that are givens just as the language is a given, and which Stephen at this age cannot possibly understand.

One such problem is that Stephen can, at this moment, only be that which is or has been offered him in language, something that also introduces another of the novel's central issues. Without language, he is nothing, but in it, he has been given a name, and that name is "baby tuckoo." There is given, along with this name, a qualifier that further identifies "baby tuckoo," and that is the idea that the person with this name is also "a nicens little boy." But here there is a dichotomy not at this moment recognizable to Stephen, yet readily apparent to the reader. This is the fact that the *name* of the "nicens little boy" and the "nicens little boy" do not share the same reality. While the "nicens little boy" refers to Stephen as he might be described in the objective world around him and thus constitutes a part of the reality of the world as-is, the name "baby tuckoo" refers to an imaginative reality that has no place in the objective world, but a reality that Stephen imagines as designating himself. But this being with the name of "baby tuckoo" is a character in a story, with no objective existence other than that accorded it through its name. In Stephen's childish mind, however, objective and fictional reality are not differentiated. The one merges easily into the other because the boundaries that would separate them in his consciousness have not yet been formed.

But although at this point Stephen cannot tell the difference between the two types of reality with which he is confronted, they are yet encoded in the way in which the language is used—whether it is used to *designate* something that already exists in the outside world, or whether it is used to create an idea that does not exist as already given in the outside world, but exists in that world only because it is given its form in language. As such, the importance of language is initially set forth in *A Portrait* in terms of referentiality, or its capacity to describe the objective world.

Objective and fictional reality in the text are thus established as undifferentiated givens, already extant in the language that the young Stephen encounters before he has had the opportunity to develop an identity in tandem with his experiences in that language. In this way, it may also be understood that the young Stephen's relationship to language at this point is derived from the outside. The cultural space that forms his existence is the same as that to which he willfully retreats to escape the "din" of voices that later offer him so many conflicting avenues of identity, and from which he begins to view exile as the only escape.

It is, however, to this aspect of existence that the novel tends through all of its linguistic explorations. The young Stephen begins as a being untouched by language, but who is also, in this silent, voiceless, pristine state, free of all of the cultural baggage that language unavoidably brings. Thus the first two chapters of the novel may be characterized as the acquisition of the cultural imprints carried in language through the interaction between language and self. The last two chapters may be characterized by the escape of the self from these cultural imprints back to the silent and voiceless state in which these cultural imprints had no control because they were not there, but with a significant difference: the newfound ability to *use* language, rather than to be used by it.

Such an understanding of *A Portrait* suggests that the third and central chapter, what critics have termed the chapter of "hell-fire sermons,"[56] is, at least in terms of its significance with regard to Stephen's relationship to language, the most important one. It is the strength of the language in this chapter that produces Stephen's most difficult battle in the fight against the cultural power of language to control the individual. Keeping in mind the prior discussion of the place of Roman Catholicism in the culture of nineteenth-century Ireland, the religious rhetoric of this chapter in *A Portrait* bears with it the weight of cultural injunction, as well as the power to generate religious fear. But the significance of the chapter is that it draws the novel's dichotomy between objective and fictional reality into the center of the conflict between religious and secular reality, so that the power of language to control is dismantled and Stephen is finally enabled to take the path to exile, through which he can (or so he thinks) escape. These four aspects of reality are linked to each other through the emotions of fear and shame, which are also linked by a very fine line. This line is the "bridge" and the "frontier" that ties the two together, the subtle, almost invisible, silent connection by which the four realities are interwoven, one into the other. And it is the severing of this line that bursts them all asunder, throws Stephen over the edge, and allows him to run toward the "freedom" of exile.

This line is to be discovered through an understanding of the nature of shame in the text. When the young Stephen is asked by Nasty Roche what his father does, Stephen makes up a lie because he is ashamed before the other boys whose fathers are all well-to-do.[57] But the motivating force of this shame is *fear*, the fear that the others will find out just what kind of man Stephen's father is and make fun of him. More than this, the power of shame is that it is inherently public—shame *must* have an audience in order to be operative. Because it must have an audience, it is essentially cultural, and therefore linguistic in nature, as society is something that, in this novel, should be understood as a linguistic construct.

But because a portion of shame is fear, it is also linked in this way to the religious rhetoric of the third chapter, which induces fear as the result of shame before God. Later in life, Stephen commits his sins of lust in private, in silence, and therefore he does not have to experience the shame he would feel if he were to be found out by his social world. But he cannot hide this shame from the eye of God, and the religious rhetoric of the third chapter allows him to understand that his sin, while silent, is yet known, exposed in all its shame and horror, to the omniscient understanding of God. The fear induced by this religious rhetoric produces in Stephen an attitude toward life that is totally in keeping with religious demands, and therefore a life lived entirely under the dominion of linguistic control in the novel, and far removed from the world of objective reality depicted therein. For the first part of chapter 4, Stephen is represented as living the life of the ideal Christian, doing everything to mortify his earthly existence in the hopes of winning everlasting life in the hereafter. Thus, fear and shame have joined forces to lock Stephen into a mode of behavior within which there is, from his developing perspective, no opportunity for individual growth or development, only a stifling sameness.

The lock that binds Stephen to the linguistic control of fear and shame is the issue of sin. If one commits a sin, one has reason to fear the wrath of God. Therefore, if one does not commit such sin, one need not be bound by the same fear. Obedience to the laws established by the religious rhetoric by which Stephen lives his life after the third chapter of the novel entails the idea of sin as a constant companion. The facility with which sins are committed requires, if they are to be avoided, a constant and rigid watchfulness on the part of the good Christian. Commission of sin reinstitutes the tyranny of fear from which living the good Christian life allows one to be free. Thus, the linguistic conundrum in which Stephen finds himself as a result of the issue of sin is one that explains away in its own terms the doubts by which Stephen would begin the long descent into a return to his prior sinful life:

> Often when he had confessed his doubts and scruples, some momentary inattention at prayer, a movement of trivial anger in his soul or a subtle wilfulness in speech or act, he was bidden by his confessor to name some sin of his past life before absolution was given him. He named it with humility and shame and repented of it once more. It humiliated and shamed him to think that he would never be freed from it wholly, however holily he might live or whatever virtues or perfections he might attain. A restless feeling of guilt would always be present with him: he would confess and repent and be absolved, confess and repent again and be absolved again, fruitlessly. Perhaps that first hasty confession wrung from him by the fear of hell had not been good? Perhaps, concerned only for his imminent doom, he had not had sincere sorrow for his sin? But the surest sign that his confession had been good and that he had had sincere sorrow for his sin was, he knew, the amendment of his life.[58]

The effect of shame is to cause Stephen to confess, but the realization that confession and a holy life would never entirely free him of his shame, that it would always be an endless repetition from which he could never escape, causes Stephen to doubt the authenticity of his faith. And in the midst of this doubt, the issue of fear comes again to the fore—if he were living this life as the result of fear and not of commitment, what then?

Religion represents the last of the voices that urge Stephen toward a path that lies still within the domain of the Irish collective, and far from the alienation and silence of exile. In this sense, the idea of alienation becomes a double bind, because it speaks both to the alienation from temporal community represented by physical exile, and also to the alienation from God that is the meaning of sin. Sin represents a permanent exile from the grace of God, and since one of the primary subjects of religious rhetoric is the idea of eternal life, it results in a powerful cultural injunction against the solely temporal freedom entailed by the embracement of exile. Thus, it is only with the same silence of soul, from the same nothingness of being with which the novel begins, that Stephen, in meeting the call of the order, can hope to escape its grasp:

> He . . . wondered vaguely which window would be his if he ever joined the order. Then he wondered at the vagueness of his wonder,

at the remoteness of his soul from what he had hitherto imagined her sanctuary, at the frail hold which so many years of order and obedience had of him when once a definite and irrevocable act of his threatened to end for ever, in time and in eternity, his freedom. The voice of the director urging upon him the proud claims of the church and the mystery and power of the priestly office repeated itself idly in his memory. His soul was not there to hear and greet it and he knew now that the exhortation he had listened to had already fallen into an idle formal tale.[59]

It is from this position of silence with regard to all of the social voices by which Stephen would be bound that the place of language in *A Portrait* is fully comprehended. Language represents all that is social and collective in this text—home, family, nation, country, religion all belong to a world of communion and brotherhood, from which Stephen stands apart. From his perspective Stephen, in order to be free, to be an individual in his own right, *must* stand apart, since within this linguistic world in which all participation in society exists as a given already in the society, there is no cultural space available that is not already imbued with a predetermining ideology, within which he can grow in the individual and unfettered freedom he seeks.

As such, the issue of sin creates an alternative narrative space within the text by separating Stephen from the religious rhetoric that is the most powerful sector of the culture from which he desires to escape. This alternative narrative space, one that symbolically represents the meaning of the politics of cultural space in Joyce's novel, is one of silence, and darkness, and it is by this that the last two chapters of the book are dominated, as opposed to the linguistic excess that dominates the first two chapters. This alternative narrative space is made evident by the way in which it is described in Stephen's surrender to the pleasures of sin in the arms of a prostitute:

> With a sudden movement she bowed his head and joined her lips to his and he read the meaning of her movements in her frank uplifted eyes. It was too much for him. He closed his eyes, surrendering himself to her, body and mind, conscious of nothing in the world but the dark pressure of her softly parting lips. They pressed upon his brain as upon his lips as though they were the vehicle of a vague speech; and between them he felt an unknown and timid pressure, darker than the swoon of sin, softer than sound or odour.[60]

Stephen's descent into sin is characterized here as a separation from language. There is no speech between himself and the prostitute, only a physical communication that takes one into hidden depths unknown to words. With this passage at the end of the novel's second chapter, the speechlessness of sin is juxtaposed in the very next chapter to the wordiness of religion, which goes on and on in depicting the horrors of a world that one cannot see and that exists alone for those who sin while still living in the world one *can* see. The world depicted in the third chapter is a world one such as Stephen cannot be certain exists, but which, if it does exist, is certainly to be feared. The silence of sin here established may be understood as the silence within which Stephen develops a relationship to language that allows him to use it for his own designs. The silence of the "swoon of sin" is also that of unconsciousness, or preconsciousness, the silence of Being without or before the intervention of language. Within it, Stephen is able to escape the cultural injunctions of language to be, and he therefore exists somewhere outside, exiled back to that zone in which he had existed at the opening of the novel, as a young child without the power of speech:

> He was destined to learn his own wisdom apart from others or to learn the wisdom of others himself wandering among the snares of the world. The snares of the world were its ways of sin. He would fall. He had not yet fallen but he would fall silently, in an instant. Not to fall was too hard, too hard: and he felt the silent lapse of his soul, as it would be at some instant to come, falling, falling but not yet fallen, still unfallen but about to fall.[61]

What begins at the end of chapter 2 with an unwilling participation, yet fascinated desire on the part of Stephen in exploring the vagaries of sinful lust, ends in chapter 4 with a conscious decision on his part to embrace the silence of sin, to embrace sin as a means to retrieve the silence by which the cultural injunctions of language could be rendered powerless over him, and the unfettered reality of exile placed within view.

What Stephen desires is freedom, something which, in light of the numerous societal voices that seek to bind him, is difficult, if not impossible, to attain. In this, Stephen's struggle recalls the problem of language, because it is on the level of language that society asserts its control over him. This problem concerns two paradoxical properties of language: the one its power to oppress, the other its power to set free. In *A Portrait*, as with Marcel in the *Recherche*, the bridge between these two properties is Stephen, whose relation to language in the text may be understood to link Joyce's physical exile to the creation of a new kind of exile, that of Stephen's artistic exile, in which the final result is reconciliation, as opposed to alienation. Thus, Stephen's desire for freedom, while it seems the same freedom sought by Joyce, is rather, a more abstract form of what Joyce asserts in his interpretation in his own life of the *non serviam*, that is, his refusal to marry, his rejection of the Church. As such, while the reader may want to regard the protagonist of *A Portrait* as merely a fictional construct intended to represent Joyce himself, it becomes clear that this is not possible because the relationship between Joyce and Stephen is far more complex than that of simple autobiography.

Though the story of *A Portrait* is told in a somewhat autobiographical form, it may be immediately recognized that there is no direct "I" narrator until the end of the novel, when the narration is continued in Stephen's strangely isolated journal entries. While the lack of an "I" narrator in itself is not strange, the fact that there is also neither a third-person omniscient narrator nor even a third person limited narrator raises an important question with regard to the text: Who then is telling the story up to the point of Stephen's journal? It is not Stephen, since at no place in the text does one find the existence of a fictional "I" other than in his journal. It is not a third-person narrator, since there is nowhere a voice within the text that functions independently of the protagonist to objectively describe him or his world. Instead, the voice by which the story is narrated speaks only in terms of Stephen's developing perceptions. This is evident through the way in which the language of the text becomes more and more complex as Stephen grows older, its increasing complexity mirroring the development of his intellectual capacities.

The only way to answer the above question is to determine that *both* Stephen and Joyce are *simultaneously* telling the story. Because the novel is narrated in terms of Stephen's perceptions, its scope remains always within the bounds of his consciousness. But because Stephen's perceptions are also arranged in a certain order in the novel, by which its form is given, and because these perceptions are not narrated by Stephen himself, but by someone outside of him who is also at the same time inside him, or his subjective perceptions could not be realized, the existence of another voice speaking in tandem with Stephen's own cannot be denied. In fact, this voice speaks for Stephen even before he can speak for himself, since, at the novel's beginning, he is a baby with very incoherent thoughts that come randomly and have no real object.

As such, the narrator of *A Portrait* may be conceived as a composite Joyce/Stephen, not entirely one and the same, nor yet entirely separate. The idea of a composite narrator Joyce/Stephen, while seeming to imply that Stephen is only a fictional cover for Joyce's autobiographical aims (much the same as Proust's narrator "Marcel" serves as a cover for similar aims on the part of Proust), is actually rather the way by which it is possible to understand how Stephen is *not* Joyce at all. Ironically, it is the extremely close connection between author and protagonist that reveals how they differ. This is because the narrative voice of *A Portrait*, since it is neither first person nor third person, but somehow a combination of both, serves to differentiate Joyce from his protagonist by granting him the aesthetic distance necessary to keep Stephen within the imaginative realm. Aesthetic distance is gained because Joyce, as the author of the voice that, if evident in the text, would have been in the third person, speaks there instead only in skeletal form, that is, as the hidden guide who determines to which of Stephen's perceptions the reader will be privy, and in what order they shall be revealed. In this way, Joyce remains a present yet silent aspect of the text, but his presence is subsumed by that of Stephen until, at the novel's end, with the entrance of Stephen's journal, he is simply eradicated and Stephen takes the stage as a full-blown "I" narrator who relates unaided his own perceptions of the world around him. But while Proust's narrator seeks to represent itself in the first-person in order to bring to light a submerged, somewhat individual cultural representation, Joyce's narrator uses the first-person in order to give voice to a silenced cultural representation of an oppressed and beleaguered, almost nonexistent, Irish national identity.

The entrance of Stephen's journal in the text represents the articulation of the alternative narrative space of freedom that he first experiences as the silence, or wordlessness, of the "swoon of sin." In Stephen's journal, one narrative voice, that of Stephen, succeeds the other. Thus, Stephen's "swoon of sin" becomes the divide by which the two attitudes toward language in the text—obedience to cultural injunction in the form of religious rhetoric and the enjoyment of artistic freedom—are separated. And when the narrative voice by which Joyce is represented is eradicated, three important things are implied with respect to the problem of language in this novel: 1), the disappearance of the guiding narrative voice leaves Stephen in control of the representation of his own perceptions; 2), Stephen's mastering of the communication of his own perceptions indicates that he controls, rather than being controlled by, the language he uses; and 3), the fact that he communicates his perceptions by way of writing rather than speech reveals how even though ensconced in almost total exile, his alienation may be used as reconciliation, through dissemination of the printed word.

In this, the idea of communion in the novel becomes very important, and much more complicated than it may seem at first glance. In understanding this, it is essential to note that at the end of chapter 3, after Stephen's confession, he is about to take communion, and the chapter ends with the line "The ciborium had come to him." However, the issue as to whether or not he actually does take communion at this moment is left in the balance. One may assume that he did, or one may assume that he did not. However, if the dual nature of the idea of "alienation" previously discussed with regard to spiritual and temporal worlds is taken into consideration, it becomes interesting to suggest that the idea of "communion" may have a similar dual meaning, and an analysis of "communion" in this way also suggests a useful way to view Stephen's attitude toward writing.

Stephen's final assumption of control over language indicates that the freedom he seeks has been attained, because his success in taking such control means that societal injunctions no longer limit him. In this way, Stephen's relation to language becomes one of "freedom" because he makes of the power of language another religion of which he himself is the master. As such, the idea of the writer may also be seen to link both Joyce and Stephen, although in different ways. Through writing from the stance of exile, Stephen may, seemingly, eradicate the societal demands that would refuse him the possibility of individuality, while leaving open the door to communicate with his countrymen, because he eradicates these cultural injunctions in print. Through writing Stephen's acquisition of the power over language that enables him (Stephen) to write in this way, Joyce achieves a level of communion with his (Joyce's) countrymen that shows how Stephen broke, and thus how others could break, the bonds of such cultural injunctions, in order to achieve Stephen's (and Joyce's) same degree of personal freedom.

The idea of communion is important here because rather than the communion of religion, in which the individual is obliged to emphasize the role he or she plays in a community subjugated to God, in *A Portrait*, Joyce describes an iconoclastic, secular communion, the communion of individual freedom, in which individual will and identity are subject only to the self in reaching out, through the printed word, to the objective community outside the self. Thus, for Joyce, the goal of literary art in this novel is to create a new cultural space for the possibility of individual existence unfettered by the social demands that would prevent individuals from engaging in the process of self-creation, thereby opening up to Irish society the very idea of "true" individuality and the possibility of achieving it. In this, the idea of the writer is quite important, because in the temporal world, it is only the writer who manipulates rather than merely receives words, and who as a result would also seem to have, like God, the power of creation.[62]

Thus, underlying Stephen's desire for freedom is one overriding question, a question that must be continually asked in the exploration into the nature and function of language in *A Portrait*: Is there truly a world beyond what we know as that created in language? This question gives rise to others that are more urgent, questions that immediately center the problem of language on the issue of the self: What is the self if it is not formed in language? Can the self exist outside of language? What is the proper relationship of the self to language? With these questions, Joyce's escape from his notion of Irish mediocrity is revealed as both deriving from and depending on Stephen's relationship to language in the novel, and the central importance of exile, both physical and social, in that relation. This relationship, which takes the whole novel to come to fruition, may be understood as the fictional representation of the connection to language that was necessary if Joyce was to create a character like Stephen: the loner, the iconoclast, the exile, through whose triumph over received cultural notions the Irish conscience would, in his view, be liberated as well. By a complex interweaving of objective and fictional, religious and secular realities through the consciousness of Stephen Dedalus, Joyce shows how each of these realities has its foundation in language, then reveals their underlying fragility by exploding their linguistic power over Stephen through the twin effects of fear and shame. In this way, language in *A Portrait* is used to create Stephen's idea of *himself*, in rejecting all possibilities of becoming any of the ideas of potential identity that are proffered in the text. Stephen's idea of himself is an isolated fiction, but his relationship to language is thus one in which *he*, rather than *it*, decides the terms of existence.

In this way, Stephen's connection to language is one that, at the end of *A Portrait*, offers Joyce a representational platform on which reality has been radically reconstructed in such a way that it becomes possible for him to write from outside the constraints of the English literary tradition, while still using the language within which it is conveyed to write himself back into it on his own terms. And it is as a result of his having positioned himself in this way, what Schorer, quoting Stephen himself, calls "refining himself out of existence,"[63] that the creative challenges to objective reality effected by Joyce in his subsequent works find their bold beginning.

The following chapter picks up where this one leaves off, expanding our view of the hidden cultural possibility in modernism and modernity by examining the impact of institutionalized viewpoints and the (vain) attempt at escape from the reality of cultural injunction—the desperate search, beyond the edge, for something that *could* be real, if only . . .

CHAPTER 5

"The Bulldog in My Own Backyard"

James Baldwin, Giovanni's Room, and the Rhetoric of Flight

> The future is not (only) monoculture.
> —James Clifford, *The Predicament*
> *of Culture*

LITERARY CRITICISM, AFRICAN-AMERICAN
LITERATURE, AND THE LEGACY OF JAMES BALDWIN

One of the most pressing difficulties for the contemporary scholar-critic who desires to discuss the fictional work of an African-American author is the opposition between what is sociological, historical, and/or autobiographical, and what is literary in many such texts. Due to the special place of the African-American in North American society, this extra-fictional triumvirate has in the past very often served to overshadow, if not entirely obliterate, the traditional issue at hand in the criticism of any fictional work: the unveiling of the complex and multifarious web of meanings and associations contained within the language by which the text is given form.

However, the cultural significance of the African-American text often reflects not only a problematic social history in view of which such texts have often become the vehicle of protest. It may also reflect the problematic relation between the African-American individual and society, since even when such texts decry the avenue of protest, the knowledge that their author is an African-American can often place them squarely back within the sociological through the particular significance that the author's race may hold for the scholar-critic, black or white—as suggested by the analysis, in chapter 2, of the role often played by ideology in critical interpretations. What this means is that very often, it has been more important to the scholar-critic to write about the African-American artist's supposed or desired relation to his or her society as a result of his or her race, than to analyze the work of that author itself with any unmixed degree of aesthetic concern.[1]

This is precisely the critical and artistic problem with which James Baldwin painfully struggled throughout his career as a novelist and essayist. As such, an elaboration of the critical terrain that he faced as an author is quite useful in beginning to understand his work in relation to the politics of cultural space and, beyond that, within a broad vision of literary modernism and modernity. By identifying the historical overemphasis of scholar-critics on the sociological, rather than aesthetic aspects of African-American texts, I do not mean to suggest that discussions of the African-American artist's racial relation to American society are not important—simply that too concentrated an attention on this single aspect of a text written by such an author often takes the critical emphasis completely off of the text itself, while at the same time helping to determine subsequent reactions to subsequent African-American texts.[2] As a result, when what is fictional in African-American literary art is forced to give way to what is sociological, such art is then forced also to take on an assignment of value determined not by its individual artistic and/or literary contribution, but by the intensity of its sociological or political impact, or the lack thereof.

Furthermore, when aesthetic value is determined sociologically, rather than artistically, all of the criteria of judgment are different from what they are for the text that is primarily judged from an the aesthetic point of view. A good example of such a reading is the following by the late Irving Howe:

> Baldwin's second novel, *Giovanni's Room*, seems to me a flat failure. It abandons Negro life entirely (not in itself a cause for judgment) and focuses upon the distraught personal relations of several young Americans adrift in Paris.[3]

Although Howe has offered a well-placed disclaimer, it is not certain that he does not find Baldwin's novel a failure because the author chose to "abandon Negro life entirely," since he does not offer any other clear reason why he has so classified it. And although this abandonment is "not in itself a cause for judgment," we are left with the feeling that in Howe's view, a novel written by a "Negro" author should in turn focus on "Negro life," and if it does not do so, it is somehow a gross misrepresentation. But a gross misrepresentation of what? What *is* "Negro life," as Howe would define it? That Baldwin *should* discuss Howe's notion of "Negro life" at all is more a sociological, than an aesthetic, judgment. One must also ask, would Howe have applied his notion of "Negro life" (which, in any case, must be his own definition of whatever that might be) if Baldwin, as the text's author, had *not* been an African-American? It seems obvious that the answer to this question is no. Though Howe wrote the above in 1963, the contemporary emphasis on highlighting cultural difference would seem in many ways to support, rather than challenge, his conclusions.

But understanding Howe's assertion is not an easy task, for it is not simply an assertion but a cultural representation of a sociological situation, one that has been largely determined, as previously mentioned, by the history of African-Americans in North American society. Leaving the slave heritage of African-Americans in the United States aside, that history has passed through a whirlwind of change during the last fifty years, change so startling that the sociological differences between the lives of the generation of African-Americans born near the turn of the twentieth century and the lives of the young African-Americans of today seem almost impossible to comprehend.

For literary criticism, however, such change is clearly revealed in the history of its racial terminology: during the first part of the twentieth century, African-Americans were referred to as "Negroes," and, as the century progressed, as "colored." During the 1960s and early 70s, with the efforts of the African-American consciousness-raising groups who preferred not to use the above terminology to refer to themselves, African-Americans came to be known as "black"; with the institutionalization of African-American studies and the development of the fields of African-American history and literature from the late 1960s to the present day, use of the terms "African-American" and "Afro-American" became more or less synonymous with the term "black." Each of these terms, however, carries with it a particular historical, political, and sociological significance, so that their use allows the reader not only to place whatever critical work makes use of them in chronological time, but by and through that placement, to understand many extra-literary things about the issues with which that work comes to grips, by virtue of the socio-historico-political situation of the time period in North America during which whatever scholar-critic is/was writing.

These changes in racial terminology also permit the contemporary scholar-critic to understand the literary criticism dealing with African-American authors that was written roughly during the first half of the twentieth century as being sometimes heavily influenced by the social climate of the times during which it was produced. In this way, just as the literary texts written by such authors are frequently overshadowed by the issue of race and the problem of protest, the literary criticism concerning these texts may reveal the weight of that history both in its choice of issues and in its manner of handling them.

A further sociological complication, one that finds its basis in historical fact, is that at least until the mid- to late 1960s, the work of African-American authors was, for the most part, written about by white journalists and academic intellectuals who had little or no social contact with African-Americans. This fact produces another kind of opposition for the contemporary scholar-critic interested in writing about African-American literature. Critical work must, of necessity, engage in a dialogue with the critical ideas that have been articulated before. But, due to the history of race relations in the United States, the scholar-critic who engages in a systematic study of previous critical work surrounding established African-American authors may find buried by the years a curious relationship between the literary work and the critical texts surrounding it. This relationship consists of the articulation of judgments made more often than not by a white and essentially separate subjectivity about a black and equally separate subjectivity. In the silent (and silenced) chasm between the two lies all of the history of race relations in America and its concomitant sociological effects, as well as whatever cultural materials need be used in the construction of stereotypical attitudes toward race and/or race relations. As many biases as may exist in such attitudes, whether they be held by critics black or white, are to be found— in any analysis purporting to look beyond (and beneath) the surface—in as many critical texts.

This situation produces a certain difficulty with regard to the establishment of a rapport between the ideas of contemporary criticism of African-American literature and that of previous years, one which becomes evident on two levels: the first is that racial sociological change in the United States in the last twenty years or so has outstripped the effects of historical racial material conditions. What this means is that while historical socioeconomic conditions (that is, the nonassimilation of African-Americans from the economic condition of slavery into the mainstream of American society) produced a particular attitude with regard to race relations, the actual material conditions of the 1990s have revealed a level of racial assimilation inconceivable in the early 1960s. The understanding of this level of assimilation must be qualified, however, to state that there are two kinds of assimilation—the public and the private. Public assimilation, that is, the types of positions and offices held in society by African-Americans, is at an all-time high, and will continue to increase as long as young African-Americans continue to take (and have the opportunity to take) the road of higher education. Private assimilation, however, while it is shown to be on the rise with increased numbers of interracial friendships and relationships, and the resulting increase in the number of magazine articles, TV shows and movies encompassing the subject of racial intermingling,[4] is still not occurring at the same rate as that of public assimilation.[5] Nevertheless, the contemporary scholar-critic must write about African-American literature within the context of a society that is substantially different, on an actual, material level, from that of, for instance, the early 1960s, when the study of African-American literature was only just beginning to open up as a possibility of a field in its own right, and much criticism on the subject began to be written.

The second difficulty with regard to the establishment of a rapport between the ideas of contemporary criticism of African-American literature and that of previous years pertains to the way in which contemporary criticism of African-American literature is handled, as well as the issues with which it is concerned. The twentieth century saw the development of African-American literature as an institutionalized field within both the areas of historical and literary studies, as well as its development as an area study. Thus, literary criticism in this field during earlier periods speaks more to the fact that the field was not as yet established. As such, its critical attitude is more one of defense and justification, seeking to elaborate strong reasons for giving isolated critical attention to the study of African-American literature which was, early on, relatively unknown, and certainly noncanonized. In this, also, prior criticism is sociological—rather than confronting the aesthetic issues raised by a minority fictional text, it was frequently more concerned with establishing a cultural mandate for the existence of such study at all. In seeking this cultural mandate, such criticism often speaks instead to the "text" formed by popular opinion, which it does not set out so much to analyze and critique as simply to oppose.

Within such a framework of prior critical endeavor, it is difficult to draw the links by which a critical continuity may be established between it and current debates on the subject. The significance of the rupture between the two critical apparatuses is that the contemporary critical apparatus with regard to African-American literature has been radically changed by the continued entry into the literary profession of talented minority literary scholar-critics, such as Henry Louis Gates, Jr., Hortense Spillers, Trudier Harris, Houston A. Baker, Jr., Cornel West, bell hooks, Deborah McDowell, Claudia Tate, Mary Helen Washington, and others. The most important way in which their contributions have changed the critical apparatus surrounding African-American literature is simple: they are intellectuals, and they are African-Americans, where before the critical domain concerning this subject was largely peopled by white scholar-critics. As such, the critical atmosphere surrounding African-American literature, once dominated by a white and, as a result of the sociohistorical situation of American society, essentially separate subjectivity, is now tempered by an African-American subjectivity whose experience of North American society is, by virtue of that fact, often much closer to that of the African-American author. The entry into the academic profession of such minority intellectuals has helped foster the change of what was once largely a white and sociologically separate critical subjectivity into one that, while it can still often be just as separate (at least on a social level), is frequently more concerned by the cultural issues currently being raised by the study of African-American literature itself, rather than by the study of its sociohistorical significance.[6]

In the current critical climate, however, debate is increasingly concentrated now more than ever before on the concept of culture, and all of the questions that the idea of culture brings to the fore, as elaborated in chapter 1. What has heretofore been considered American culture is, in its traditionally Anglo-American aspect, decried by many as "monocultural," because it has for so long been presented as "the" American culture. This representation of "the" American culture took place in spite of the fact that American culture has always, in actual reality, been pluralistic, due to the ethnic diversity that is the historical foundation of American society.[7] In this, the debate on canon revision and culture studies has become of paramount importance in the effort to find a way to allow the plurality of American society to be revealed as a substantial part of the American cultural heritage, so that that heritage may be more truthfully and adequately represented by making it part of the larger body of common knowledge. In this attempt, it must ask, among others, two fundamental questions: if American society is, in actual fact, pluralistic, how can it as a nation espouse a cultural heritage that is monocultural, that is, primarily Anglo-American? And if it bases notions of its national identity and cultural heritage on a monocultural idea not true to its social reality, what effects will such a situation have on the future development of American culture, and what difficulties will it pose for any revisionist concerns?

While such questions would require the culture studies project to remain at least somewhat sociological in emphasis in this regard, there is a major difference between the way in which literary criticism espousing this approach handles African-American literature and the way in which the literary criticism of the 1950s and 1960s handles it, in terms of sociology. This difference is that while earlier literary criticism often concerns itself with the sociological in African-American literary texts as an important area of exploration due to the need to justify such study to begin with, contemporary culture studies approaches are concerned with the sociology of culture itself, that is, how and why aesthetic value is ascertained, who ascertains it and why, and which criteria are important and which are not in the process of ascertaining it. Thus, critical culture studies analyses would necessarily ask questions that are in one sense sociological, because they are concerned with determinations of culture, but that are in another sense aesthetic, because they require actual and direct textual confrontation if they are to be answered.

Among the questions that might come under the rubric of such an approach in this regard are those concerned with the "place" of minority literature in American literature, as well as the idea of calling minority literature "minority" at all. What role does "minority" literature play in American literature? What does its traditional exclusion from mainstream American literature reveal about that literature? What does such exclusion say about American culture in general?[8] What does the term "minority" mean? To whom does it refer? What is the relationship between the production of literature, who produces it, the type of literature produced, and the way in which that literature is classified? How does the meaning of the term "minority" affect the reception of literature classified as such?

This last question becomes very important when considering the basic assumptions of the entire culture studies project, particularly as it relates to the study of African-American literature. The meaning of the term "minority" is accompanied by any number of extra-literary associations that perpetuate the critical emphasis on the sociohistorical and/or autobiographical in such texts. When a text is classified as "minority," it is also viewed as "alien," "other," as existing somehow outside the general idea of the order of things.[9] As such, the politics of cultural space may be understood as operative here in the powerful effects that such predetermined significations exert over institutionally sanctioned interpretations. In the context of such a formulation, this type of text is already no longer regarded simply as an instance of artistic creation, but as a statement that has a certain place in the social scheme, and it is this "place" that reinscribes the sociological within the literary critical endeavor.

The most significant way in which the term "minority" brings about this reinscribing of the sociological is in the fact that it applies not to the text itself, but to the *author* of the text, a situation already discussed in chapters 1 and 2. As a result, the idea of the "place" of "minority" literature within American literature is itself in some ways representative of the idea of the "place" of minorities within American society. In this way, the handling of texts written by minority authors replicates the situating of minority groups within American society through categorizing them as "other," and therefore alien to what is considered mainstream. Such cultural locating of a text with regard to the *social status* alone of its author, rather than the interrelationship between such status and the *cultural context* in which the text was created, automatically brings a degree of sociological baggage to the interpretation of that text. This is because in such a case, the particular social situation of the author, as a minority, may color the reader's expectations before he or she has even begun to read the book.[10]

A good way to look at how this works may be to compare the literary critical apparatus surrounding James Baldwin to that surrounding James Joyce. While seemingly incongruous, at least from a traditional perspective due to the different canonical status of the works of both authors, such a comparison may in actuality be made because although Joyce is not an American author, and did not write during the same time period as did Baldwin, the similarities between the social positions of both authors vis-à-vis their respective societies and the cultural contexts within which these may be understood reveals both the inner workings and the power of the literary critical apparatus in creating critical perspectives on literary works and their authors—or the institutionally sanctioned articulation of the politics of cultural space. The most striking similarity between the two authors is that both Joyce and Baldwin represent the experience of a form of involuntary exile (as explained in chapter 1) that leads to a voluntary exile by which their situations of involuntary exile come to be understood within a much broader perspective which is then made use of in literary creation. While the involuntary exile experienced by Joyce does not have to do specifically with race, it does have to do with the same kind of perceived cultural difference that is, in America, inscribed by race. This difference is the historical difference that pertains between British culture and Irish culture, something which, because of the historical British occupation of Ireland, may serve to produce much the same relationship between opressor and oppressed as does racial prejudice in American society. There are, of course, certain important dissimilarities between American racial prejudice and the historical British occupation of Ireland, such as, for example, the fact that the Irish remain on the soil that belonged to their forebears, while African-Americans are culturally exiles twice-removed, since they were originally stolen from their homeland, then exiled a second time, because of their race, in the country in which they were forced to make their home. Both of these instances are similar, albeit in a different way, to the cultural difference identified in chapter 3 between the cultural subtext of homosexuality in Proust's *Recherche* and the novel's primary theme of the search for social acceptance. All three are concerned with cultural situations of oppression that create striking similarities in the cultural situation of the oppressed, one that centers on language and the way in which language is used, as wa Thiong'o elaborates:

> The choice of language and the use to which language is put is central to a people's definition of themselves in relation to their natural and social environment, indeed in relation to the entire universe. . . . Language, any language, has a dual character: it is both a means of communication and a carrier of culture. . . . Culture is a product of the history which it in turn reflects. . . . Language as culture is thus mediating between me and my own self; between my own self and other selves; between me and nature. Language is mediating in my very being. . . . Language is . . . inseparable from ourselves as a community of human beings with a specific form and character, a specific history, a specific relationship to the world.[11]

In this way, it may be understood that the way in which language is used becomes a powerful force both in the creation of a people and in the mastery of a people. For Marcel Proust, language becomes not only the means by which he is oppressed, but the vehicle of deception as well as the road to "freedom" through the possibility of confession. For James Joyce, the problem of language becomes the necessity to use English as opposed to Gaelic, and the resulting menace to the survival of Irish culture of such linguistic hegemony, so that his literary project encompasses the desire and the imperative to force the English language to mean in a distinctly Irish way. For James Baldwin, the problem of language is not only the necessity to use English, but the fact that English is the only language that *can* be used, since for him, the language of his African forebears has long since been lost. But, more important, the problem of language in Baldwin's case, as in that of Joyce, concerns also the uses to which language is put. This refers directly to the label "minority" discussed above, and all of its concomitant sociological baggage.

But where the comparison between the social positions (and their requisite cultural contexts) of these authors and the effects of these on their work becomes even more interesting is in the comparison between the North American critical apparatuses surrounding both Joyce and Baldwin. Since that apparatus surrounding Joyce has already been elaborated in the preceding chapter, it will suffice to say here that, particularly in its earliest manifestations, it is characterized by a keen admiration of Joyce's genius that quickly mushrooms into veneration. Under the cover of veneration and the intensity of critical concentration on Joyce's artistic prowess and technical mastery, the cultural context of Joyce's work (aside from its references to Catholicism) has been, for the most part, ignored—hidden and silenced by the dominant Euro-American modernist discourse to which Joyce's work has, from midcentury, largely been assimilated.

In the case of James Baldwin, however, the proliferation of critical essays concerning the question of identity reveal the crushing weight of the sociological in relation to the ethnicity of the author, while simultaneously forming a particular viewpoint with regard to his work and creating, also based on his ethnicity, a particular place for his work within the cultural imagination, one that indelibly marks any analysis of its cultural context.[12] This is not to say that such critical work is not valuable in and of itself, but rather, that the volume of work on the problem of identity with regard to Baldwin serves as proof that the sociological aspect of the life of an ethnic writer can often become more important than, if not completely obfuscate, the aesthetic contribution of his or her work, while at the same time codifying its cultural context in terms of a particular sociologically determined perspective. With Baldwin, this is also exacerbated by the fact that his own work, in the form of his numerous essays, also serves to reinscribe him, as an author, into such a singular, sociologically determined view. The fact that such reinscription can complicate the determination of aesthetic contributions with regard to the fictional work of "minority" authors becomes very important when considering, as in the case of a comparison between Marcel Proust, James Joyce, and

James Baldwin, three authors whose canonical status, with regard to modernism and modernity, exists on both ends of the traditional spectrum (while Baldwin is certainly a canonical writer when considered from the perspective of African-American literature, his work has not commonly been considered in the context of or in relation to modernism and modernity).

It is here that the uses to which language is put when discussing the significance of language with regard to oppressor and oppressed is most clearly understood. This is because one of the most important functions of literary criticism, which is to comment on the meaning and contribution of literary works, serves also, in so doing, to create culture. That is, literary critical judgments of individual literary works serve either to build or to destroy the reputations of such works and their authors and, in this way, to regulate the size of their reading audiences. At the same time, these judgments determine the ways in which the reading audiences they help to create will think about the texts representing the concerns of such judgments. As such, when sociological concerns become an overly important part of the literary critical act, they can operate in such a way as to force literary criticism to maintain the status quo through the concerns with which it occupies itself—thereby building and reinforcing cultural assumptions that also simultaneously create and assign textual value according to extra-literary criteria. One example of such an extra-literary criterion is the relation between the ethnicity of an author and the critical reception of his or her work. On the one hand, such critical reception, translated into literary critical knowledges disseminated in the university, creates an institutionalized body of knowledge about given texts that affects all of those who enter the university and learn about them; on the other hand, translated into newspaper and magazine reviews and/or articles, such critical reception has a very important impact, positive or negative, on the attitudes toward particular texts of reading audiences in the public at large outside the university.

While culture studies approaches also place somewhat of an emphasis on the author, their bent is to recuperate, reveal, reinterpret and reevaluate, rather than to classify, alienate and/or categorize.[13] The culture studies approach to this difficulty can, nevertheless, still be problematic in some ways. This may be understood in that even while such approaches seek to offer a different perspective with regard to literature traditionally considered as existing outside the cultural mainstream, and even though they may ask questions that interrogate the very foundations of that cultural mainstream, they may also often continue to operate, specifically with respect to African-American literature, within the same conceptual framework of "black" and "white," or binary opposition. While this framework may take various forms, such as "ethnic" and "mainstream," "minority" and "majority," "marginal" and "central," "colonized" and "colonizer," all are different ways of saying essentially the same thing. What is said also takes various forms, but in the case of African-American literature, the concepts "black" and "white" each carry with them certain connotations by which they may be defined, and these connotations also carry hidden sociological implications. The fact that culture studies approaches, while somewhat confrontational, often operate within the same general conceptual framework with which "minority" texts have always been approached reveals that they can also be, on a very profound level, simply a permutation of the idea of protest.[14] This becomes the case when such approaches are solely based on the very idea that they seek to invalidate: that there are texts that are considered "mainstream" and others that are considered "minority," and that this situation must be changed.

Thus, while questions often asked by culture studies approaches may bring us closer to an aesthetic consideration of African-American texts, they do not always escape the underlying idea that the world is divided into "black" and "white." This is of course largely due to the fact that *de facto* social realities indicate in some ways that this is so, but the continual replication of such cultural realities also serves to perpetuate them. Yet if the goal of culture studies is to escape the rigidity of ethnic division and achieve a new understanding of today's multiple cultural identities, it must first offer such a possibility itself. This, however, can only be done through the realization that the *ideas* that culture studies puts forward with regard to such newfangled cultural understanding are not the same thing as this cultural understanding itself. Is it not possible that continued discussion of multiplicity, hybridity, and the like as *ideas* could serve, rather, to help us distance ourselves from the difficult process of restructuring and reassessment they will demand in terms of social, critical, and institutional change, just enough so that nothing really has to change except the surface reality for each of these contexts? For true change to take place, the retreat into discussion must sooner or later give way to the creation of a cultural space within which such change may begin to develop, and without which, it never will.[15]

The division of American social reality into "minority" and "majority" offers a situation in which everyone, not just racial or ethnic minorities, is trapped. These categories, with their connotative baggage, prescribe of what, according to where one falls on the ethnic continuum, one's identity should consist, and this occurs in rigid and well-defined ways. Within the social framework that classifies American reality into "majority" and "minority," a crisis of identity is discovered, a crisis that is commonly ascribed only to the "minority" (particularly the African-American "minority"), but which may also be understood as a crisis that includes the "majority," or the white mainstream, as well as all other ethnic-American groups (who are also usually classified as "nonwhite" or "other"). If the conceptual framework "black"/"white" is understood in terms of its connotative meanings, and if these connotative meanings are believed to constitute or to partially constitute individual identity with regard to ethnicity, then the connotative meanings in American society of the terms "black" and "white" may also be understood as mutually exclusive. What this means is that what is considered "white" cannot be considered "black," and vice-versa. Where this poses a problem is not just in the attempt to describe individual identity, which is by its nature unclassifiable in static terms, but in the attempt to embrace the idea of cultural multiplicity. The problem is that personal differences are summarily rejected, forcing the individual, "minority" or "mainstream," into a kind of supermarket conformity or, in the event that such conformity with the prescribed and polarized "identities" of these authorized collectivities is rejected, an intense alienation where, too often, only silence reigns. Into this silent cultural space fall many different voices, cultural experiences, and cultural realities, all of which share one important characteristic—they know the pain and difficulty of silence. Yet it is only within such silence, in reading this silence into words, that the cultural space that would allow for the understanding of the cultural reality of multiplicity, changeability, hybridity, and instability may be found. And it is also here that the difficult excavation of this buried cultural space of silence, alienation, otherness, and shifting ground must inevitably begin.

This is so because in doing this, it is necessary to come out of rigidly prescribed, sociologically determined ideas as to what exactly constitutes ethnic American cultural identity and to embrace a new idea of such cultural identity that can explain the larger ethnic picture of the American, and more broadly, the Western, social reality.[16] The attempt to do this is, however, often extremely difficult, because of the fact that popular belief as to the way in which racial identity is constituted particularly in North America is inscribed within the connotative meanings of the conceptual framework, described above, on which the relationship between the races is based. Because of the historical relationship in America between the white mainstream and African-Americans (what the black sociologist, W. E. B. DuBois, in his seminal work, *The Souls of Black Folk*, recognizes as "the color line")[17] this conceptual framework also operates between the two social groups in a potentially alienating fashion.[18]

As a result, when the situation is viewed from its most polarized extreme, each attempt on the part of the white mainstream to protect what it conceives as its cultural identity takes the possibility of full American identity away from African-Americans, because that of the white mainstream relies on its identification of itself as "not black," that is, not any of those adjectives commonly associated with "blackness." Concomitantly, each attempt on the part of African-Americans to gain full American identity takes the possibility of such identity away from whites, because it would force a change in the social connotations of those adjectives by which the idea of "white" is commonly described.[19]

In the case of the African-American identity, this problem is complicated by the fact that if the connotations of the idea of "black" within the conceptual framework have been accepted by the African-American, he or she also cannot aspire to full American identity. This is because aspiring to full American identity rather than simply African-American identity would immediately negate what he or she conceives as the idea of being "black." This is due to the fact that any conception that would fall outside of the way in which "black" is described within the accepted American racial conceptual framework must, of necessity (within that framework), refer to what is "white," as the framework is dichotomous, and allows for no other interpretation. This leaves only the possibility of searching for the roots of African-American identity particularly in West Africa, or the idea of using only African cultural materials in its establishment. The difficulty facing this endeavor is that even though there have been some who have found many West-African survivals in African-American culture, such identity is in many ways now largely more specifically racial, rather than directly cultural, in the material sense, due to the African-American history of six generations of exile on the North American continent.[20] Such problems help to illuminate the idea that the question of cultural identity in America can seem a continual push/pull between opposing forces that offers little hope of resolution unless the idea of such identity itself, and American identity in particular, is put into question, intensely examined, and redefined.

It is here that the voice of James Baldwin becomes most illuminating, in its elucidation of the politics of cultural space in this circumstance. From his first collection of essays, *Notes of a Native Son*,[21] Baldwin begins the elaboration of a new attitude toward the meaning of race in America that begins with a reexamination of what it means to be an American, black *or* white. Dating from the time of his self-imposed exile in France in 1948, the essays of *Notes* encompass subjects from the idea of the "protest novel" in American fiction to the social position of people of color in Paris, to the problematic relationship of the individual in exile both to homeland and to the new country. But the primary contribution of *Notes* is to introduce not only different ways of understanding the meaning of color and race in America, but to question the idea of "Americanness" itself, as well as race, in relation to the culture of the European continent.

As aforementioned, in the case of James Baldwin, the fact of exile exists on two levels: one is voluntary and the other involuntary, and in this sense his relationship to exile offers a complexity that both parallels and comments on the exile of the two authors previously discussed. This complexity centers on that aspect of Baldwin's exile that is involuntary, that is, his racial relation to American society. After learning that his good friend Eugene Worth had committed suicide at the age of twenty-four by throwing himself off of the George

Washington Bridge, Baldwin's dissatisfaction with the racial situation in America reached a level he could no longer endure. He felt that the unrelenting racial pressures of New York had killed his friend, and he blamed the city for his death. More important, this death had such an impact on Baldwin that after it, he became numb, and it gradually became clear to him that the only way he would be able to preserve his sanity was to leave America. After much deliberation, he decided to go to France.[22] Thus, for Baldwin, involuntary exile leads to voluntary exile; one form of exile informs the other, and vice versa. What this means is that Baldwin's voluntary exile (his flight to France) is what allows him a broader, more universal perspective on the experience of involuntary exile, that is, the American racial prejudice of his time. This broader perspective not only provides the foundation for the writing of *Giovanni's Room*, but also becomes one of the most important ways by which Baldwin is linked to the other authors with which the present text is concerned, and by which his work contributes to a broad vision of literary modernism and modernity, one that would seek to analyze the significance in modern culture of multiple and hybrid identity.

As such, Baldwin's legacy to literature in general, and to American literature in particular, is to be found in the central message of *Giovanni's Room*: what is the price that must be paid for the achievement of brotherly love?[23] The idea of brotherly love and of the need for such love espoused in *Giovanni's Room* speaks to the necessity of dismantling stereotypes and demystifying differences in order to come to some point of reference by which rapport rather than division in cultural multiplicity may be attained. In the radical separation produced by the cultural silence and isolation of exile, Baldwin reveals the fundamental concerns of human existence (those with which the two previous authors here discussed are also involved) in bas-relief: the relationship between identity, the individual, the society in which the individual must live, the relation of the individual to that society, and the influence of that society on the development of individual identity. In *Giovanni's Room*, all of these rely on the attitude taken toward the issue of brotherly love. In this way, the text represents a radically modern approach toward an issue of long-standing controversy in American letters—the place, role and status of "minority" contributions to the American literary canon, and the definition of "minority" itself.

THE FLIGHT INTO MODERNITY

In a recent essay on Richard Wright's *Native Son*, Craig Werner elaborates a number of ways by which African-American literature may be understood in relation to the experimental movement of Euro-American modernism:

> At least since Du Bois produced *The Souls of Black Folk*, Afro-American culture has explicitly addressed the central concerns of

modernism: fragmentation, alienation, sense-making. . . . the central problem confronted by Afro-American culture closely resembles that confronted by mainstream modernism: the alienated individual experiences a profound sense of psychological and cultural disorientation in a world characterized by an accelerating rate of change; he or she subsequently attempts to regain some sense of coherence by articulating the experience of disorientation. The difference lies in the tendency of many Euro-American modernists to experience their situation as individual and, to some extent, ahistorical, while Afro-American modernists generally perceive a communal dilemma deriving from historical and political forces.[24]

Here, the familiar conceptual framework of "black/white" elaborated above may again be found, this time in terms of the way in which the modern cultural situation is perceived. In Werner's view, on the one hand, Euro-American modernists experience a sense of alienation as individual, as something happening only to them, or only to a few others whose ideas and beliefs are aligned with them. On the other hand, the African-American modernists, alienated because of their skin, recognize in addition that they are one of an entire people who, possessing the same genetic makeup, experience daily a similar form of alienation. It is the fact of community which, in Werner's formulation, reintroduces the idea of struggle into his conception of African-American literature, and perpetuates the problem of historical (and historicized) incommensurable difference that continues, albeit in ever more subtle ways, to divide America along predominantly racial lines in virtually all realms of human existence—historical, cultural, economic, and social. Thus, while the formulation of Euro-American modernism Werner expands does indeed reveal a thematic similarity to what have commonly been the concerns of African-American literature, it does not entirely escape the pitfall of returning to the sociological aspect of that literature by which to explain it. This is clearly understood in Werner's idea of the way in which Wright's work carves a niche for itself within literary modernism and modernity:

> Like the popular discourses, the leading aesthetic discourses of the 1930s exclude important aspects of Bigger's—and Wright's—experience. Nonetheless, the very attempt to include the discourses, or more precisely fragments of these discourses, in the text of *Native Son* highlights Wright's close relationship to a modernism grounded—though Wright would almost certainly not have thought of his work in these terms—in the blues.[25]

With this passage, the creation, much like that suggested in chapter 2 with de Certeau's articulation of the notion of space, of a "bridge" and a "frontier" between a mainstream aesthetic movement, that is, literary modernism, and a "minority" text is realized. But although the foundation for this "bridge" and "frontier" has been laid thematically, as revealed in the first quoted passage from this essay, and although it is quite reasonable to understand the blues as a representation of literary modernism, understanding Wright's *Native Son* in terms of a modernism grounded in the blues requires a sociological leap tenable only if one is not interested in questioning the assumptions making such a leap would require, or exploring the problems it may present. Why is it that, in considering Wright's work in relation to literary modernity, one might first make a connection between modernism and the blues? The answer to this question seems immediately evident: because modernism and modernity have traditionally been perceived as belonging to Euro-American culture, or the Western tradition, and the blues has been an important part of African-American culture. While this connection may also be viewed in the positive light of reclamation and recuperation, in creating a viable African-American literary tradition, still it poses an important problem: the attempt to bridge the distance between the cultural space of African-American literature and that of Euro-American modernism may indeed bring us to a new consideration of African-American literature, but it cannot by itself take such literature out of the realm of the sociological and put it into Euro-American modernism's aesthetic economy, nor can it bring to light the submerged operations of the politics of cultural space that have made Euro-American modernism what it is in the contemporary critical imagination, and that have historically excluded African-American literary contributions from that perception.

One difficulty here is that the structure by which this distance is bridged is one which, while attempting to articulate a purely African-American modernist position, does so in a way that replicates a distinct and separate Euro-American understanding of literary history, that is, as a tradition representing a cultural and national chronological continuity.[26] Thus, this fact produces a question that challenges the very manner by which we are accustomed to organize and understand our world: Why must a "tradition" include a search for origins that are exclusive of influences outside the national or genetic makeup of a people? Particularly in America, such a concept of tradition becomes problematic, since even those authors whom we are accustomed to think of as constituting the American literary tradition take a step closer to disparate European heritages with each century that one reaches backward.

As such, the attempt to think about African-American literature in relation to literary modernism and modernity has more than simply artistic significance—it has a social and a cultural significance as well. While current debates concerning Euro-American modernism argue, as elaborated in chapter 2, as to whether or not it constitutes a historical period (by which it has also been classified as a tradition), the consideration of previously excluded authors within this distinctly Euro-American modernist tradition can also help radically to change our idea of that tradition itself within a larger conception of literary modernism and modernity, as our readings of Proust and Joyce in chapters 3 and 4 have revealed.

We can understand the way in which this may take place by trying to answer yet another question. Why is it that those to whom we refer as canonical modernists are well-known, and many of those considered "other," such as women and minorities, are not? To become well-known, an author must gain the attention of the literary critical world, and to ensure that his or her reputation will survive, that author must become institutionalized, as was seen in chapter 4, in the discussion of the history of Joyce criticism. But once well-known, an author's work must, in traditional terms, also compete with the work of other authors, based on determinations of its aesthetic value, that is, its contribution to one or more of technique, style, narrative structure, characterization, and so on. And it is precisely because of this fact that any consideration of the literary contributions of African-Americans in relation to those of the Euro-American modernists, if it is to be both viable and lasting, *must* be made on aesthetic, as opposed to sociological, grounds. What is meant by "aesthetic" here, however, is not the aestheticism of the discourse of colonialism that is, as we have seen in chapter 2, a hidden yet important part of traditional conceptions of Euro-American modernism. It implies instead a valorization of what whichever text is in question may have to tell us about life in general, rather than emphasizing a form of value derived from the politics of cultural space, or the struggle over control of the space of legitimized cultural representation. It has been asserted that if culture studies approaches are to bring about the understanding of cultural multiplicity that is their primary purpose, they must themselves create, in more than a surface manner, the cultural space in which such an occurrence may take place. And it is with James Baldwin, in terms of African-American literature, that the beginnings of such a cultural space in literary modernism and modernity are to be found. In its difference with the traditional conceptual framework of black/white, Baldwin's work locates itself in the heart of the aforementioned American crisis of identity. There, it paves the way for the recognition of another cultural space beyond the polarized cultural location within which, as an African-American author, he necessarily finds himself. In this new space, Baldwin's work writes the silence of cultural multiplicity and, in so doing, challenges the polarized conceptual framework that would silence the multiple cultural locations from which he speaks, lending authorized voice to only one.

In James Baldwin, the alignment of Euro-American modernism with African-American literature finds an almost ready-made aesthetic bridge, through the intensity of Baldwin's interest in the work of the Euro-American modernist Henry James, as Lyall H. Powers elaborates in a recent essay:

> Coupling Henry James and James Baldwin may still seem to be an odd undertaking, but there is ample justification for doing so. In Baldwin's list of the ten novels that had helped him "break out of the ghetto," two are by Henry James—*The Portrait of a Lady* and *The Princess Cassamassima.* . . . And in Baldwin's published work there is explicit encouragement for coupling him with James. The first essay in his early collection *Nobody Knows My Name* (1961), for instance, begins: "It is a complex fate to be an American," Henry James observed . . .[27]

Powers, however, seems more concerned with establishing echoes of James' work in Baldwin's, to reveal a certain "indebtedness," and calling what he terms Baldwin's "preoccupation with the problem of identity" a "Jamesian theme."[28] In essence, however, the result of this is to take from Baldwin's work the credit for originality by which its aesthetic properties may be properly explored. Beyond this, however, it represents the refusal to read "on the edge," to read for understanding of the cultural significance of Baldwin's work in a new and unfamiliar, unlegitimized context. If, as in this vein, a study of Baldwin is undertaken instead in terms of the *effects* of such artistic influence, not to show what he *owes* to that influence but rather, to reveal the *results* of that influence in his work, one finds that Baldwin's interest in Henry James opens up a new cultural path within the framework of African-American literature, by which it may advance far beyond the idea of "protest" into a cultural future in which its artistic parameters are no longer determined exclusively by traditional notions of "black" and "white" when engaging with issues of "self" and "other." This is because such a study would, of necessity, show how Baldwin makes use of his cultural surroundings in a way that is very different from what would be revealed through seeking, as sociologically created expectations might demand, to determine how he continues or manages to fit into an African-American literary tradition, racially defined, yet nationalist in form. Baldwin himself explains why this may be so:

> I know, in any case, that the most crucial time in my own development came when I was forced to recognize that I was a kind of bastard of the West; when I followed the line of my past I did not find myself in Europe but in Africa. And this meant that in some subtle way, in a really profound way, I brought to Shakespeare, Bach, Rembrandt, to the stones of Paris, to the cathedral at Chartres, and to the Empire State Building, a special attitude. These were not re-

ally my creations, they did not contain my history; I might search in them in vain forever for any reflection of myself. I was an interloper; this was not my heritage. At the same time I had no other heritage which I could possibly hope to use—I had certainly been unfitted for the jungle or the tribe. I would have to appropriate these white centuries, I would have to make them mine—I would have to accept my special attitude, my special place in this scheme—otherwise I would have no place in *any* scheme.[29]

Through this statement, Baldwin's "special" position vis-à-vis the American literary tradition is clearly understood. Though he does not say it, the conflict here represented in which Baldwin is engaged is the conflict between what Henry Louis Gates, Jr., calls "cultural geneticism," a defining of culture based on one's genetic makeup, and, in Baldwin's opinion, the near impossibility of directly possessing such a cultural affiliation—at least in European terms—when one is an exile twice-removed, as is the African-American.[30] Baldwin's decision to abandon the genetic idea of culture and embrace the cultural framework within which he was engendered represents the transformation of his position from passive to active with regard to the aesthetic bridge by which his work is initially linked to Euro-American modernism, because it is only as a result of this mind-set that he is able to understand what the work of Henry James has to tell him.[31]

The message James's work holds for Baldwin is none other than the exploration of what it means to be an exile, to speak necessarily from multiple cultural locations, and the problematic relationship between exile and identity. What is important here, however, is the idea of exile, because it is the fact of exile that takes Baldwin's work out of the more isolated problem of the search for African-American identity and into the more universal problem of the relationship between the individual and society.[32] This in turn also leads into one of the central problems of literary modernism and modernity, which is the relationship of the artist to tradition, a problem that may also be viewed as taking the same general form as that of the problem between the individual and society. This is evident in the way in which the conflict between the individual and society is elaborated in James's work, as Powers describes:

> James's fiction regularly develops the Emersonian theme of self-reliance. For the Jamesian hero, the prerequisite to self-reliance is self-knowledge—achieving and accepting a sense of self in order safely to trust and to rely on that self . . . The problem of achieving a sense of self is constantly presented in James's international fiction as the struggle between the demands of individual integrity and the demands of social conformity—all the strictures of

tradition, convention, "manners" that swaddle the nascent individual, grasp his conscience, and dictate to him his "duty."[33]

In James, this struggle, that between "individual integrity" and "social conformity," is also complicated by the problem of "Americanness," which in both James and Baldwin is translated into the problem of national identity. In James, the problem of national identity complicates that of individual identity, whereas, in Baldwin, the same difficulty forces the problem of individual identity out of the narrow confines of the relationship between "black" and "white" and into the larger, universal human concerns of personhood in whatever context. The significance of "Americanness" in the work of the two authors is, however, as Newman points out, that both "realized early that the American fabric is not subject to European tailoring, that America has no culture in European terms."[34] This realization is particularly important for Baldwin, as it is because of it that his exile in France becomes so important for his work. This is due to the fact that, as a result of his state of exile, he was able not only to realize for the first time what it was to be an *American*, as opposed to simply an *African*-American (whose rights in his own country were severely and broadly truncated), but also that the problem of multiple identity faced (but not always recognized and acknowledged) by the African-American within his or her own country was a problem quite similar to that of Americans in general, both because of the country's short-lived history and because of its relation to that history in terms of the ethnic variety of its inhabitants, whether white, black, or other.[35] This Baldwin could only come to understand against the European backdrop, as he explains in another early essay:

> If the American found in Europe only confusion, it would obviously be infinitely wiser for him to remain at home. Hidden, however, in the heart of the confusion he encounters here is that which he came so blindly seeking: the terms on which he is related to his country, and to the world. This, which has so grandiose and general a ring, is, in fact, most personal—the American confusion seeming to be based on the very nearly unconscious assumption that it is possible to consider the person apart from all the forces which have produced him. This assumption, however, is itself based on nothing less than our history, which is the history of the total, and willing, alienation of entire peoples from their forbears. What is overwhelmingly clear, it seems, to everyone but ourselves is that this history has created an entirely unprecedented people, with a unique and individual past. . . . It is the past lived on the American continent, as against that other past, irrecoverable now

on the shores of Europe, which must sustain us in the present. The truth about that past is not that it is too brief, or too superficial, but only that we, having turned our faces so resolutely away from it, have never demanded from it what it has to give. . . . From the vantage point of Europe . . . [the American] discovers his own country. And this is a discovery which not only brings to an end the alienation of the American from himself, but which also makes clear to him, for the first time, the extent of his involvement in the life of Europe.[36]

This passage suggests that Baldwin has made one very important conceptual leap: from the isolated and bewildered African-American searching for a past long lost, to the confused and unconscious American, who refuses to allow the past the importance it must have if he is ever to understand himself. For Baldwin, the position of the African-American vis-à-vis the white American majority is, conceptually, the same in many ways as the position of the white American vis-à-vis the cultures of Europe: both are rendered culturally problematic, depending on the context within which they are viewed. And it is at this juncture, where Baldwin comes to a deeper understanding of cultural multiplicity in terms of his relation to both American-ness and African-Americanness, that the significance of his relationship to the work of Henry James becomes almost evident, and the terms upon which his work is related to the problems of modern culture most clear.

In his book, *Stealing the Fire*, Horace Porter reads the link between Baldwin and Henry James in an entirely different way. While he recognizes Baldwin's immense admiration for James' artistic prowess, Porter describes what he sees as Baldwin's initial success as his attempt to achieve what he explains as James' "sense of the ideal of detachment," or the separation of the artist from the man.[37] Porter focuses, however, on the significance of this relationship specifically with regard to American, not modern, culture. For Porter, Baldwin fails in his desire to approach James' artistic accomplishment because rather than continuing to develop his work along more "Jamesian" lines, he allows himself to become too embroiled in the American cultural politics of his time. With the 1963 publication of *The Fire Next Time*, Porter writes, "Baldwin is typecast as an angry spokesman—'a black Tom Paine,' as *Time* magazine put it."[38] For Porter, then, Baldwin becomes a representative of the African-American population in precisely that fashion that his early work eschews. This conclusion forms a large part of the foundation of Porter's reading of *Giovanni's Room*—perhaps Baldwin's most controversial novel—not in terms of what Baldwin achieves from a cultural perspective in writing beyond socially determined racial imperatives, but, rather, in terms of what Porter reads as echoes of Richard Wright's *Native Son* and the tradition of the protest novel against which Baldwin so vehemently pitted himself, as evidenced in the novel's (*Giovanni's Room*) subtle interwining of race and homosexuality.

Yet this is also where Porter completely overlooks a crucial aspect of Baldwin's cultural endeavor. For not only does Baldwin percieve the problems of homosexuality and race as inherently intertwined, but it is through this very relationship that he catapults his work into the modern—by using it to comment not specifically on race in America, as literary convention would demand, but on the larger difficulty represented by American society and its confrontation with "otherness." Baldwin's earlier works tell us that he knows he is black. But they also tell us that, through having confronted his place in American history against the European backdrop, he understands something even more profound: the separation of the *man* from the *black* man. It is this which gives him the perspective he needs in order to understand Henry James' ideal of detachment from his own special vantage point, and it is also this deeper understanding which *allows* him, rather than *compels* him, to write so passionately, with such amazing clarity and vision, about the social problems of America in his later work. And it is within this nexus, through his understanding of the relations between white and black in America in terms of a shared silence about a shared past and a shared positional circumstance with regard to the past, that Baldwin is able to break through the received conventions of the African-American literary tradition and take flight, in effecting the technical and artistic achievement that resulted in his own version of a modern novel: *Giovanni's Room*.

In *Giovanni's Room* literary modernism and modernity engage head on with the quintessentially modern difficulty of cultural multiplicity—the need and/or necessity to speak from multiple cultural locations in artistic expression. Here, Baldwin uses his newfound understanding of "Americanness" in such a way that he is able to see far enough beyond the communal obligation to write about race (something he discusses in "Autobiographical Note" in *Notes of a Native Son*) that he frees himself to write about another, and in some ways, for him, more pressing problem—that of homosexuality.[39] But more important, he frees himself to write about the cultural significance of homosexuality in terms of the culturally sanctioned silence surrounding it, the historical disavowal of homosexuality as a viable social identity and the difficulties faced by the individual in coming to terms with the conflict between personal desire and the communal obligation to eschew an identity not authorized by social consensus.[40] But what Baldwin actually achieves in doing this is the possibility of writing not about race, nor really about homosexuality, but rather, about character. And it is this, when considered in terms of Baldwin's problematic relationship with the African-American literary tradition, that ultimately links his work, aesthetically, to a new conception of the modern beyond that traditionally elaborated in terms of Euro-American perspectives of modernity. This is because in freeing himself in this way, he also cuts through the layers of social expectation within which from his perspective an African-American artist must exist, to discover the freedom to explore, more or less unencumbered, the motivations of character alone. The choice of David as the novel's white American protagonist serves as the means by which the problem the novel treats is kept pure, free of sociological interference—at least in terms of race. Because David is a white American, the problem of homosexuality can neither be obfuscated by the problem of race, nor its cultural significance. And because of David's own personal dilemma, which seems ostensibly to be about homosexuality, but is in reality about the consequences of self-deception, the problem of homosexuality becomes not a motive for protest in the novel, but rather a metaphor for society, in the form of social injunction, of what one is not, at all costs, to be.[41] By breaking through established preconceptions pertaining to both of these traits, Baldwin not only creates a new vision of the modern; he also shows the common plight of the oppressed, those who, silent and silenced as a result of their multiple cultural locations, cannot make themselves part of the ideas by which mainstream society is constituted. This he achieves in part *because* of his emphasis on homosexuality: while the problem of homosexuality is not any more acceptable to the mainstream American society of his time than that of race, it does not possess the same sociologically isolating characteristic as does race. Anyone of any race, of any class, of either gender, and of any nationality can be a homosexual.

Thus, with this novel, Baldwin changes the terms that cohere to writing from outside the mainstream in America—as well as altering the socially determined and externally imposed understanding of what a "black" writer *should* be, and what he or she *should* write about. And in so doing, he builds his own aesthetic bridge to the modern by bringing the problems of living on the outside, living in the cultural space of silence, directly into the center of mainstream American life, by dealing with a mainstream American's difficulty in maintaining personal integrity while in conflict with the values of his society. In this he (Baldwin) also directly challenges that society, which would demand conformity with one authorized collective identity, and the silencing of all other cultural locations from which he (or his protagonist) might feel the need to speak.

For David, to all external appearances, *is* a part of mainstream American society. He is tall, blond, and comes from a decidedly middle-class background. Yet he lives at the moment in France, and on the inside, he is not what he seems. It is from within this divide that the novel derives its form and, through its concentration on the distortion of fictive reality through the narrator's subjective dilemma of cultural multiplicity, its unconventional modern perspective. Despite the narrator's efforts to force his personal reality to conform to what appearances would suggest that it is, true reality in the text is always to be found elsewhere, a nasty and hidden undercurrent that the narrator denies (tries to silence in keeping with cultural injunction) each time he is confronted with it. As such, reality in the text takes on a strange, unreal character, something which is partially a result of the fact that the narrator also tells the story from two separate perspectives at the same time (an objective indication of his cultural multiplicity): one being the perspective of the experienced David after the events of the novel have taken place; the other being the perspective of the David who lives in silence and denial, the David whose voice is the rhetoric of flight, in which only silence—and silencing—are his constant companions.[42]

Reality in the text is thus distorted because it has itself been subsumed by the rhetoric of flight, since the novel opens with the narrator looking at his reflection in the window of his rented house in the south of France. It is almost as if the only solid ground for the locus of reality in this text is the narrator's reflection. As a reflection, even that has a questionable reality, and it is this porous, wavering insubstantiality by which Baldwin builds a bridge to the modern in this text. But it is only through the narrator's watching himself that the reader gets any idea that the reality of flight, which surrounds the narrator with an eerie cultural silence and places him in perpetual motion, will ever find a destination. Will the narrator ever stop running? Will he ever confront and come to terms with that cultural silence from which he is in flight? The fact that the text opens as it does, with the narrator physically in the exile to which his flight has brought him, but standing still and watching his reflection through which, since it is a reflection in a darkening window, he can also see the landscape of the foreign country spread out before him, suggests that the painful process of increasing self-awareness from which self-acceptance may eventually be developed, has begun. It is not where the narrator finds himself, but how he thinks of himself that is important:

> I repent now—for all the good it does—one particular lie among the many lies I've told, told, lived, and believed. This is the lie which I told to Giovanni but never succeeded in making him believe, that I had never slept with a boy before. I had. I had decided that I never would again. There is something fantastic in the spectacle I now present to myself of having run so far, so hard, across the ocean even, only to find myself brought up short once more before the bulldog in my own backyard—the yard, in the meantime, having grown smaller and the bulldog bigger.[43]

In this passage, one finds all of the elements upon which the novel is structured, and upon which its aesthetic relation to the modern may be based. First, there is the "I" narrator speaking from the distance of the future about a past which it is too late to change. Through the idea of repentance, that past is made an agonizing part of the present, continually held up to view and continually something by which the present is distorted. As a result of this, the present can never be simply the present, but is throughout the novel always something in danger of being stolen by the past. Thus, the experienced narrator speaks with self-conscious irony in terms of the novel's rhetoric of flight, and one finds in this passage all of the text's contradictions with regard to reality, the relationship between reality and belief, the relationship between self and society and society and personal integrity, all problems with which the modern individual must grapple. The narrator's description of his flight across the ocean as "something fantastic" outlines the extent to which the rhetoric of flight, of which he makes use throughout the novel, has done nothing to change what he was running from, nor has exile given him the freedom from his own personal beliefs about his relationship to reality. Instead, that flight, in which he sought salvation, has only distorted his imaginary reality, that of conformity to social edicts, to the point of ridiculousness, while at the same time destroying what he believes was and should have been his actual reality, that is, his life with Giovanni.

The fact that the novel begins with a lie—yet another form of silencing—that the narrator had never slept with a boy, is the basis for the division between the real and the imaginary and, as such, the conventional opening to the modern in the text. The narrator's decision that he would never again sleep with a boy is the origin of the text's imaginary reality, from which the rhetoric of flight takes its impetus. It is the narrator's idea of what he *wants* his reality to be and the impossibility of giving form to this idea in actuality that give the novel its paradoxical, and conventionally *un*conventional modern reality:

> For I am—or I was—one of those people who pride themselves on their willpower, on their ability to make a decision and carry it through. This virtue, like most virtues, is ambiguity itself. People who believe that they are strong-willed and the masters of their destiny can only continue to believe this by becoming specialists in self-deception. Their decisions are not really decisions at all—a real decision makes one humble, one knows that it is at the mercy of more things than can be named—but elaborate systems of evasion, of illusion, designed to make themselves and the world appear to be what they and the world are not. This is certainly what my decision, made so long ago in Joey's bed, came to. I had decided to allow no room in the universe for something which shamed and frightened me. I succeeded very well—by not looking

at the universe, by not looking at myself, by remaining, in effect, in constant motion.[44]

Even here, the narrator speaks from two perspectives, the one the voice of experience, the other the voice of flight. The idea that personal will can force reality to be something other than what it actually is also speaks to the narrator's surveillance of his own reflection at the novel's beginning. What he is looking at, in the window of his home in exile, is not so much a reflection of himself as it is the flimsy substance of what he tried to make of himself in actual reality. That reflection is the testimony to what the constant motion of David's continual self-deception and self-silencing has made of his actual reality, and it is also the core of Baldwin's vision of the modern individual. For in truth, a mere reflection of himself is all that David has left, after the events of the novel have taken place. He has alienated himself from his cultural past through exile, from his personal past in that he has alienated himself also from his own actual reality, and he has destroyed all further possibility of truly intimate connection with another person in life, through having destroyed Giovanni, something which he realizes, but too late: "I was beginning to think of Giovanni dying—where Giovanni had been there would be nothing, nothing forever."[45] Even in the state of self-awareness that it seems he will move toward at the novel's beginning, the horror of what he has done and of what is about to happen leaves David still desiring his haven of self-deception, in which actual reality never has to be faced, but may be continually evaded, altered, subdued, or silenced by his own imagination. But his isolation in the rented house in exile leaves him painfully aware of his own self-deception even as he attempts to continue it, as seen in his effort to understand its origins, which derive from that long-ago summer when he experienced his first homosexual adventure with that boyhood friend named Joey:

> I began, perhaps, to be lonely that summer and began, that summer, the flight which has brought me to this darkening window.
> And yet—when one begins to search for the crucial, the definitive moment, the moment which changed all others, one finds oneself pressing, in great pain, through a maze of false signals and abruptly locking doors. My flight may, indeed, have begun that summer—which does not tell me where to find the germ of the dilemma which resolved itself, that summer, into flight. Of course, it is somewhere before me, locked in that reflection I am watching in the window as the night comes down outside. It is trapped in the room with me, always has been, and always will be, and it is yet more foreign to me than those foreign hills outside.[46]

While he seeks to analyze his motivations in order to find the beginnings of his difficulties, David finds a self-deception deeper and more silent even than that self-deception of which he is already aware, one that began to take place long before he knew he was deluding himself, that is, the "maze of false signals and abruptly locking doors." The origins of what became his flight, therefore, are only the culmination of prior years of denial and silencing of the problem itself. What created actual, physical flight was the external manifestation of an internal quandary of which the narrator was not even aware, though the indications must have been there for quite some time.

Even as he regards his reflection in the window, David yet attempts to run away from what he knows is the truth, though he knows that this truth will always remain with him and has always been with him. But he seeks to evade its reality in trying to believe that a truth so intimately connected with his personal reality, one which has been for so long connected in this way with his personal reality, is also one which is "yet more foreign" to him than the French countryside beyond the window in which he is watching himself. In this he speaks again from two voices, the one of experience, the other of flight. These two voices are woven together in a sophisticated fictional tapestry that, in its technical achievement, reveals the essential ambiguity and cultural multiplicity of the narrator's position—as a 1950s mainstream white American male who is also a homosexual—while simultaneously suggesting, through the fluctuating reality they create, a new understanding of the modern representation of character and experience. Such ambiguity could also be realized if the author simply *said* it, but in *Giovanni's Room*, it is part of the very fabric of the text, because the two voices are almost one and the same. It is through this complicated narrative voice that Baldwin also, like Proust, maintains the aesthetic distance necessary to create in *Giovanni's Room* a text that maintains a firm grip on the artistic and the imaginative—making of it a fictional, rather than a purely autobiographical, treatment of the plight of the homosexual in the middle of the twentieth century.

This complicated narrative voice and its shifting perspective from one to the other recalls yet again the double "I" narrator of *A la recherche du temps perdu*, which was detailed in chapter 3. There is here, however, another important difference. While the narrator in *Giovanni's Room* is also a double narrator, in that he speaks with two voices, both voices are *simultaneously* a part of the story. In Proust, the voice of the "I" narrator masks the voice of the author, so that at the crucial moment, the author can speak with authenticity, without sacrificing the protective cover provided by the fictional "I" narrator. It is, in fact, because of this undoubtedly fictional "I" narrator that the *Recherche* keeps its hold on the domain of the artistic and imaginative, thus maintaining the aesthetic distance necessary to escape the snare of autobiography. It is almost the same thing here with regard to James Baldwin. The difference is that in *Giovanni's Room*, the narrator's voice does not mask that of the author. Rather, the author's voice is split in two, each voice speaking almost simultaneously, yet separated by a radical divide, or edge, visible only to the reader—that of silence.

This shifting perspective also causes a peculiar tension in the novel that centers on the problem of desire and the relation of desire to reality, which suggests yet another nuance in the articulation of the modern in *Giovanni's Room*. In this novel, reality becomes paradoxical because within the private world of the narrator, desire functions to transform the actual into the imaginary and to create in its place a new world of actuality. The fact that the novel concerns the issue of homosexuality provides the grounding for the above assertion, since in order to understand this transformation it is necessary also to understand how another world of actuality can be created by something that destroys the world thought to be actual by the mainstream society, which is heterosexual. What *Giovanni's Room* depicts is the other, silent (and silenced) side of the heterosexual actuality of marriage and children, or the homosexual actuality that lives without these, on the silent fringes of heterosexual society. In this, the novel seems to be asking a number of questions that have much larger implications than the isolated problems of its protagonists, issues that lead the reader far beyond the significance of homosexuality alone, to focus on a number of more broadly defined universal difficulties: when two or more conceptions of cultural reality clash, and one is intolerant of the other, how are they to be reconciled? Must they be reconciled? What are the consequences if they are not? What happens when multiple conceptions of cultural reality meet in one individual? What are the consequences of not coming to terms with such reality, and with the fact that in the world, there are many different realities, many different ways of looking at and living in the world? But the most crucial line of questioning seems to be this: Is reality something that is determined by one's surroundings, or is it something one carries in one's head, in terms of beliefs? Is the reality of belief the same as actual reality? Is actual reality always the same, regardless of what one believes? What is the difference between actual reality and cultural reality, the reality of human life at its lowest common denominator, and the reality of cultural affiliation? These are essentially the same difficulties with which mainstream modern artists are confronted—yet while traditionally these problems are aestheticized, here they are brought directly to the fore.

Giovanni's Room seems to invite the exploration of such questions since the narrator is himself in exile. The fact that the narrator is living in Paris serves to emphasize the idea that the reality of belief, while it may seem actual when considered in relation to a group sensibility, is really only a matter of personal conviction. But what is important for the narrator in terms of belief are the cultural strictures that may be placed on him with regard to belief by the people he knows, that is, the possibility that he is really "just an

American boy, after all, doing things in France which . . . [he] would not dare to do at home."[47] As such, his exile in Paris is meant to set him free from the family (social) pressures that would force him to look at himself as he really is, that is, homosexual, but he ends up faced with his homosexuality anyway, because the same cultural pressures exist in his own mind, as he reveals through his understanding of his nightly sexual experiences with his girl-friend, Hella, with whom he contracts an engagement in spite of his leanings toward men:

> And these nights were being acted out under a foreign sky, with no one to watch, no penalties attached—it was this last fact which was our undoing, for nothing is more unbearable, once one has it, than freedom. I suppose this was why I asked her to marry me: to give myself something to be moored to. Perhaps this was why, in Spain, she decided that she wanted to marry me. But people can't, unhap-pily, invent their mooring posts, their lovers and their friends, any-more than they can invent their parents. Life gives these and also takes them away and the great difficulty is to say Yes to life.[48]

In this passage, the voice of denial, or flight, and the voice of experience collapse into one another. The idea that the narrator asks Hella to marry him in order to give himself "something to be moored to" could only be true if he were not already trying to hide something from himself and from her: the fact of his homosexuality. In this sense, his relationship with Hella, which is already a farce, becomes even more so, since in the mode of flight, the narrator cannot admit to himself that what really frightens him about the magnitude of freedom under a foreign sky is not the freedom itself, but what he might or could do with it—the fact that he might actually succeed in eradicating the silent divide in his life, and exist as one person whose identity is formed from multiple cultural locations. The loosening of the bonds that hold him to an outward reality of conformity could make it all the easier for him to lose sight of what for him is an imaginary reality, to lose the willpower necessary to conform so that he could begin to live the life of a 1950s white American homosexual in Paris, and his inner and outer realities could become one. Being engaged to Hella would thus replace the outer connection with heterosexual society and its demands (something he lost in leaving home and family) in a way that would prevent him from taking, as time passed, full advantage of the cultural freedom offered him by his physical exile.

But out of the voice of flight comes the voice of experience, which states that whatever one may decide about who and how one will love, one has, ul-timately, no control over the matter. One can only live, and try to take advantage of what life offers. In this sense, the narrator himself reveals the gap between reality as one desires it to be and reality as it actually is, which is also the same gap that exists between the reality of human life at its lowest common denominator and the reality of cultural affiliation—the difference between life itself and numerous other ways of life, multiple modes of being.

The difficulty of saying "Yes to life" is one of the central problems of this novel, because it elaborates the way in which cultural affiliation can prevent one from living life to the fullest degree (as was also suggested by the dilemma of Joyce's protagonist, Stephen Dedalus in chapter 4), since its cultural injunctions can often force one not only to dehumanize other people, but to deny the humanity even of those one could like and would enjoy spending time with if it were not for the interference of intolerance rooted in cultural belief. In a sense, the narrator's inability to say "Yes to life," choosing instead to embrace silence in trying to force himself to follow the path of cultural belief, a path which for him is devoid of any personal meaning, shows that the attempt to live in the imaginary realm can offer a safe haven for only a short time. When that time has passed, the reality of life is still there, but it may, however, be irrevocably, and painfully, changed.

In the case of David, his sojourn in the imaginary world he creates for himself in order to protect himself from endangering his personal integrity forces him to damage that integrity in a much more serious way than he would have had he simply said "Yes" to the possibility of a life with Giovanni.[49] With Hella's departure to Spain, his last link in exile to the heterosexual world, the last objective fetter between him and complete, lawless freedom, disappears, and when he meets Giovanni, he succumbs to his inner reality. But for him, this surrender is accompanied by a sensation of disequilibrium. Rather than feeling the calm stability that is usually implied by the idea of marriage (which could, in David's mind, accompany the process of heterosexual falling in love), David senses danger. At this point, that danger is a part of the cultural injunctions that David carries in his own head, because the imaginary reality he has constructed for himself is suddenly being threatened in a way more real than the threat posed by subjective desire alone:

> I saw myself, sharply, as a wanderer, an adventurer, rocking through the world, unanchored. I looked at Giovanni's face, which did not help me. He belonged to this strange city, which did not belong to me. I began to see that, while what was happening to me was not so strange as it would have comforted me to believe, yet it was strange beyond belief. It was not really so strange, so unprecedented, though voices deep within me boomed, For shame! For shame! that I should be so abruptly, so hideously entangled with a boy.[50]

In fact, the threat posed by Giovanni is none other than the threat already posed by Joey, from whom David took flight across the ocean. The presence of Giovanni, and his desire for Giovanni, are the same external manifestation of David's secret, silent (and silenced) inner dilemma as was his desire for Joey and their subsequent affair. The fact that at the moment he meets Giovanni, Hella is in Spain, leaves David without the protection of cultural injunction she represents before the intensity of his desire for Giovanni. Here again, the two narrative voices are operative. In one sense, David understands that what he is feeling is neither strange nor unprecedented, but in another sense, he insists that it is "strange beyond belief." He would have felt "comforted" if he could believe in its strangeness, thereby also being able to understand himself as conforming to social edicts. But knowing that he does not really find it so strange as those edicts would demand of him, he also, at the same time, hears their warning— "For shame!" and longs to run.

The realities of these two voices are also represented externally by Hella, David's father, and America on the one hand, and Giovanni, France, and Giovanni's room on the other. The conflict between the two realities reaches its culmination while David is still living in Giovanni's room. When Giovanni is fired and David realizes the extent of Giovanni's utter emotional dependence on him, he has just received a letter from Hella agreeing to marry him, and he is, as a result, suddenly torn by the two directions that his life is objectively trying to take. At this point, it is his love for Giovanni that triumphs, yet it does not succeed in obliterating the dividedness of his character:

> Neither my father nor Hella was real at that moment. And yet even this was not as real as my despairing sense that nothing was real for me, nothing would ever be real for me again—unless, indeed, this sensation of falling was reality.[51]

But the difference is that David's inner dilemma has now become an outer dilemma, in that he has allowed both desires to be manifested in actual life, without paving the way for external cultural acceptance of his multiple identities. He has still continued to live in his imaginary world of self-deception, silence, and flight—he has remained in constant motion while his passage through the lives of two people have caused them both to stop at his doorstep, each for different reasons, and each expecting vastly different things from him. Through this it is possible to see that, while David was living in the "safe" haven of silence and self-deception, the reality of his actual life was gradually changing. He asked Hella to marry him, he began to live with Giovanni. Both actions—each of which demanded a certain kind of solidity on the part of David—were made in the absence of such solidity, and two people trusted that such solidity was there. As such, both Giovanni and Hella began to live their lives with David, but the David with whom they thought they were living did not exist, since his self-deception made of him, in terms of reality, no more real than the reflection of himself that he is watching at the novel's beginning. At this point, however, his actions have had no serious consequences, and though it may be messy, he can still put things right. But this cannot be done until or unless he is able to see through his own self-deception to a reality which would allow him to take a firm stand on his dilemma—the acceptance of multiple cultural locations. Without having taken a firm stand, he is just allowing himself to be buffeted by circumstance like a piece of driftwood in the ocean, thus "nothing was real."

But the problem with silence and self-deception here is that David does not overcome them before it is too late, before he does irrevocable damage to the lives of two people. As long as his dilemma remains a silent (and silenced) internal problem, it can only do harm to himself. But as soon as that problem is made manifest in the external world through his objective choices and actions, it can hurt other people. And it is because of this that David's personal integrity is, in the end, more damaged by not having said "Yes" to his life with Giovanni than it would have been had he simply surrendered to his homosexuality.

It is also because of this that the consequences of his actions are irreversible. Giovanni will die, Hella has been irreparably damaged. David finds himself utterly alone. In this situation, he is totally unable to continue the silencing self-deception that originally brought him to this pass:

> I pour myself a very little drink, watching, in the window pane, my reflection, which steadily becomes more faint. I seem to be fading away before my eyes—this fancy amuses me, and I laugh to myself.[52]

The reflection in the window, a mere representation of who he has been in exile, a transparent apparition that had no substance to begin with, fades away as David is forced to look at the reality of what his denial, his flight, his perpetual motion, have done to his life and to his future. And as this apparition disappears, it is replaced by another, more substantial image. Still alone, David is forced to look for the first time at himself as he is, whole in his multiplicity, with no subterfuge and no place to run or to hide:

> I walk into the bedroom where the clothes I will wear are lying on the bed and my bag lies open and ready. I begin to undress. There is a mirror in this room, a large mirror. I am terribly aware of the mirror. . . . The body in the mirror forces me to turn and face it. And I look at my body, which is under sentence of death. . . . And I do not know what moves in this body, what this body is searching. It is trapped in my mirror as it is trapped in time . . . I long to crack that mirror and be free. I look at my sex, my troubling sex, and wonder how it can be redeemed, how I can save it from the

knife. . . . the key to my salvation, which cannot save my body, is hidden in my flesh.[53]

The image in the mirror is of David alone, not mitigated by a world outside. It is within the world outside that David recognized his dilemma as such and sought release from it, but here it is made evident that the only release possible for him is to be found within himself. His reference to his body as "the body" as well as "my body" yet seeks to objectify it, to put distance between it, that is, his body, and him. Yet his reference to "my sex, my troubling sex" reveals an understanding that there will be no chance of escape from his body's demands. And it is because of the impossibility of escape from the certainty of homosexuality, coupled with the impossibility of escape from the damage he has done to his personal integrity through the destruction caused by his silence and self-deception, that David must also bear with him forever the memory of Giovanni, though he throws away the blue notice of Giovanni's execution:

> I take the blue envelope which Jacques has sent me and tear it slowly into many pieces, watching them dance in the wind, watching the wind carry them away. Yet, as I turn and begin walking toward the waiting people, the wind blows some of them back on me.[54]

In this sense, Giovanni becomes the opposing pole within the text, the pole by which its actual reality is given not only form, but depth, meaning, and acceptance. And it is the loss of that more profound reality (by the fact of Giovanni's death), yet the impossibility of escape from the meaning of that reality on the part of the narrator (as represented by the blowing back on him of some of the torn pieces of the execution notice) that brings David's four realities, American and French, heterosexual and homosexual, and his two narrative voices of experience and flight, into one unified focus.

While the new cultural path within African-American literature that Baldwin creates in writing *Giovanni's Room* would seem to center on the most obvious traditionally "modern," or experimental aspect of the novel— the fact that David, the protagonist, is a white, rather than a black, American—he in fact creates in this text an entirely new relationship to literary modernism and modernity, one that moves beyond that described in Euro-American modernism to posit multiplicity, difference, hybridity, and above all, silence, silencing and the relation of these to cultural forgetting as some of the most important, yet almost completely ignored, grounds of modern experience. By considering the conceptual leap Baldwin was enabled to take through exile and through his understanding of the work of Henry James, it is easy to see how, in relating many aspects of his own life—that is, his exile in Paris, his homosexuality—he could have had no problem transposing them into the life of a white American protagonist. David's color is, as such, only a small part of what is modern about this text, and does not offer much with regard to the idea of Baldwin's development of a new modern cultural space in this novel.

In addition, while one could yet understand *Giovanni's Room* in terms of protest by discovering in Giovanni the problems of the African-American, in David, the problem of the white American enculturated to deny the humanity of the African-American, and in the problem of sexual identity, the same problem of racial and national identity that is often the subject of Baldwin's essays, it would be a protest so much more sophisticated than the traditional idea of protest that it would shock the few and miss the many.[55] This would be, instead, a "protest" against what has been the invariably enforced and rigidly policed silencing of multiple identities derived from multiple cultural locations in modern life.

What is much more pertinent to an understanding of this novel with regard to its articulation of literary modernism and modernity is the theme of flight. Although this theme is normally subsumed by discussions of the seemingly more compelling problem of identity with regard to Baldwin's work,[56] a closer look at its significance in the text reveals that the rhetoric of flight in *Giovanni's Room* links this novel to Euro-American modernism through its similarity to that attitude toward the role of the past; yet it also moves beyond this conception, into a larger reconceived notion of literary modernism and modernity, in that it creates a dichotomous, paradoxical reality within the text that reveals the significance of the past in the present (represented by the blowing back onto the narrator of the torn pieces of the execution notice). This significance is not simply a sense of nostalgia for what has been lost, but a representation of how the past both alters the present and, in turn, impacts the future—a subject which, in traditional Euro-American modernist formulations, has too often formed a part of that silent (and silenced) cultural excess that it has been this book's task to unearth and read.

It is also only through a concentrated analysis of the role of the past in the present that any more truly tolerant attitude toward "minority" literature in conceptions of literary modernism and modernity may be developed. And only from such a vantage point can we begin to form those much needed questions without which the answers that can direct the tide of cultural change in American, and more broadly, Western, society will not be found. What are the ways in which our problematic social history may be explored in relation to the cultural heritage presented by our literature(s)?[57] What conclusions may be drawn or understandings reached through such comparison? Can "minority" or ethnic literature be understood through the gaps in canonical literature, through what is not said, shown, or revealed by and in that literature—that is, through what is and/or has been silenced there? In this, the importance of the historical context must be reemphasized, since it is only through a historical consciousness that such silences, silencings and gaps may be identified at all, not just in relation to literary modernism and modernity, but in the larger context of literary study itself.

We must search, then, for a new way of cultural understanding, one that would not simply recodify literary modernism and modernity into the very cultural constrictions from which it tried, even in its Euro-American context, to break free. Perhaps our modern cultural alienation, produced by our flight from our shared modern past, could light the path toward recognition of the richness of our multiple and hybrid present, now silenced by our ever-increasing contemporary desire for selective ethnic remembering and consensual collective cultural forgetting. And perhaps—perhaps—this could even herald the cultural space of modernity (read in and through its "others") as the literary horizon of a new and transformative world order— that edge beyond which the as yet unimagined social realities (and possibilities) of a world growing smaller and smaller are only just beginning to be explored.

CHAPTER 6

Conclusion

In many American universities, the frequent right-thinking
response to the demands of newly empowered marginal
groups was to say "show me the African (or Asian, or feminine) Proust . . ."
—Edward Said, *Culture and Imperialism*

CANONS, CANONICITY, CANONIZATION:
LITERARY "CULTURE" AND THE PROBLEM OF OTHERNESS

In his book *Loose Canons: Notes on the Culture Wars*, Henry Louis Gates, Jr., identifies one of the central themes with which the present book has been concerned:

> In 1903, W. E. B. DuBois could write, prophetically, that the prob-
> lem of the twentieth century would be the color line. We might well
> argue that the problem of the twenty-first century will be the prob-
> lem of ethnic differences, as these conspire with complex differ-
> ences in color, gender, and class. As actual cultural differences
> between social and ethnic groups are being brought to bear to jus-
> tify the subordination of one group by another, the matter of mul-
> ticulturalism becomes politically fraught. Until these differences are
> understood in an era of emergent nationalism, the challenge of mu-
> tual understanding among the world's multifarious cultures will be
> the single greatest task that we face.[1]

As Gates describes it here, the social and cultural differences that pertain to race, ethnicity, gender, class, and/or nationality are one and the same. In this regard, then, what I have identified in previous chapters as the notion of literary "culture" must also, inevitably, be viewed as intricately and undeniably connected to the social world from which it emanates. What this means is that in many ways literary "culture," in its examination of human life and motivations, replicates the social divisions, complexities, and difficulties of the surrounding world of which, though it may often take the form of critique, it must still be considered a part. But what exactly is meant here by the notion of literary "culture?" Does such "culture" exist simply by virtue of the creative texts of which it consists? Or is literary "culture" something that must be constructed, through the inculcation of institutionally sanctioned and, therefore, legitimized *readings* of those texts into a literary "tradition"—something that will also often interpret such creative texts as representations of a singular and, more important, specifically national, idea?

When, for example, the idea of literary "culture" is construed broadly enough to encompass critical as well as creative texts, then the notions of "canons," "canonicity," and "canonization," all of which have been fundamental to our traditional understanding of literary tradition(s), become extremely important. The critical texts that serve to interpret and/or explain creative works have also traditionally functioned to construct and uphold a fundamental idea of literary "culture" as necessarily historical. This is because the notion of a literary tradition is itself historical, in that it serves to authorize certain cultural representations in certain ways through reliance on the authority of longevity. With regard to literary "culture," such longevity, like literary culture itself, has also traditionally been determined, more often than not, in terms of nationality, as a symbolic representation of a distinct national character and/or idea.

As such, it is not difficult to understand why traditional notions of literary "culture" in particular may be disturbed by the entrance of "other" voices and cultural representations into the space of "culture." If "culture," specifically literary "culture," is a means of describing and understanding a national character, and if whatever nation in question has defined that character as existing in an essentially "pure" state, undisturbed by "other" cultural influences, then such "other" cultural voices must necessarily pose a substantial threat: they cannot, in such an event, be considered simply as representative of different ways of viewing, understanding, and interpreting cultural phenomena. They also represent different ways of viewing history itself, and the way in which it has been interpreted and encoded into truth. In other words, they represent separate and often violently conflicting visions of cultural and social reality.

"Other" cultural representations open up entirely new ways of looking at and understanding the world, viewpoints that also often pose a direct challenge to established worldviews and their authority. When the subject at hand is specifically literary history and its relation to the notion of "culture," what this means is that the entrance of "other" literary representations into the space of "culture" must necessarily demand an alteration in the way in which such "culture" has to that point been read, interpreted, and understood. It requires, then, an intense reexamination of its very foundations, and of what such "culture" has come to mean and represent in terms of its influence in the larger social and political world. When literary "culture" is construed as a specifically national idea, it is also inescapably, albeit covertly, political, and when that national idea is then linked with the forcible suppression of "other" cultural representations, such "culture" is thus implicated in the notion of power, one by which such "other" representations must, in their search for recognition, find themselves necessarily opposed.

Such opposition is strongest at the level of the literary canon, the fundamental structure on which most of the traditional literary disciplines and fields have been based.[2] Because the canon in whatever context represents a list of texts chosen for what is determined beforehand as their literary and aesthetic value, it is not just a random list. And because determinations of aesthetic value are inevitably subject to the vagaries of taste, it is not difficult to see how such determinations could also (as were reading and interpretation, examined in chapter 2) find themselves linked to questions of ideology—especially when they are considered in relation to the concept of nationalism, in terms of the role of the literary canon in the symbolic representation of a largely homogeneous, nationally defined idea or character.

It is here, then, that Gates's comparison above (between DuBois's "problem of the color line" and Gates's own "problem of ethnic differences") becomes significant. The "problem of the color line" was, for DuBois, the problem of social, cultural, economic, and political subordination, which he understood as being based on an assumption of essential and incommensurable racial difference. In his view, the cultural hegemony of the West resulted in the cultural subordination of women, of blacks (both native Africans and those of the black diaspora), as well as of other "minorities." When dealing with the issue of race in particular, however, it must be recognized that this racial hegemony was expressed in DuBois's time not only in relation to culture, but in all areas of social life, and it resulted in the near silencing, during that time, of all cultural representations deemed "other" as a consequence of the racial origin of their creators. "Culture" became the domain primarily of Euro-Americans, and the bulk of "other" cultural representations were effectively excluded, as Said points out:

> Because the West acquired world dominance . . . Westerners have assumed the integrity and inviolability of their cultural master-

pieces. Their scholarship, their worlds of discourse; the rest of the world stands petitioning at our windowsill.[3]

Thus, DuBois describes a world made up of those who stand inside the framework of "culture" and those who must remain outside, petitioners at its windowsill, irreconcilably divided due to the power of a cultural subordination justified by race.

By contrast, the contemporary situation Gates describes is much more broad, extending itself beyond the problem of racial difference to include those of ethnicity, gender, and class. As such, in Gates's formulation, the fundamental problem remains that of difference, but "difference" as he defines it is not singular, as might seem the case when it is described only by race, but plural, as it must be considered when all the subtle gradations of culture, nationality, race, class, and gender are taken into account. What Gates has described as an "era of emergent nationalism" is precisely that historical moment when those cultural voices long suppressed across the world, having become aware of collective identities (an awareness that is often, but not always, nationalist in expression), begin to speak from that central understanding.[4] In this book, I have articulated a cultural perspective different yet again from this one, emphasizing the importance of the multiplicity, hybridity, instability, and inherent difference of multiple cultural locations, the silent cultural space that stands apart from the polarized debate on canon revision and culture studies and is, by virtue of that debate's emphasis on singularly defined ethnic identity, in many ways also silenced by it.

When locating the most intense opposition to cultural change at the site of the traditional literary canons, it is significant to discuss literary modernism and modernity in particular. Here, a number of social factors have initially converged, in particularly interesting ways, to bring about the cultural confrontation with difference that has resulted in the crisis in representation manifested in the debate on canon revision and culture studies. Canonical power and influence in this instance is, however, more clearly understood if it is viewed in relation to the broader historical context of the national/international conflict that I described in chapter 2 as a central aspect of critical formulations of Euro-American modernism, which has been traditionally understood as the sole means by which literary modernism and modernity were to be articulated in critical formulations.

While some felt that the rise of internationalism in the early twentieth century would sponsor a greater contact between nations that could bring about the development of a "universal civilization," many others felt that such contact could only have the opposite effect, as Kern explains:

> [One] response to the shrinking distances and the growing proximity was conflict. Its most visible manifestation was imperialism, and its

most explicitly written expression, the imperialist tracts of its defenders. The English and French who first staked out empires and the Germans and Americans who came later shared the same assumptions, values, and fears—that the new technology had greatly facilitated the exploration and seizure of vast empires, that the command of territorial space was essential to national greatness, that such command was morally defensible, and that the imperialist scramble would eventually lead to war, especially after all the "virgin land" had been taken. Internationalism and imperialism coiled around the staff of the new technology and around one another like the snakes of a caduceus.[5]

What Kern identifies here is precisely the subtle underlying difficulty that the encounter with cultural difference poses to literary canons in general, and the Euro-American modernist literary canon in particular—namely, that the rise and development of *inter*national culture, or any situation in which the encounter with cultural difference is encouraged (such as that found in multiculturalism), often has nationalistic or at least culturally hegemonic ends similar to those of cultural nationalism as its underlying motive. Thus, the international (or multicultural) may be understood as inextricably implicated in the national, in its imperialistic form, and vice versa. In this regard, then, nationalism and internationalism may be often understood to go hand-in-hand, through the connections held by each to imperial culture. In Said's view, what he calls this "geographical element" must be privileged in any discussion of the difference between Western and non-Western cultural representations because, as he explains, imperialism "is an act of geographical violence through which virtually every space in the world is explored, charted, and finally brought under control."[6] In this context, then, the conflict inherent in geopolitics, engendered by the interaction between nationalism, internationalism, and imperialism, and given material expression in terms of the battle over geographical space, may also be viewed as finding symbolic expression in terms of the politics of cultural space, in the form of the battle over the authorization and legitimization of cultural representations, whose material representation has traditionally been the literary canon.[7]

When literary canons are viewed from this vantage point, the reason that canon *revision* is, as Gates describes above, "politically fraught," becomes very clear. Because the act of revising the canon does not substantially interrogate the structure of the canon itself, it accepts that structure as is, and in doing so, simply ignores those cultural representations that cannot be placed under its rubric, or automatically relegates them to a necessary and inviolably marginal status within whatever canon is in question. This occurs, as Said points out, because of the silent imperialistic aims that may often be concealed in traditional literary canons under the guise of nationalism:

The modern history of literary study has been bound up with the development of cultural nationalism, whose aim was first to distinguish the national canon, then to maintain its eminence, authority, and aesthetic autonomy. Even in discussions concerning culture in general that seemed to rise above national differences in deference to a universal sphere, hierarchies and ethnic preferences (as between European and non-European) were held to.[8]

If the traditional literary canon is understood in these terms, then the political nature of multiculturalism as Gates has described it above, and particularly in terms of American literature, must be understood as being motivated by the ideological underpinnings of its development as a discipline, as discussed in chapter 2: initially created by a select group of white, upper-class males, those who could go to college at all in the 1920s, the canon of American literature was originally constructed in such a way as to support their worldview, which included across-the-board recognition of the cultural achievements neither of women nor of those of their compatriots who belonged to what they deemed minority groups—or, for that matter, large-scale recognition of the cultural context of any literary works at all. Nor did it substantially recognize the cultural significance of those cultural representations derived from multiple cultural locations, in America or elsewhere.

In the event, then, that such a canon is not itself questioned in terms of the values, assumptions, and historical attitudes it represents, how is the mere *inclusion* of such "minority" texts, or the mere recognition of cultural representations derived from multiple cultural locations, to represent a true revision of that canon? When viewed in this context, the way in which we have heretofore perceived the notion of canon revision must be understood as having little to do with the idea of revising our notion of "canons" themselves. In the absence of a substantial revision of the very notion of "canons" and their role, function and relationship to the literature we read, the debate on canon revision and culture studies may be running very fast in order ultimately to go nowhere at all.

The problem, then, as previously discussed in chapter 1, is not really the issue of "inclusion" versus "exclusion," around which critical debate about canon revision and culture studies has traditionally centered, but the question What does the notion of "canon" really mean? How has it traditionally been construed? What is its significance in literary study? What happens when our traditional notions of what canons are and what they are meant to do are radically questioned? Such questions must necessarily lead us as well to pose others, having to do with the covert, but no less influential, properties of canons, that is, the notions of "canonicity" and "canonization."

For example, as Gates discusses in *Loose Canons,* in connection with the organization of his group project to edit the *Norton Anthology of African-American Literature,* the notion of "canon" is not self-evident, but rather, a function of the interaction between the creative texts that are its central focus and the critical, interpretive texts that surround it:

> My pursuit of this project has required me to negotiate a position between, on the one hand, William Bennett, who claims that black people can have no canon, no masterpieces, and, on the other hand, those on the critical left who wonder why we want to estab-lish the existence of a canon, any canon, in the first place. On the right hand, we face the outraged reactions of those custodians of Western culture who protest that the canon, that transparent de-canter of Western values, may become . . . *politicized.* . . . That peo-ple can maintain a straight face while they protest the irruption of politics into something that has always been political from the be-ginning—well it says something about how remarkably successful official literary histories have been in presenting themselves as nat-ural and neutral objects, untainted by worldly interests.[9]

What Gates is speaking of when he mentions "official literary histories" is nothing other than those critical interpretations legitimized within the uni-versity, and thereby lent the authority of truth, in the process described in chapter 2. In this way, the interaction between such interpretations and the creative works they discuss may be understood as functioning to a large de-gree to create that canon. Where a large, legitimized body of such literature is not available, as was originally the case of African-American literature, then the very existence of such a canon is subject to question, as Gates has elaborated above. Yet when this situation is reconsidered in terms of the cur-rent discussion of the often ideological and perhaps implicitly imperialistic properties and aims of traditional literary canons and canon formation, then it is not difficult to understand the nonexistence of such interaction in a given instance as something that may be explained through the politics of cultural space—the operations of legitimation and institutionalization (or the lack thereof) within the university.

The difficulties Gates identifies above with regard to the development of a specifically African-American literary canon have to do with determi-nations of the "canonicity" of such literature—in other words, whether or not it possesses those properties necessary for canonical inclusion, or "can-onization." If this discussion is continued in terms of the line of thought elaborated above, it is clear that if the activity of canon revision is to be suc-cessful, our current notions (as they have been traditionally established) of the idea of "canons" must also take into account the ideological residue that may be embedded in the notions of "canonicity" and "canonization," which are automatically implied by the notion of "canon" itself. When these concepts are not substantially interrogated, all that is suggested by the canonical inclusion of previously silenced voices is the need to compare those marginalized voices just entering the canon to those already forming it, on the basis of "canonicity," or their "qualifications" for inclusion. Since, as we have seen, these qualifications are subject to the passage of time, the vagaries of taste, and any number of social and political influences, determinations of "canonicity" from traditional points of view cannot be considered unbiased because the notion of "canonicity" itself, as well as its companion terms "canon" and "canonization," have not themselves been interrogated and revised. As Gates goes on to suggest, we must also study "the history of the idea of the 'canon,' which involves . . . the history of literary pedagogy and . . . the history of the school."[10] Without such a prior, or at least concomitant, analysis of the notion of "canon," and its history, both in relation to literature and in relation to the institution, the activity of "canon revision," at least in terms of the effort to recognize the significance of the contemporary multiplicity of cultural representations, will remain ineffective at best, and incomplete at worst.

CULTURAL STUDIES OR TRANSCULTURAL STUDIES?

> Texts are protean things; they are tied to circumstances and to politics large and small; and these require attention and criticism.
>
> —Edward Said, *Culture and Imperialism*

The foregoing discussion of the role of "canons," "canonicity," and "canonization" in relation to the activity of canon revision is meant to underscore the primary goals of *Reading on the Edge* as a text, and the larger implications of its critical analysis. The powerful influence of traditional notions of "canons," "canonicity," and "canonization" not only in established perceptions of Euro-American modernism, but in our conception of literature and literary study in general, cannot be denied. If these terms are understood in relation to the current discussion, a conventional reading of, for example, James Baldwin, that would seek to situate his work within the context of literary modernism and modernity, broadly defined, would necessarily fail if it were approached in an uncritical manner, and if Euro-American modernism itself were not subjected to intense questioning as well.

This is because, as all three of these notions (of literary modernism, literary modernity, and Euro-American modernism) have been construed to the present time, they have not adequately confronted the difficult question of how to accommodate radical cultural difference. While Euro-American modernism, as it has been articulated in its international form, has indeed been involved with cultural difference in terms of its engagement with the cultural products of authors (and other types of artists) from various nations, that engagement of difference, as we have seen, is also one that was deeply implicated in the system of imperial expansion, or colonialism. In this regard, then, its encounter with difference went only to a point: it was ultimately contained by a gendered and racialized boundary, even as it crossed other boundaries that were national and linguistic.

I have sought in this text to analyze the implications of reading beyond these tightly controlled boundaries, serving to keep "other" cultural representations submerged below an overtly nationalistic surface that would, in many ways, silence them out of existence. In this respect, *Reading on the Edge* has not been an attempt at canon revision in the traditional sense, as such an attempt would also involve an uncritical acceptance of the notion of "canon," and, as a result, necessitate a justification, in this instance, of James Baldwin's qualifications for inclusion under an uninterrogated rubric of Euro-American modernism. Instead, what has been examined here are the implications of exploring and analyzing the politics of a cultural space whose surface presentation would indicate that such a politics did not actually exist. What such an exploration reveals in the end is that if we want to get the "right" answers, we also have to ask the "right" questions. As Guillory so clearly puts it, the "question before us is . . . how the revaluation of particular authors alters the set of terms by which literature as a whole, or what we . . . call the canon, is represented to its constituency, to literary culture, at a particular historical moment."[11]

In the present case, the authors under consideration have been revalued, but not in a conventional sense: such revaluation is usually one-sided, usually involving the upgrading of a marginalized cultural voice to the status of those considered legitimate. Revaluation undertaken in circumstances such as these not only subtly devalues itself by taking traditional terms as an unquestioned starting point, that is, that the text in question must naturally begin as an inferior text if only because it has historically been articulated as such, but also adopts a defensive posture that seeks to prove the worth of such cultural products by comparison rather than by virtue of their own merits. When this happens, the text itself may often be bypassed, as more emphasis is placed on what must be proven than on what the text itself may have to offer.

The readings undertaken here have sought, rather, to enact such revaluation with regard to all three texts involved, and, in so doing, to suggest a radical revaluation of our traditional understanding of the idea of the literary "canon" itself, as well as the concepts of "canonicity" and "canonization" that it necessarily implies, in addition to suggesting a rearticulation of our conception of literary modernism and modernity along these lines. In a sense then, part of the present discussion of the politics of cultural space has been an effort to show how such politics is more a matter of culturally authorized and institutionally sanctioned readings of texts and their relationship to the notion of "canon" than it is inherent to the texts themselves—to show how interrogating traditional canonical divisions in order to create the possibility of reading disparate texts *differently* can also produce radical, and potentially illuminating, results. By examining these texts outside of the cultural constructs they normally inhabit, we have been able to understand them in ways that were silenced, hidden, and/or obfuscated by those cultural constructs and, in doing so, learn more about those constructs themselves, as well as about the texts that were examined. In a sense, then, what we have been studying is, as Graff explains, that which the structure within which literary study is currently effected has for the most part tended to obscure:

> The disconnection between the divisions that organize the literature department and the university tends to efface the larger cultural conversation to which works of literature refer. The cultural text tends to fall into the cracks separating periods, genres, and fields, criticism, creative writing, and composition. Nobody is responsible for it since it is nobody's field—or else someone is responsible for it only as one field among others. . . . That there is no agreement over how the cultural text should be understood, or whether it should come into play at all in the teaching of literature, seems to me an argument for rather than against a more explicitly historicized and cultural kind of literary study that would make such disagreements part of what is studied.[12]

It is this "larger cultural conversation" that is of interest here, in gaining a complete understanding of how *Reading on the Edge* reads the work of Proust, Joyce, and Baldwin—what Graff, following Robert Scholes,[13] has identified as the "cultural text." If this cultural text is viewed in the terms set out above, as something forcibly submerged by a seemingly hegemonic, double-edged impulse (as represented by the polarized debate on canon revision and culture studies) committed to the articulation and authorization only of *certain* types of cultural experience and understanding, then it is only natural that it should be something that must remain in the no-man's land of the "cracks" between the boundaries of established literary disciplines.

When, as Graff suggests, this cultural text becomes a part of literary study rather than something silent, hidden, and obscured, it must also inevitably carry with it a discord that has been strangely absent not only from literary discourse per se, but from the structure of the academic institution itself. What this means is that while scholar-critics engage in numerous debates within their various disciplines and fields, these debates historically have not concerned themselves with the way in which the university and/or the department itself is structured, and what this may have to tell us about how we understand literature and literary study and its contemporary cultural significance. These structures are usually taken as given, and usually remain uncontested. When they are not disturbed or questioned, however, the cultural text also remains safely outside their confines—silent, hidden, and obscured. It is not something to be discussed, as it does not possess a context that would authorize such discussion. Lacking a legitimized cultural space, then, the "larger cultural conversation" is something that is elided, neglected, or simply ignored—that is, silenced. When this happens, creative literary texts are, to a certain extent, often taken out of context—they are not viewed in terms of the cultural complexities by which their authors may have been surrounded during their production, but are instead *read* into another context that, because it has a particular agenda (e.g., the elaboration of a national or nationally defined idea or character) is also interested only in whatever aspect of the text in question will support this agenda.

The significance of a given "text" may be understood, then, as something that may change according to the way in which it is *read*, and according to the context within which such reading is undertaken. Whether we discover more or less about what given texts have to offer is thus founded on these two premises. If a text is understood thus, as a "protean thing," as Said identifies, then the "cultural text" becomes something of paramount importance, especially if the study of literature is to be understood within the broader context of humanistic study in general. This is why I have suggested in this conclusion that perhaps what must be questioned is our notion of "culture" itself; perhaps "culture" is not one thing, to be acquired only through education and assiduous study, but many things, never to be reconciled, yet endlessly fascinating in their multitudinous variety. Perhaps the point is not reconciliation, or the desire to retrieve the semblance of some sort of singular idea, but rather, the identification and appreciation of what we may possibly learn from the infinite and multiple variations of cultural difference.

It is in this respect that the notion of the politics of cultural space is most important: it suggests that "culture" has always been a matter of controversy, something that only becomes overtly *political* when that controversy is forcibly silenced. In the case of literary "culture," this controversy has often been muffled by the structure of the university and the department which, through the demands of "professionalization," have succeeded in relegating it to and keeping it in a subordinated state. Moving beyond this becomes, as West describes, no simple matter:

> As cultural critics attuned to political conflict and struggle in-
> scribed within the rhetorical enactments of texts, we should relate
> such conflict and struggle to larger institutional and structural bat-
> tles occurring in and across societies, cultures, and economies. . . .
> The key here is not mere interdisciplinary work that traverses ex-
> isting boundaries of disciplines, but rather the more demanding ef-
> forts of pursuing dedisciplinizing modes of knowing that call into
> question the very boundaries of the disciplines themselves.[14]

This does not mean that the literary disciplines and fields such as they are
can and should no longer exist. Rather, it suggests that in addition to these,
the cultural text can and should be given credence. Moreover, it suggests that
an adequate exploration of this cultural text (what I would like further to describe as the identification and recognition of multiple cultural representations in all of their variety) cannot occur without a concomitant recognition
of the essentially political nature of studying it in relation to prior established structures within which it was not given credence, a version of what
Said calls "contrapuntal"[15] reading. And it is only by questioning the stasis
suggested by the established boundaries that separate the disciplines, what
West calls here "dedisciplinizing modes of knowing" that this cultural text
may be brought back into critical debate. This is because the refusal to hold
such boundaries inviolate necessitates the posing of very different questions
from those that may be suggested from within established disciplines believed to possess more stable boundaries.

   As stated in chapter 1, a major emphasis of this book has also been the
analysis of culture studies. The development and gradual recognition of this
burgeoning field as a viable literary critical approach is evidence, as aforesaid, that the literary profession is currently, and subtly, undergoing a major
paradigm shift that seems to be focusing on the (re)determination of its object of study. Culture studies approaches suggest that this object is no longer
to be simply the "text," which is not to be "studied for its own sake, nor
even for the social effects it may be thought to produce, but rather for the
subjective or cultural forms which it realises and makes available."[16] Yet because what I have been describing in this book seeks not only to read beyond
but also to critique disciplinary boundaries in the effort to explode our traditional (historical) notions of "culture" (whether literary or otherwise), as
well as those notions of "canon," "canonicity," and "canonization" on
which it relies, it could be asserted that there exists an immutable bond between it and such culture studies approaches. In their emphasis on social effects, however, culture studies approaches may also be seen by many to
sidestep the difficult questions that may be asked only at a textual level,
those questions pertaining to the way in which texts have been and will be

interpreted, and how these interpretations (or readings) will in turn affect and/or serve to create our cultural understanding. What really does it mean to view texts from disparate cultures outside the boundaries set up by the established literary disciplines? Why are these boundaries so tightly drawn? What are we protecting? What does it mean to cross boundaries? To be an exile? To have a transnational identity?[17] Can we learn about these from the way in which we read texts?

This is the goal of the type of textual analysis and reading that has been undertaken here, what I will call a sort of "transcultural studies." While in this type of reading, there are indeed to be found many links with culture studies, the goal, and hopefully the end results, of both projects are to some extent different. While culture studies seeks to explore the notion of "culture" in all of its forms, "transcultural studies" would seek to take this exploration even further, by examining how different cultural representations from disparate cultural origins interact with each other, and thereby influence our understanding both of those that are familiar and those that are not. It is, essentially, interested in analyzing and interpreting—in *reading*—that cultural space which exists between the established disciplines, between cultures as they are nationally defined, so that their borders, now politically fraught, might become instead the intellectual watershed taking us over the edge, moving toward our critical (and cultural) future.

As previously discussed in this book, questions from the border are sometimes very risky and, in this respect, quite challenging. But they may also, as a result, lead us down less well-trodden, and thus very fruitful, intellectual paths. In this context, literary study can become an endeavor that may not point in such clear-cut directions as has traditionally been the case, but this does not mean that what may be learned is any less valuable or any less enlightening. The project may be challenging, but it may also prove the oft-repeated notion of the greater the risk, the greater the potential reward.

Reading on the Edge is a text that has tried to travel such a road. In focusing on the way in which the politics of cultural space relates through the figure of exile to the work and experiences of the three authors whose texts it has examined and to a new conception of literary modernism and modernity, it reveals that the study of literature is (or should be) in many ways similar to that same experience: an exilic journey into the unknown, looking for something one thinks one knows but realizes in the end one never did, where the familiar is left far behind, perhaps never to be recovered, and the daily challenge is to succeed in adapting to the implications of continual discovery. As Said writes:

> Once we accept the actual configuration of literary experiences overlapping with one another and interdependent, despite national

boundaries and coercively legislated national autonomies, history and geography are transfigured in new maps, in new and far less stable entities, in new types of connections. Exile, far from being the fate of nearly forgotten unfortunates who are dispossessed and expatriated, becomes something closer to a norm, an experience of crossing boundaries and charting new territories in defiance of the classic canonic enclosures.[18]

Thus, if we seek to understand literature and literary study themselves as possessing far more importance than the cultural politics they often symbolically represent in the form of more local and particular determinations of cultural superiority and/or inferiority, we can move beyond notions of cultural difference as inherently conflictual, and begin to see new, unimagined possibilities in studying how such cultural difference may be potentially enhancing. And perhaps in this way, we may also begin to perceive how, through the study of culturally and ethnically disparate texts in greater proximity than commonly permitted by traditional disciplinary divisions, the cultural and social significance of difference itself may be radically altered, in ways that can only enrich both our critical readings and our cultural understanding of those texts, and the cultures from which they derive.

Notes

PREFACE

1. Wlad Godzich, "Afterword: Religion, the State, and Post(al) Modernism," in *Institution and Interpretation* by Samuel Weber, Theory and History of Literature, Vol. 31 (Minneapolis: U of Minnesota P, 1987) 157.

2. This is, however, also largely due to the fact that African-American literature did not exist at all as a discipline until the early 1970s, and even then, its existence as a discrete discipline was due to the efforts of the first wave of African-American critics in the academy.

3. See Rodolphe Gasche, "Introduction," in Andrzej Warminski, *Readings in Interpretation: Holderlin, Hegel, Heidegger* (Minneapolis: U of Minnesota P, 1987).

4. Contemporary Marxist theory has questioned the reliance on experience as a means to establish individual identity. This problem will be discussed in more detail in Chapter 1.

5. D. Emily Hicks, *Border Writing: The MultiDimensional Text*, Theory and History of Literature, Vol. 80 (Minneapolis: U of Minnesota P, 1991) xxxv.

6. Ibid.

7. Hicks xxvi.

8. An interesting representation of this type of experience is to be found in Maxine Hong Kingston, *The Woman Warrior: Memoirs of the Girlhood Among Ghosts* (New York: Vintange, 1975).

9. Hicks xxvi.

1. INTRODUCTION

1. See Gates, Clifford, Torgovnick, Morrison, Said, and JanMohamed. This is by no means meant to be an exhaustive bibliography of ex-

isting discussions of this subject, but rather a suggestion of the great variety with which it is currently being handled. Both anthropology and its subfield, ethnography, deal entirely with this issue. Each of these fields has recently come under attack because of feminist and poststructuralist rearticulations of the notion of the subject, which have served as well to critique the stability of the boundaries between "self" and "other."

2. By "authorized group identity" I mean to suggest those cultural locations of identity that are recognized by particular, largely homogeneous (or giving the impression of homogeneity), collective consensus, whether that be defined by nation, ethnicity, religion, race, or gender. Cultural representations produced in keeping with such collectivities become the objects of literary study and thus the ground of cultural knowledges about these group identities. Cultural representations and identities derived from outside of these recognized collectivities do not fit easily within the frameworks established by and supporting such "authorized" identities and representations.

3. See Bhabha, *Location*.

4. Gilroy 2. Gilroy writes: "Regardless of their affiliation to the right, left, or centre, groups have fallen back on the idea of cultural nationalism, on the overintegrated conceptions of culture which present immutable, ethnic differences as an absolute break in the histories of 'black' and 'white' people. Against this choice stands another, more difficult option: the theorisation of creolisation, metissage, mestizaje, and hybridity. From the viewpoint of ethnic absolutism, this would be a litany of pollution and impurity. These terms are rather unsatisfactory ways of naming the processes of culturation and mutation and restless (dis)continuity that exceed racial discourse and avoid capture by its agents." While Gilroy's work focuses on the embattled traditional relationship between "black" and "white" and the issue of cultural difference, I expand this view in the present text to encompass the meaning of cultural difference in numerous cultural binaries stretching across the multiple forms and contexts he identifies (e.g., in this text such cultural binaries could also be viewed in terms of Catholic/Protestant, citizen/expatriate, heterosexual/homosexual, Jewish/Gentile, rich/poor, etc.). See also Lionnet.

5. See note 2 above. For a variety of conservative cultural viewpoints, see Bennett, Schlesinger, Bloom, and D'Souza.

6. See Bourdieu. Bourdieu's analysis of cultural production will be discussed in greater detail in chapter 2.

7. In the study of English literature, however, this is currently undergoing a radical alteration, specifically in the field of American literature. The increasing recognition of diverse populations of ethnic minorities in the United States has brought about a very energetic movement toward comparatist studies of American literature. See, for example, Spillers; Perloff, "Living"; Fitz; and Firmat.

8. For a detailed history of the development and institutionalization of comparative literature, see Wellek; Schultz & Rein; Warren & Wellek; Weisstein; Koelb & Noakes; Gossman; Spariou; Owen; and Jost. For an analysis of contemporary issues in comparative literature, see Bernheimer; see also *World Literature Today* 69.2 (Spring 1995), special issue on comparative literature.

9. Perloff, "Modernist" 172. Perloff separates modernism into its "first phase" (which she calls "mainstream modernism"), having its development mostly prior to 1914 and its end somewhere around 1918, with the end of World War I; and its later phase, stretching into the 1930s and beyond. All subsequent references to Euro-American modernism should be understood to represent this distinction, as well as both periods.

10. Smithson and Ruff 1. See also Appadurai and Featherstone. Both of these scholars discuss the cultural implications of globalization.

11. For an elaboration of this burgeoning field, see Smithson & Ruff 1–22 and Johnson; for a broad range of cultural studies perspectives, see Grossberg, Nelson & Treichler.

12. See note 11 above.

13. See note 11 above. See especially Smithson & Ruff 4–5. They write: "In the 1990s, English studies/culture studies investigates . . . how literary canons are formed; the conventions that have defined some texts as "literary"; why some histories and interpretations prevail while others struggle to get into print; the differences made by gender, sexual orientation, ethnic background, and political and economic power in the writing, publication, and reading of texts; writers, texts, and readers as cultural commodities; the roles of educational and other institutions in defining objects, methods, and values of education; and the relations among educational institutions, governments, business interests, and other cultural components. The present text is a study constructed to some extent along these lines.

14. Smithson 1.

15. Ibid.

16. Ibid.

17. The study of English literature, which had been used by the British in India as a means to "homogenize" the Indian elite into a British mode of life and cultural understanding, had ousted the study of classics in the British curriculum only in the late nineteenth century. It was then used for the same purpose in America, where it found a competitor, albeit not a strong one, in the rise of American literature in the 1920s. In both cases, the new literature was viewed as a means to bring about cultural homogenization. See Viswanathan; see also Lauter.

18. Smithson 10–11. For a more detailed discussion of the New Criti-

cism, see Brooks & Warren; Brooks, Warren & Purser; Wimsatt & Beardsley; and Wimsatt & Brooks.

19. Something many scholar-critics exploring what has now come to be called the exlusionary legacy of Euro-American modernism often forget to consider is that modernism was, at its beginning, and for a long time thereafter, a nontraditional literary art form, viewed as a threat in established literary cultural circles of the time. See Karl xvi. He writes: "What Modernism has done, historically, has been to connect countries and cultures that otherwise had little in common. With the spread of modern ideas, culture bulged across borders. The old idea of a national literature which was defined in the nineteenth century with Fichte and Herder can no longer obtain. Nations now become linked, whatever their divergence of official policies, by way of modern ideas in literature, music, art, and technology. As a consequence, Modernism for many countries . . . becomes a dangerous code word in political terms. For not only does it introduce into nations ideas that might be anathema ideologically, it also forces linkages with alien cultures." See also Perloff, "Modernist"; Bradbury & McFarlane.

20. It is also interesting that Euro-American modernism's critical institutionalization was instigated by early comparatists, such as Harry Levin and Edmund Wilson. For an analysis of modernism as a subversive movement, see note 19 above.

21. For an elaboration of this issue, see Calinescu; for an in-depth history of Euro-American modernism, see Bradbury & McFarlane; for an analysis of its intellectual background, see Ellmann, *Modern*.

22. Graff; see also Scholes, *Rise*.

23. Culler, *Framing* 33.

24. For various perspectives on the function of the university in society, see Readings, Guillory, Newfield, and Bourdieu.

25. Because this text adheres even more closely to the American version of the culture/cultural studies model, all references to this approach will subsequently be to "culture," rather than "cultural," studies.

26. Gilroy 37–38.

27. For various perspectives pro and con regarding this issue, see Bernheimer; see also *World Literature Today* 69.2 (Spring 1995), special issue on comparative literature. Traditional notions of comparative literature are very much intertwined with this emphasis on "literariness," which also implies a particular type of valuation of the literary text.

28. A more in-depth analysis of the notion of space, the politics of cultural space, and the relation of these to literary modernism and modernity will be undertaken in chapter 2.

29. See Ross 668.

30. Clifford 10. I am suggesting here, with Clifford, that "culture," at

least as we have come to know it in terms of literature, may very well be a sort of fiction, developed with the establishment and maintenance of certain kinds of values in mind. See also Viswanathan.

31. Kern 223–40.

32. Clifford 13–14.

33. See Perloff 168. Here, Perloff identifies the issue of substitution with regard to canon revision as "canon reversal." The problem of substitution may also in this instance be compared to the "master-slave" dialectic described by the nineteenth-century German philosopher, G. W. F. Hegel. See Hegel, chapter IV. The polarized nature of the debate on canon revision and culture studies is itself the progenitor of this problem of substitution. As in the "master-slave" dialectic, this debate is engaged in a figurative hand-to-hand, life-or-death struggle in which, from the perspective of either side, there can be only one true winner.

34. See Kern 223-40. See also Said; Viswanathan; Althusser.

35. Ibid.

36. See note 23 above.

37. Kenner 367.

38. Torgovnick 188. Following Lukacs, Torgovnick describes the site of exile as that which represents "transcendental homelessness" which, in Lukacs's formulation, describes the Western mind, which yearns for a return to "immanent totality." See also Lukacs.

39. For an in-depth analysis of the development of modern notions of nationalism, see Anderson; see also Hobsbawm.

40. Guillén, *Entre* 42; Guillén, *Challenge* 27.

41. Guillén 28.

42. Guillén 20.

43. Guillén 3.

44. Guillén 4.

45. Ibid.

46. Yet the current debate on canon revision and culture studies has brought about an emphasis on the role, methods, and importance of comparatism in literary studies never before seen in the relatively short history of the field. Whether comparatism be undertaken in relation to culture and globalization, diasporic communities, migration, emergent literatures, postcolonial theories, feminist theories or any number of burgeoning contexts for the study of literature and culture, comparatist methods and assumptions have been and are being pushed increasingly to the forefront of literary critical debate. See, for example, Pratt, Lionnet, Gilroy, Higonnet, Felski, and Torgovnick.

47. "Similarity" here is not meant to suggest that the cultural experiences of each of the authors to be studied are the "same," and therefore in-

terchangeable. I maintain here the difference between "sameness" and "similarity." *The American Heritage Dictionary*, 2nd College Ed., defines "same" as "being the very one; identical . . . conforming in every detail," while it defines "similar" as "related in appearance or nature; alike though not identical." Thus, in this instance, "similarity" allows for a certain likeness that provides the ground for comparison.

48. Laclau 110–11. Recent Marxist theory problematizes the notion that lived experience is an adequate foundation on which to construct a notion of stable identity. Ernesto Laclau and Chantal Mouffe write: "If we accept . . . that a discursive totality never exists in the form of a simply *given and delimited* positivity, the relational logic will be incomplete and pierced by contingency. . . . A no-man's land thus emerges, making the articulatory practice possible. In this case, there is no social identity fully protected from a discursive exterior that deforms it and prevents it becoming fully sutured. Both the identities and the relations lose their necessary character. As a systematic structural ensemble, the relations are unable to absorb the identities; but as the identities are purely relational, this is but another way of saying that there is no identity which can be fully constituted." Following Guillory (10), who writes that the establishment of canonical or noncanonical status based on the social identity of the author as gounded in his or her "experience of a marginalized race, class, or gender identity" is not a viable option precisely because, as Laclau and Mouffe have outlined, identity and experience are not one and the same, I argue that it is precisely *because* identity and experience are loosely related that it is indeed possible to argue against the boundary separating all three of these authors in traditional literary critical formulations. None of these authors possesses a singular cultural identity, nor do any of them possess only that identity given to them as a by-product of literary critical "readings." What *Reading on the Edge* seeks, then, is to establish the cultural space in which these "other" (or multiple) identities may be given voice in tandem with the authorized cultural identities assigned to them in such literary critical readings.

49. See note 47.

50. Marino 118.

51. See Gilroy xi. Although Gilroy attempts to do precisely this in his influential book, *The Black Atlantic*, the present text is substantially different from that work. In *The Black Atlantic*, Gilroy makes a case for the inclusion of specifically African-American cultural contributions in a redefined concept of literary modernism and modernity. Although he does make repeated avowals that he is not trying to articulate a space within modernism and modernity that will reinstitute essentialized racial categories, his emphasis on specifically black cultural materials (although within the broader framework of his conception of diasporic cultural identity) yet serves to rein-

scribe such a racialized category. He writes: "[It] . . . is my hope that the contents of this book are unified by a concern to repudiate the dangerous obsessions with 'racial' purity which are circulating inside and outside black politics. It is, after all, essentially an essay about the inescapable hybridity and intermixture of ideas." While Gilroy has indeed written about the importance of hybridity in modern thought, his emphasis has not been the analysis of the cultural significance of that hybridity in all of its heterogeneity, the subject with which the present text is concerned. Gilroy limits his discussion to the analysis of hybridity specifically within a racially defined cultural context. The present text analyzes the impact of hybridity in terms of its multiple cultural locations and significance.

52. See note 47.

53. Said, *Culture* 188. Said notes that "many of the most prominent characteristics of modernist culture, which we have tended to derive from purely internal dynamics in Western society and culture, include a response to the external pressures on culture from the *imperium* . . ." Such responses may be found in particularly overt form in the work of both Baldwin and Joyce.

54. See Bourdieu. Bourdieu identifies this as the process of legitimization. This subject will be examined in more detail in chapter 2 as it relates to Euro-American modernism and the politics of cultural space.

55. Kenner 367.

56. For various analyses of this issue, what may be termed Euro-American modernism's legacy of exclusion, see Baker, de Jongh, Scott, Felski, Benstock, Gilroy, and Doyle. This issue will be discussed in greater detail in chapter 2.

2. (AN)OTHER MODERNISM

1. See Wilson.

2. See Levin.

3. See chapter 1, note 54.

4. Jameson 1. This discussion of the relationship between modernism and postmodernism is further elaborated below.

5. Jameson, "Modernism," 43–66.

6. Kalaidjian 4.

7. See the section on the New Criticism in chapter 1.

8. Ibid.

9. See Scott, Benstock, Baker, Gilroy, Kalaidjian, Felski, de Jongh, Huyssen, and Tratner.

10. Kalaidjian 2–4.

11. Guillory 136. Guillory writes: "[Literature possesses] specificity . . . as an ideological form, namely, its capacity in concrete institutional contexts

to produce ideological effects *through form.*" For Guillory, this "ideological effect" is a consequence only of the way in which literature is filtered through the university which, in turn, implies its relation to literary criticism. See also chapter 1.

12. See Kermode 93–124.

13. de Certeau 124.

14. Clifford 10. James Clifford writes here of such "stories," in suggesting that "ethnographic texts are orchestrations of multivocal exchanges occurring in politically charged situations. The subjectivities produced in these often unequal exchanges—whether of "natives" or of visiting participant-observers—are constructed domains of truth, serious fictions." Clifford's discussion of ethnography highlights the fact that since ethnography is the domain within which the West has traditionally studied those cultures deemed "other" to the Western imagination, its authority to (re)create such "others" has gone largely uncontested. The ideas disseminated under its rubric, then, have become "domains of truth" that have an extremely powerful influence over the linguistic structuring of reality that has shaped the West's understanding of such cultural "others." But in emphasizing their quality as "serious fictions," Clifford is also suggesting that such (re)creations are not real in fact, but have been mediated through the screen of values and cultural assumptions of the ethnographer, and are therefore also, to some extent, fictions created about the real. This is the sense in which I would like here to suggest that the narratives within which our traditional ideas of "modernism" acquire their form may be viewed as stories. These narratives, then, are the "serious fictions" by which "modernism" has been encoded and inscribed in literary history. See also White.

15. de Certeau 126.

16. See de Certeau 127. Here he suggests that "bodies can be distinguished only where the "contacts" . . . of amorous or hostile struggles are inscribed on them. This is a paradox of the frontier: created by contacts the points of differentiation between two bodies are also their common points." If the boundary that I have identified as existing between the two narratives of modernism is understood as both "frontier" and "bridge," then this boundary is a point of contact that must be viewed as simultaneously positive and negative. Because it represents a point where two opposing forces meet, it must also be recognized as the site of an enormous struggle. It is because of this struggle that traditional formulations of modernism may be understood to produce the "semantic confusion" discussed above. And it is also through this struggle that we may begin to explain why the almost mythical presence of the narrative of international modernism must be described in terms of power, and why that notion of power then forms the hub

or nexus around which our discussion of modernism and the politics of cultural space must be centered. See note 33 in chapter 1 and note 12 above.

17. See Kermode.

18. Johnson 58. Johnson writes: "There is . . . a sense in which . . . we can speak of texts as 'productive' and a much stronger case for viewing reading or cultural consumption as a production process in which the first product becomes a material for fresh labour. The text-as-produced is a different object from the text-as-read." What I am suggesting here is that the knowledges centered within the university, as "readings" (or interpretations) of a given literary text, represent the text as "product"—something which is, in the end, very different from the lived experience of reading.

19. Guillory 59. Guillory explains the function of the university in society as a system of exchange in which texts are "consumed" by the university, that is, processed in its system of accreditation, then redisseminated into the social world from which they originally came: "Individual works are taken up into this system (preserved, disseminated, taught) and confront their receptors first as canonical cultural capital. There is no other access to works: they must be confronted as the cultural capital of educational institutions . . . The school functions as a system of credentialization by which it produces a specific *relation* to culture. That relation is different for different people, which is to say that it reproduces social relations." The end result is that the university not only serves as the "producer" and facilitator of literature's "ideological effect," but in endowing that effect with cultural value through credentialization, it sanctifies its authority, translating this into the relation of power from which I have derived the notion of a politics of cultural space. For an in-depth analysis of ideology, see Althusser.

20. Lauter 23–28. Lauter also views literary canon formation in terms of the potential of its normative influence. For Lauter, the canon "encodes a set of social norms and values; and these, by virtue of its cultural standing, it helps endow with force and continuity . . . The literary canon is, in short, a means by which culture validates social power." In Lauter's view, the parameters of this power are identifiable along the lines of class, race, and gender.

21. Guillory 135. He writes: "The effects of ideology are generated around the conceptualization of literature itself, which is to say around the discursive/institutional form by means of which literary works are disseminated."

22. In this regard, "culturally dominant" does not mean the oftassumed "domination" of white (Euro-American) cultural representations and ideas over black (African, African-American) ones. These issues are so sensitive that the language that is often used to refer to them is so heavily loaded it becomes almost impossible not to imply these significations through linguistic connotation. In this case, what is meant is simply what-

ever culture in whatever instance happens to be the dominant one, something that can also take many forms depending on the culture in question.

23. de Certeau, "Reading," 157. De Certeau writes: "The use made of the book by privileged readers constitutes it as a secret of which they are the 'true' interpreters. It interposes a frontier between the text and its readers that can be crossed only if one has a passport delivered by these official interpreters, who transform their own reading (which is *also* a legitimate one) into an orthodox 'literality' that makes other (equally) legitimate readings either heretical (not 'in conformity' with the [accepted] meaning of the text) or insignificant (to be forgotten). From this point of view, 'literal' meaning is the index and the result of a social power, that of an elite. By its very nature available to a plural reading, the text becomes a cultural weapon, a private hunting reserve, the pretext for a law that legitimizes as 'literal' the interpretation given by *socially* authorized professionals and intellectuals (*clercs*)." De Certeau also writes here that the freedom of interpretation enjoyed by intellectuals and other professional "readers" is summarily denied to "students (who are scornfully driven or cleverly coaxed back to the meaning 'accepted' by their teachers) or the public (who are carefully told 'what is to be thought' and whose inventions are considered negligible and quickly silenced)." See also Chambers, Bennett, Mailloux, Fetterley, and Culler, *On*; Said 66.

24. Geertz 220. Geertz includes, as a type of ideology, the social attitudes involved in racism, in the form of segregation.

25. Geertz 198. Here, Geertz refers to Talcott Parsons's analysis of ideology, in which he suggests that "ideology arises when there is a *discrepancy* between what is believed and what can be [established as] scientifically correct." The quote here cited refers specifically to Parsons's conclusion that "'deviations from [social] scientific objectivity' emerge as the 'essential criteria of an ideology': 'The problem of ideology arises where there is a *discrepancy* between what is believed and what can be [established as] scientifically correct.'" This quote represents one of the two types of such deviation or discrepancy outlined by Geertz in this regard. See also West 200. West writes: "The literary objects upon which we focus are themselves cultural responses to specific crises in particular historical moments. Because these crises and moments must themselves be mediated through textual constructs, the literary objects we examine are never merely literary, and attempts to see them as such constitute a dehistoricizing and depoliticizing of literary texts that should be scrutinized for their ideological content, role and function. In this sense, canon formations that invoke the sole criterion of form . . . are suspect."

26. Guillory 15. Guillory problematizes the notion that such exclusion can be based on the minority social status of such writers. He writes: "By defining canonicity as determined by the social identity of the author, the

current critique of the canon both discovers, and misrepresents, the obvious fact that the older the literature, the less likely it will be that texts by socially defined minorities exist in sufficient numbers to produce a 'representative' canon. Yet the historical reasons for this fact are insufficiently acknowledged for their theoretical and practical implications." Although Guillory's observation may indeed be true, in using it to support the assertion that canonical exclusion cannot be based on the social identity of those excluded, he neglects to analyze the possibility that the fact that "minority" texts may exist in insufficient numbers to warrant canonical inclusion may be a result of precisely the sort of exclusion he is arguing against. In addition, and as is often the case, he perhaps defines the notion of "minority" racially, when it can also be considered from the perspective of minority groups that are defined not by race, but by some other nondominant characteristic. This is the type of "otherness" with which the present text is engaged.

27. See note 47 in chapter 1.

28. Bourdieu 42.

29. There are important similarities between this struggle and that described in chapter 1 in terms of Hegel's "master-slave dialectic" and the problem of substitution (note 47, chapter 1). Like that one, this struggle is one of life and death, represented in terms of literary legitimacy: Which narrative will take precedence over the other? This is the central question in both instances of struggle.

30. Bourdieu 50–51. Bourdieu identifies three principles of legitimacy, the most important of which for the purposes of the present discussion is that "corresponding to 'bourgeois' taste and to the consecration bestowed by the dominant fractions of the dominant class and by private tribunals, such as *salons*, or public, state-guaranteed ones, such as academies, which sanction the inseparably ethical and aesthetic (and therefore political) taste of the dominant."

31. Guillory 6.

32. See Godzich, "Afterword" 157. He writes, as mentioned in the Preface, "Interpretation, beholden as it is to the institutional framework that both authorizes and empowers it, finds itself indebted to the instituting act that enables it." Thus, each new interpretive moment is always a subsequent moment, necessarily linked to prior interpretive possibilities, taking these necessarily as the ground from which to "institute" themselves. In this way, the reproduction of the power relations of the social world finds itself automatically inscribed within the interpretive act, unless the examination and analysis of this process is also made part of such acts.

33. Guillory 33–34.

34. For a brief elaboration of this relationship, see Calinescu 58–68.

35. See Foucault.

36. For elaborations of the various parameters of postmodernism, see Jameson, Lyotard, Calinescu, Hutcheon, and McHale.

37. Jameson, *Postmodernism* 1.

38. Jameson, *Postmodernism* 3–4.

39. Traditional definitions of "difference" would describe it in terms of variations between large, ostensibly homogeneous, nationally, religiously, ethnically or racially constituted; nontraditional definitions of "difference" would include any of those multiple unorthodox cultural locations or variations thereon which are the subject of this text.

40. Jameson, *Postmodernism* 6.

41. Jameson, *Postmodernism* 5.

42. Jameson, *Postmodernism* 6.

43. Jameson, *Postmodernism* 48.

44. For a fine analysis of the permutations of Western modes of "us/them" thinking, see Torgovnick.

45. See note 47 in chapter 1.

46. See note 30 in chapter 1.

47. See Lyotard. Even in its international form, the older Euro-American modernist "narrative" may be described as a singular hegemonic cultural perspective, as a result of its emphasis on Euro-American culture and perspectives to the exclusion of those that lie outside its domain.

48. Hutcheon 170.

49. Hutcheon, "Downspout," 152.

50. Hutcheon, "Downspout," 150.

51. Hutcheon, "Downspout," 161.

52. Said, *Culture* 243. Said writes: "A huge and remarkable adjustment in perspective and understanding is required to take account of the contribution to modernism of decolonization, resistance culture, and the literature of opposition to imperialism." See also Torgovnick.

3. MARCEL *mondain*, "MARCEL," AND THE HIDDEN DIASPORA

1. Michaud 79. Michaud discusses the common juxtaposition of Proust's reputation as dilettante man-of-the-world and serious writer, Proust the flatterer and social-climber and Proust the guilty, secretive recluse. A brief history of the critical representation of these oppositions may be divined in the following works: Painter 55. Painter remains the classic examination of the relation between Proust's life and his creative work, here identifying the creation of the *Recherche* with the death of Proust's mother, which he described in Proust's experience as a spatial divide: "On the far side of the barrier [Mme Proust's death] was the lost time in which his [Proust's] mother continued to

give and withhold her infinite love; on the hither side he was alone in an un-real, ghostly and posthumous present which could be given meaning only by a recovery of the time he had squandered"; Bree 142. Here Bree discusses Proust's personality as being "split" with reference to the narrator's discussion with Albertine about her "vice"; Vigneron 13. Vigneron identifies a cultural split in Proust's heritage, the Beauceron and the Jew, revealing him as being "constantly torn between conflicting heredities"; Poulet 51. Poulet describes the split in Proust's personality as an "inclusion-exclusion, which splits exis-tence in two, like a wall of which it is impossible to perceive at one and the same time the internal face and the external face"; Fernandez 15. Fernandez argues that it is the split between normal life and Proust's nocturnal habits that became the foundation for the creation of *A la recherche du temps perdu*, as-serting that "cette originalité était le résultat d'un défaut de *prescence* dans la vie normale, d'un défaut d'habitude de la vie normale . . ."; Rivers 107. Rivers describes these oppositions in terms of Proust's homosexuality, on the one hand his embracement of his own nature, and on the other, his culturally con-ditioned idea of homosexuality as "unnatural, degrading, and shameful."

   2. See chapter 1.

   3. See Cain 105. He writes: "The New Criticism appears powerless, lacking in supporters, declining, dead or on the verge of being so. No one speaks on behalf of the New Criticism as such today, and it mostly figures in critical discourse as the embodiment of foolish ideas and misconceived techniques. But the truth is that the New Criticism survives and is prosper-ing, and it seems to be powerless only because its power is so pervasive that we are ordinarily not even aware of it. So deeply ingrained . . . are New Crit-ical attitudes, values, and emphases that we do not even perceive them as the legacy of a particular movement. On the contrary, we feel them to be the nat-ural and definitive conditions for criticism in general. It is not simply that the New Criticism has become institutionalized, but that it has gained accep-tance as the institution itself. It has been transformed into "criticism," the essence of what we do as teachers and critics, the ground or given upon which everything else is based."

   4. Brady 114. Brady cites a book on this question: Paul Jay, *Being in the Text: Self-Representation from Wordsworth to Roland Barthes* (Ithaca, N.Y.: Cornell UP, 1984).

   5. See above reference.

   6. Painter 126.

   7. For a more detailed examination of the autobiography debate, see Mehlmann; for the opposing viewpoint, see Milly.

   8. For an analysis of the weaknesses of Painter's work, see Thomas.

   9. Hindus 8–20.

   10. Brady 111–21.

11. Beginning with Rivers, which is the classic work on homosexuality in Proust, there are a few essays spanning a number of years that are specifically concerned with this issue and its relationship to the text as a whole: see O'Brien; Carter; Grosskurth; Ellison; Rosello; Greenburg; McGinnis; Levin & O'Brien; Guenette; Viti; and Litvak. Another early work is March.

12. Sansom 59.

13. Stambolian and Marks 26.

14. Brée 8–9.

15. Brady 114–17.

16. Brady 115.

17. Brady 115.

18. Painter, vol. 2, 34–37.

19. Painter, vol. 2, 105–07. Painter documents Proust as having spoken "to Robert Dreyfus of a plan to write a topical article, in which he would use the Eulenburg Affair as the pretext for a general discussion of homosexuality." Prince Philip von Eulenberg was one of the Knights of the Round Table or the Camarilla, who were the intimate friends of Kaiser Wilhelm II in turn-of-the-century Germany. This group was hated by the Pangermanist war party, who attacked Eulenburg in October 1907 through Maximilian Harden, a right-wing journalist. Eulenburg was guilty, was discovered in a later criminal prosecution, and his political career was ruined. The Kaiser no longer trusted his friends and had only militarists to advise him, and this situation became one of the minor causes of the First World War.

20. Painter, vol. 1, 126.

21. Michaud 81–83.

22. Michaud 83. Michaud here misreads Martin-Chauffier's essay by referring to the double "I" narrator alone as a screen existing between Proust the man and Proust the author. In actuality, Martin-Chauffier writes that the double "I" narrator, as well as Proust the man, act as a screen behind which Proust the author controls the story.

23. Michaud 83.

24. Guenette 229.

25. For a discussion of early critical responses to this issue, see Alden; also, see Hodson. Other useful texts are Bonnet, vols. 1 and 2; Spagnoli; Kopp; Auchincloss; May 16–29.

26. See de Diesbach.

27. Shattuck 82.

28. Jephcott 251.

29. Kopp 16.

30. This withdrawal is descriptively documented in Brée. She writes: "'Every artist,' remarks the narrator of Proust's long novel . . . 'seems to have

come from an unknown land which he has forgotten, a native land, different from that of any other artist.' In the most literal sense, more especially in the period between 1908–09, when he seems definitely to have started on his novel, and 1922, when he died, Marcel Proust did indeed live among his contemporaries as though he belonged to some other world. His eccentricities have become legendary: a nocturnal creature who slept by day and worked by night, roaming the city streets, calling on friends or receiving them around midnight . . . a semi-recluse in ever-precarious health, voluntarily confined to a comfortless cork-lined room whose tightly shuttered windows let in neither light nor air."

31. May 3.

32. Sansom 13–14.

33. Guenette 245–46. Remarking on the nature of this difficulty, Guenette writes: "There has to be more to the masquerade than public relations, as becomes obvious when the *Recherche* is considered as the fictional autobiography of a homosexual writer. The narrator wants to write, but he is homosexual, and, as such, is hampered in his chosen task by the ban society has placed on the bulk of his erotic experience." Guenette thus shows both how quickly a study of the *Recherche* concerning the issue of homosexuality can collapse into the social, and how the social/biographical/historical is never very far away from this text.

34. Painter 312–14.

35. Rivers 107.

36. Rivers 23.

37. Proust, Tome I, 3. All subsequent references to the novel will be made from this edition, and cited in the text. All translations of the French text are derived from Marcel Proust, *Remembrance of Things Past*, ed. C. K. Scott Moncrieff and Terence Kilmartin, 3 vols. (New York: Vintage-Random, 1981).

38. See Heidegger.

39. Proust, *Remembrance*, Vol. I, 3.

40. Proust, *Remembrance*, Vol. II, 635–36.

41. Proust, *Remembrance*, Vol. I, 187.

42. Zenou 157–164.

43. For the purposes of differentiation, from this point on "Marcel" will refer to the fictional narrator of the *Recherche*, and Marcel, without quotation marks, will refer to Marcel Proust, the author.

44. Rudinow 176.

45. Proust, *Remembrance*, Vol. I, 172.

46. Proust, *Remembrance*, Vol. I, 174–77.

47. Proust, *Remembrance*, Vol. I, 173.

48. Proust, *Remembrance*, Vol. II, 815.

49. Proust, *Remembrance*, Vol. II, 1152.

50. Proust, *Remembrance*, Vol. II, 862.

51. Proust, *Remembrance*, Vol. II, 832.

52. Proust, *Remembrance*, Vol. II, 861–63.

53. Proust, *Remembrance*, Vol. I, 244.

54. Proust, *Remembrance*, Vol. I, 825.

55. Proust, *Remembrance*, Vol. I, 825.

56. Proust, *Remembrance*, Vol. II, 862.

57. Proust, *Remembrance*, Vol. II, 831.

58. Proust, *Remembrance*, Vol. II, 623–56.

59. Georges Poulet, *Proustian Space*, trans. Elliott Coleman (1963; Baltimore: Johns Hopkins UP, 1977) 51.

60. Proust, *Remembrance*, Vol. II, 623.

61. Proust, *Remembrance*, Vol. II, 626.

62. Proust, *Remembrance*, Vol. II, 629.

63. Proust, *Remembrance*, Vol. II, 629. "greatly annoyed."

64. Proust, *Remembrance*, Vol. II, 629–31.

65. Proust, *Remembrance*, Vol. II, 638.

4. STEPHEN DEDALUS AND THE "SWOON OF SIN"

1. See Beja.

2. For introductory explications of this idea, see Kenner 152, and Magalaner 116.

3. Although such a conclusion might be suggested by the obvious connections throughout Joyce's work in terms of Dublin, recurring characters, Irish customs, and so on, it is yet not fully articulated in his work itself that it does and should represent one whole.

4. Parrinder 151. Parrinder writes: "To speak of Joyce's rejection in England between 1914 and 1930 may sound tendentious. After all, he began this period as a literary unknown and ended as one of the most famous . . . writers of his time. 'Rejection,' however, is in certain ways more adequate than the conventional cliché 'reception' to describe this process. If Joyce's name was well known in the England of 1930, it was as a writer widely regarded as unreadable, whose masterpiece—thanks to the operations of the censor—could not be lawfully read."

5. See Ellmann. The above publishing history of *Dubliners*, *A Portrait of the Artist as a Young Man* and *Ulysses* is elaborated in Ellmann's biography. Specific page references are numerous and distributed throughout the text, so I will reproduce them here in chronological order for each work discussed: for Dubliners, see pages 219, 220, 267, 310, 313–15, 322–33, 329–32, 334–35, 349, and 353; for *A Portrait of the Artist as a Young Man*, see pages 270, 353, 355, 384, 400, 404, and 406; for *Ulysses*, see pages

264–65, 357, 421, 443, 486, 497, 503-04, 523, 641 and 653. All subsequent references to Ellmann's biography will be made from this edition.

6. The foregoing publishing history has failed to detail that of *Chamber Music* and *Finnegans Wake* because it needs only the three texts that it has discussed in order to offer an understanding of Joyce's reception in the English-speaking world—*Dubliners* because it was his first book-length work, *A Portrait* because it was his first novel, and *Ulysses* because it was the work that established Joyce as a world figure.

7. Benstock 211.

8. See chapter 1.

9. See note 2, chapter 2.

10. Levin, *Critical* vii.

11. See Kain.

12. Gaiser 255.

13. Staley 109.

14. Beja 114.

15. Herring 131.

16. See Dunleavy.

17. Hayashi ix.

18. Gaiser 248.

19. Benstock, "Joyce Industry," 212.

20. Gaiser 248.

21. Senn 26–27.

22. Gaiser 250–55.

23. Beja and Benstock x.

24. Beja xv.

25. See, for example, Brown; Cheng, "Of Canons"; Cheng, *Joyce;* Duffy; Herr; McGee; Norris; and Valente.

26. See chapter 2.

27. Collins 37.

28. Beja xiii.

29. See Staley, "Following" 267.

30. Buttigieg 18.

31. Goldman vii.

32. In this, like Joyce, in the spirit of Joyce's individual creativity, the scholar-critic is to use his or her own sensitivity and perspective in interpretation, viewing whatever text in question from this vantage point.

33. *The Compact Edition of the Oxford English Dictionary*, Vol. II (Oxford: Oxford UP, 1971) 586.

34. *The American Heritage Dictionary*, 2nd college ed. (New York: Houghton-Mifflin, 1982) 1056.

35. For discussions of the nature of autobiography in *A Portrait* and

Joyce's work in general, see Levin 45. Levin sees the *Portrait* as straight autobiography, "based on a literal transcript of the first twenty years of Joyce's life"; Kelly 26–27. Kelly identifies Stephen's shame of his home and family with Joyce's shame of his own father; Tindall 8. Tindall equates Joyce's desire for freedom with his creation of an exile in the character of Stephen Dedalus; Sullivan 6, 12. Sullivan reiterates the idea that while Joyce's work did not exactly constitute the work of autobiography, he constantly used autobiographical material, but that does not mean that "the story of Stephen Dedalus may be read as the history of James Joyce"; Noon 58–59, 73–74; Noon depicts Stephen as "a kind of alter ego of Joyce," describing his mind as a reflection of that of Joyce and of turn-of-the-century Ireland. He sees Stephen's ideas as representing an "early voice" of Joyce as a young man, showing how Joyce's early notebooks and papers at Cornell University corroborate the fact that real events that took place in Joyce's life make up many of the events of Stephen's life; Brown 8. Brown represents Stephen as having begun as a disguise for Joyce, who ended up as a fiction; Manganiello 14. Manganiello identifies Stephen as the cognitive locus of Joyce's concern with the individual and the effects of society on the individual through Stephen's understanding of the fall of Parnell and the maturation of his political consciousness in tandem with his artistic consciousness; Wright 8. Wright views the autobiographical nature of the *Portrait* as self-reflexive—through the character of Stephen Dedalus, Joyce explores the development of Stephen as artist and the relationship of himself as artist to his own material, that is, Stephen as fictional character; and finally, Harper x–xi. Harper equates the autobiographical impulse in Joyce's work with the artistic concern of the question of "individual identity in terms of one's past."

36. Wright 8.
37. Ellmann 3. All subsequent references will be made from this text.
38. Boyce 115–36.
39. Boyce 115–36.
40. See Joyce, *Dubliners*, 278–96.
41. Manganiello 20–25.
42. Ellmann, Vol. II, 48.
43. Ellmann, *Letters*, 53.
44. Manganiello 20.
45. Deane 175.
46. wa Thiong'o 16.
47. Boyce 130.
48. Joyce, "Ireland," 162.
49. Joyce, "Ireland," 166. James Joyce, *Scritti italiani*, a cura di Gianfranco Corsini e Giorgio Melehiori, Milano, Arnoldo Mondadori Editore, 1979.

50. Joyce, "Ireland," 173.
51. MacCabe xi. MacCabe writes, "It was never simply formal questions of language that were at stake in Joyce's writing. Joyce's deliberate aim had always been the writing, forging of an Irish consciousness which would throw off the twin yokes of British imperialism and Roman Catholicism. Such a project brought home to Joyce more clearly than the other modernists how such political liberation went hand in hand with questions of sexuality and cultural identity, questions which could not be considered independently of language."
52. For further explication of the significance of the *non serviam*, see Reilly 45–52.
53. Joyce, *Portrait* 83–84. All subsequent references to this text are taken from this edition.
54. The articulation of this world beyond language represents the heart of Joyce's rebellion against the colonial cultural imposition to which he was opposed—when the language one speaks is that of the colonizer, better to have no language at all.
55. Joyce, *Portrait* 1.
56. See Boyd 561–71.
57. Joyce, *Portrait* 9.
58. Joyce, *Portrait* 153.
59. Joyce, *Portrait* 162.
60. Joyce, *Portrait* 101.
61. For an explanation of this, see all of *Portrait*, chapter 4.
62. It must be reiterated here that Joyce's difficulty was not with Catholicism and religious injunction per se, but rather with what he saw as the combined effect on the Irish national identity of Catholicism and British imperialism. To escape the one (imperialism) he felt he had to eschew the other (Catholicism).
63. Schorer 67–87.

5. "THE BULLDOG IN MY OWN BACKYARD"

1. See Gates, "African-American."
2. While such an assertion may seem to conflict with the positive stance toward culture studies approaches taken earlier in this text, it in fact does not. In the case of African-American literature, the culture studies emphasis on the importance of the cultural context becomes somewhat complicated. This text argues that African-American literature has too often been read through a lens that forces it into a narrow cultural context defined specifically by authorized articulations and expectations of racial and/or ethnic identity. Culture studies approaches would broaden this cultural lens to encompass African-American experience in contexts that exceed this narrow

lens, embracing cultural representations derived from any range of cultural experiences not necessarily linked to any authorized consensus of group identity, as well as analyses of such authorized consensus itself, its relation to society and its institutions (such as the university), its role and function in the articulation of culture, and its relation to the politics of cultural space.

3. Howe 179.

4. Two good examples of these are the currently very popular TV show "Ally McBeal," which features the protagonist, Ally, as having a black roommate, and "Chicago Hope," which emphasizes the close friendships between its white and black characters, and often features these interracial relationships in intimate, personal social interaction. See also the periodical *Interrace*.

5. Morganthau 54. Morganthau writes: "Since 1964 white America has essentially accepted guilt for the original sin of slavery, and it has tried to make amends, through the mechanism of the law, for 350 years of racism. De jure segregation has been abolished and affirmative action adopted—and if today many whites and at least a few blacks contend that affirmative action has its drawbacks, few can doubt that it has brought millions of African-Americans into the economic mainstream. Specifically, about 40 percent of all black families nationwide can now be regarded as middle class or better, and many have left the ghetto for good." Secondary literature on this topic is quite broad, but a good place to begin is Takaki.

6. See Gilroy, especially chapter 1.

7. For an analysis of how one ethnic group handled its ethnicity in relation to the imperatives of the larger American society, see Ignatiev, *How*.

8. See Morrison.

9. This is so even though in the current critical climate, the study of "minority" literature would seem to be moving closer and closer to the center. Yet the often-ascribed appellation, "minority," as well as the structural complexities frequently encountered in the endeavor to study nontraditional cultural representations would seem to give the lie to this assumption.

10. This is in many ways the situation surrounding the writing of the recent novel *Memoirs of a Geisha*, written by Arthur Golden, a white, Western man who lived in Japan for some time and researched the world of the geisha in order to write the book.

11. wa Thiong'o 4–16.

12. For various analyses concerning the issue of identity in Baldwin's work, see Levin, "Baldwin's," 239–47; Redding 57–70; Standley; Klein; Bell; Dance; Taylor; Powers; Bieganowski; Bigsby; Jackson; Nelson; Soyinka; and Weatherby.

13. For a detailed examination of the issues discussed above, see Gates, "'Ethnic.'"

14. "Protest" is used here in the same vein as that described by James Baldwin in his essay, "Notes of a Native Son."

15. See Lefebvre; see also Buttigieg. The present text also seeks to open up such a cultural space.

16. See Shorris, especially chapter 11. Shorris describes here the dizzying complexity and minute detail of racial classification and ethnic variation among Latino and Chicano populations in America.

17. See DuBois.

18. DuBois's notion of the "color line" also describes a social situation that becomes of utmost importance in maintaining the antebellum socioeconomic conditions on which the whole idea of problematic race relations in America is based.

19. See Morrison; see also Ignatiev, *How*, 1–3.

20. The difficulty represented by this circumstance is that concerning any diasporic community, in which two or more cultures are involved, in the construction of a cultural identity—that of cultural translation and the risk of romanticization of the motherland as the result of nostalgia and/or the lack of direct personal experience with its culture.

21. Baldwin, *Notes*. All subsequent references are taken from this text.

22. Weatherby 68–71.

23. See Gibson 11.

24. Werner 121.

25. Werner 134.

26. See Gilroy.

27. Powers 651; see also Newman 56; Weatherby 95–99.

28. Powers 656.

29. Baldwin, "Autobiographical," 6–7.

30. See Gates, "'Ethnic,'" 294.

31. This particular creative move, however, sparked immense controversy in the American literary milieu of Baldwin's time, none more heated than Eldridge Cleaver's "Notes on a Native Son."

32. See Washington, Zahorski, and Pratt 48. Pratt discusses the notion of universality in terms of what he calls the "negative connotations" it has taken on because of its association with "the values of the dominant racial group." Here, as in Pratt's formulation, the reference to universality does not suggest the attempt on the part of Baldwin to make his work more palatable to the white majority, but rather his attempt to be, in his own words, "an honest man and a good writer." ("Autobiographical Note," *Notes of a Native Son*) and to speak more clearly and specifically to the human, rather than simply the black, condition. Hence, it is understandable why his novel, *Giovanni's Room*, which eschews the conventions pertaining to black writing at this time, would be marginalized in Baldwin's corpus. It is also in this

regard that Baldwin can be considered in relation to modernism and modernity, both in terms of his knowledge of the early modernists and his connections with *The Partisan Review*. I am indebted to Robert von Hallberg for this observation.

33. Powers 653.

34. Newman 46.

35. See Zahorski 201.

36. Baldwin, "A Question," 136–37.

37. Poter 129.

38. Porter 165.

39. See Washington; Davis 20–21. Baldwin seems to have felt a lot of ambivalence about this, as the homosexual content of this work sparked much controversy (see Campbell, Cleaver, Lash, Fiedler, and Weatherby). His ambivalence was perhaps due to the fact that he intended his work to speak to precisely the difficulty between universal human desires and the mainstream refusal to grant the validity of such desires to certain segments of the population. See also Adams 35. Adams writes: "Baldwin's identification with . . . minorities has sometimes brought his status as an artist into question; to regard him as a 'black' writer or as a 'homosexual writer' is to suggest limits on his individuality and on his treatment of his chosen subject matter. Such labelling underlines the tenacity of the very stereotypes Baldwin fights. A racial or sexual identity which does not coincide with that of the majority is frequently presumed to disqualify a writer from entering into territories beyond that minority experience."

40. See Nelson, "Continents."

41. See Leeming, "Henry James," 55.

42. For other elaborations of the significance of dividedness in this text, see DeGout, Bigsby, and Summers 174. For a brilliant elaboration of the problem of flight in the text, see Summers 178–79.

43. Baldwin, *Giovanni's*, 10–11. All subsequent references are taken from this text.

44. Baldwin, *Giovanni's* 30–31.

45. Baldwin, *Giovanni's* 35.

46. Baldwin, *Giovanni's* 16–17.

47. Baldwin, *Giovanni's* 142.

48. Baldwin, *Giovanni's* 9–10.

49. See Leeming, "Henry James," esp. 55.

50. Baldwin, *Giovanni's* 84.

51. Baldwin, *Giovanni's* 147.

52. Baldwin, *Giovanni's* 220.

53. Baldwin, *Giovanni's* 221–23.

54. Baldwin *Giovanni's* 224.

55. This idea has indeed been broached by at least two critics. See Rupp 141, Fabre 205.

56. Levin, "Baldwin's"; Redding; Standley; Klein, *After;* Bell, "Dilemma"; Dance; Taylor; Poers; Bieganowski; Bigsby; Standley & Burt; Jackson; Nelson; Soyinka; and Weatherby.

57. See Sundquist. This is a brilliant analysis of the interwoven relationship between the traditional canons of American and African-American literature. See also Morrison.

6. CONCLUSION

1. Gates xii.

2. While the national literatures have been based on literary canons of works taken to represent a national literary and cultural heritage, the discipline of comparative literature has not. Its relation to canons has been indirect, in that it encompasses those canons previously established in two or more literatures.

3. Said, *Culture* 259.

4. For a brilliant analysis of the process of national self-realization, see Fanon.

5. Kern 232.

6. Said 225.

7. See Guillen 89. He writes: "Events and literary movements considered as international phenomena are stimulated by analogous historical developments in the social life of peoples as much as by reciprocal cultural and literary contacts between them." See also chapter 2 in the present text.

8. Said 316.

9. Gates 33.

10. Gates 33–34. See also Guillory.

11. Guillory 135.

12. Graff 10 and 258.

13. See Scholes, *Textual.*

14. West 200.

15. Said 66.

16. Johnson 62.

17. See Spivak, "Making," 791. Spivak discusses the analysis of transnational identity as necessarily studied within what she calls the structure of a "transnational study of culture," or "a revision of the old vision of Comparative Literature" emphasizing the study of colonial and postcolonial discourse, interdisciplinarity and a language requirement expanded to include study "in at least one colonized vernacular."

18. Said 317.

Bibliography

Achebe, Chinua. *Morning Yet on Creation Day: Essays*. New York: Anchor, 1975.

Adams, Robert M. *James Joyce: Common Sense and Beyond*. 1966. New York: Octagon, 1980.

Ahmad, Aijaz. "Jameson's Rhetoric of Otherness and the 'National Allegory.'" *Social Text: Theory, Culture, Ideology* 17 (Fall 1987): 3–25.

Alden, D. W. *Marcel Proust and His French Critics*. Los Angeles, Calif.: Lymanhouse, 1940.

The American Heritage Dictionary. 2nd College Ed. New York: Houghton-Mifflin, 1982.

Aldridge, Owen, Ed. *Comparative Literature: Matter and Method*. Urbana: U of Illinois P, 1964.

Althusser, Louis. "Ideology and Ideological State Apparatuses (Notes Toward an Investigation) (January–April 1969)." In *"Lenin and Philosophy" and Other Essays*. Trans. Ben Brewster. New York: Monthly Review, 1971: 127–86.

Anderson, Benedict. *Imagined Communities: Reflections on the Origin and Spread of Nationalism*. London: Verso Books, 1983.

Appadurai, Arjun. "Disjuncture and Difference in the Global Cultural Economy." *Theory, Culture, Society*. 2.3 (June 1990): 295–310.

———. *Modernity at Large: Cultural Dimensions of Globalization (Public Worlds, V.1)*. Minneapolis: U of Minnesota P, 1996.

Attridge, Derek. *The Cambridge Companion to James Joyce*. Cambridge: Cambridge UP, 1990.

Auchincloss, L. "Proust's Picture of Society." *Partisan Review* 27.4 (Fall 1960): 690–701.

Baker, Houston A., Jr. *Modernism and the Harlem Renaissance*. Chicago: U of Chicago P, 1987.

191

Baldwin, James. "Autobiographical Notes." In *Notes of a Native Son.* Boston: Beacon, 1955: 3–9.

———. "Everybody's Protest Novel." In *Notes of a Native Son.* Boston: Beacon, 1955: 13–23.

———. *Giovanni's Room.* New York: Dell, 1956.

———. *Notes of a Native Son.* Boston: Beacon, 1955.

———. "A Question of Identity." In *Notes of a Native Son.* Boston: Beacon, 1955: 124–37.

Barksdale, Richard K. "Alienation and the Anti-Hero in Recent American Fiction." *College Language Association Journal* 10.1 (September 1966): 1–10.

Barthes, Roland. "The Death of the Author." In *Image—Music—Text.* Trans. Stephen Heath. New York: Noonday, 1977.

Baugh, Albert C., and Thomas Cable. *A History of the English Language.* 3rd ed. Englewood Cliffs, N.J.: Prentice-Hall, 1978.

Beckett, Samuel. *Proust.* New York: Grove, 1931.

Beja, Morris. "Synjosium: An Informal History of the International James Joyce Symposia." *James Joyce Quarterly* 22.2 (Winter, 1985): 113-29.

Beja, Morris and Shari Benstock. Introduction. In *Coping with Joyce: Essays from the Copenhagen Symposium.* Columbus: Ohio State UP, 1989: ix–xv.

Bell, George E. "The Dilemma of Love in *Go Tell It on the Mountain* and *Giovanni's Room.*" *College Language Association Journal* 17.3 (March 1974): 397–406.

Bennett, Tony. "Text, Readers, Reading Formations." *Modern Literary Theory.* Ed. Philip Rice and Patricia Waugh. London: Edward Arnold, 1989: 206–220.

Benstock, Bernard. "Inscribing James Joyce's Tombstone." In *Coping with Joyce: Essays from the Copenhagen Symposium.* Columbus: Ohio State UP, 1989.

———. *James Joyce.* New York: Frederick Ungar, 1985.

———. "The James Joyce Industry: An Assessment in the Sixties." *Southern Review* 2.1 (Jan. 1966): 210–28.

———. *James Joyce: The Undiscover'd Country.* Dublin: Gill, 1977.

Benstock, Shari. *Women of the Left Bank: Paris 1900–1940.* Austin: U of Texas P, 1986.

Bernheimer, Charles. *Comparative Literature in the Age of Multiculturalism.* Baltimore, MD: Johns Hopkins UP, 1995.

Bersani, Leo. *Marcel Proust: The Fictions of Life and Art.* New York: Oxford UP, 1965.

Bhaba, Homi K. *The Location of Culture.* New York: Routledge, 1994.

Bieganowski, Ronald. "James Baldwin's Vision of Otherness in 'Sonny's

Blues' and *Giovanni's Room.*" *College Language Association Journal* 32.1 (September 1988): 69–80.

Bigsby, C. W. E. "The Divided Mind of James Baldwin." In *Critical Essays on James Baldwin.* Ed. Fred L. Standley and Nancy V. Burt. Boston: G. K. Hall, 1988: 94–111.

Bloom, Allan. *The Closing of the American Mind.* New York: Simon and Schuster Trade, 1988.

Bolt, Sydney. *A Preface to James Joyce.* New York: Longman, 1981.

Bone, Robert. *The Negro Novel in America.* New Haven: Yale UP, 1968.

Bonheim, Helmut. *Joyce's Benefictions.* Berkeley: U of California P, 1964.

Bonnet, Henri. *Marcel Proust de 1907 à 1914.* Paris: Nizet, 1971.

———. *Le progrès spirituel dans l'œuvre de Marcel Proust.* 2 vols. Paris: Vrin, 1947–1949.

Bourdieu, Pierre. *The Field of Cultural Production: Essays on Art and Literature.* New York: Columbia UP, 1993.

Boyce, D. G. *The Revolution in Ireland, 1879–1923.* Dublin: Gill, 1988.

Boyd, Elizabeth F. "Joyce's Hell-Fire Sermons." *Modern Language Notes* 75 (Nov. 1960): 561–71.

Bradbury, Malcolm and James McFarlane, eds. *Modernism: 1830–1930.* 1976. New York: Penguin, 1978.

Brady, Patrick. "The Present State of Studies on Marcel Proust." *Claudel Studies* 16.1–2 (1989): 111–21.

Brandabur, Edward. *A Scrupulous Meanness: A Study of Joyce's Early Work.* Urbana: U of Illinois P, 1971.

Brée, Germaine. *Marcel Proust and Deliverance From Time.* New York: Grove, 1958.

———.*The World of Marcel Proust.* Boston: Houghton-Mifflin, 1966.

Brooks, Cleanth and Robert Penn Warren. *Understanding Fiction.* New York: Appleton-Century-Crofts, 1943.

———. *Understanding Poetry: An Anthology for College Students.* New York: Holt, 1938.

Brooks, Cleanth, Robert Penn Warren, and John Purser. *An Approach to Literature: A Collection of Prose and Verse with Analyses and Discussions.* New York: Crofts, 1938.

Brown, Homer Obed. *James Joyce's Early Fiction: The Biography of a Form.* Cleveland: Case Western Reserve UP, 1972.

Brown, Richard. *James Joyce and Sexuality.* New York: Cambridge UP, 1985.

Bucknall, Barbara J. *The Religion of Art in Proust.* Urbana: U of Illinois P, 1969.

Burgess, Anthony. *Here Comes Everybody: An Introduction to James Joyce for the Ordinary Reader.* London: Faber & Faber, 1965.

————. *Joysprick: An Introduction to the Language of James Joyce*. London: Andre Deutsch, 1973.

Buttigieg, Joseph. *A Portrait of the Artist in Different Perspective*. Athens: Ohio UP, 1987.

Cain, William E. *The Crisis in Criticism: Theory, Literature, and Reform in English Studies*. Baltimore; London: Johns Hopkins UP, 1984.

Calinescu, Matei. *Five Faces of Modernity*. 1977; Durham: Duke University, 1987.

Caranfa, Angelo. *Proust: The Creative Silence*. Lewisburg: Bucknell UP, 1990.

Carter, William. "Proust's View on Sexuality." *ADAM International Review* 413–415 (1979): 56–62.

Cattaui, Georges. *L'amitié de Proust: Les cahiers Marcel Proust, VIII*. Paris: Gallimard, 1935.

Certeau, Michel de. *The Practice of Everyday Life*. Trans. Steven F. Randall. Berkeley: U of California P, 1984.

Chambers, Ross. *Room for Maneuver: Reading the Oppositional in Narrative*. Chicago: U of Chicago P, 1991.

————. *Story and Situation: Narrative Seduction and the Power of Fiction*. Minneapolis: U of Minnesota P, 1984.

Chantal, René de. *Marcel Proust: critique littéraire*. Tome II. Canada: Les Presses de L'Université de Montréal, 1967.

Chefdor, Monique. "Introduction: Marcel Proust and the Modern Reader." In *In Search of Marcel Proust: Essays from the Marcel Proust Centennial Colloquium at the Claremont Colleges*. Claremont: Scripps College and Ward Ritchie Press, 1973: 3–14.

Cheng, Vincent. "Of Canons, Colonies and Critics: The Ethics and Politics of Postcolonial Joyce Studies." *Cultural Critique* 35 (Winter 1996/97): 81–104.

————. *Joyce, Race and Empire*. Cambridge: Cambridge UP, 1995.

Cixous, Hélène. *The Exile of James Joyce*. Trans. Sally A. J. Purcell. New York: David Lewis, 1972.

Clifford, James. *The Predicament of Culture: Twentieth-Century Ethnography, Literature, and Art*. Cambridge: Harvard UP, 1988.

Collins, Ben L. Ph.D. "The Created Conscience: A Study of Technique and Symbol in James Joyce's *A Portrait of the Artist as a Young Man*." Diss Ab. U of New Mexico, 1962. In *James Joyce: Research Opportunities and Dissertation Abstracts*. Ed. Tetsumaro Hayashi. Jefferson, N.C.: McFarland, 1985.

The Compact Edition of the Oxford English Dictionary. Vol. II. Oxford: Oxford UP, 1971.

Culler, Jonathan. *Framing the Sign: Criticism and Its Institutions*. Norman: University of Oklahoma Press, 1988.

———. *On Deconstruction: Theory and Criticism After Structuralism.* Ithaca: Cornell UP, 1982.

Daiches, David. "James Joyce: The Artist as Exile." *College English* 2.3 (December 1940): 197–206.

Dance, Daryl C. "You Can't Go Home Again: James Baldwin and the South." *College Language Association Journal* 18.1 (September 1974): 81–90.

Davis, Walter A. *Inwardness and Existence: Subjectivity in/and Hegel, Heidegger, Marx and Freud.* Madison: U of Wisconsin P, 1989.

Deane, Seamus. "Joyce and Nationalism." In *James Joyce: New Perspectives.* Ed. Colin MacCabe. Sussex: Harvester, 1982: 168–83.

DeGout, Yasmin. "Dividing the Mind: Contradictory Portraits of Homoerotic Love in *Giovanni's Room.*" *African-American Review* 26.3 (Fall 1992): 425–35.

Deleuze, Gilles. *Proust et les signes.* Perspectives critiques. Paris: Presses Universitaires de France, 1964.

Deming, Robert H. *A Bibliography of James Joyce Studies.* Lawrence: U of Kansas P, 1964.

———. *A Bibliography of James Joyce Studies.* 2nd ed., Revised and Enlarged. Boston: G. K. Hall, 1977.

Derrida, Jacques. *Of Grammatology.* Trans. Gayatri Chakravorty Spivak. Baltimore: The Johns Hopkins UP, 1974.

Diesbach, Ghislain de. *Proust.* Paris: Perrin, 1991.

Dostoevsky, Fyodor. *Crime and Punishment.* Trans. David McDuff. Harmondsworth: Viking, 1991.

Doyle, Laura. *Bordering on the Body: The Racial Matrix of Modern Fiction and Culture.* New York: Oxford UP, 1994.

DuBois, W. E. B. *The Souls of Black Folk.* Boston: Bedford Books, 1997.

Duffy, Enda. *The Subaltern Ulysses.* Minneapolis: U of Minnesota P, 1994.

Dunleavy, Janet Egleson. *Reviewing Classics of Joyce Criticism.* Urbana: U of Illinois P, 1991.

Eagleton, Terry. *Literary Theory: An Introduction.* Minneapolis: U of Minnesota P, 1983.

Edelman, Lee. "Homographesis." *The Yale Journal of Criticism: Interpretation in the Humanities* 3.1 (Fall 1989): 189–207.

Ellison, David R. "Comedy and Significance in Proust's *Recherche*: Freud and the Baron de Charlus." *MLN* 98.4 (May 1983): 657–74.

Ellmann, Maud. "Polytropic Man: Paternity, Identity and Naming in *The Odyssey* and *A Portrait of the Artist as a Young Man.* In *James Joyce: New Perspectives.* Ed. Colin MacCabe. Sussex: Harvester, 1982.

Ellmann, Richard. *James Joyce,* new and rev. ed. 1959. New York: Oxford UP, 1982.

——. *Letters of James Joyce.* 2 vols. New York: Viking, 1966.

Fabre, Michel. *From Harlem to Paris: Black American Writers in France, 1840–1980.* Urbana: U of Illinois P, 1991.

Fanon, Frantz. *The Wretched of the Earth.* 1961. New York: Grove, 1991.

Farrell, James T. "Joyce's *A Portrait of the Artist.* In *James Joyce: Two Decades of Criticism.* Ed. Seon Givens. New York: Vanguard, 1948: 177–97.

Featherstone, Mike. *Undoing Culture: Globalization, Postmodernism and Identity.* London: Sage Publications: 1995.

Feehan, Joseph. Introduction. *Dedalus on Crete: Essays on the Implications of Joyce's Portrait.* Los Angeles: Immaculate Heart College, 1956: 7–10.

Felski, Rita. *The Gender of Modernity.* Cambridge, Mass.: Harvard UP, 1995.

Fernandez, Ramon. *Proust, ou la généalogie du roman moderne.* Paris: Grasset, 1979.

Fetterley, Judith. *The Resisting Reader: A Feminist Approach to American Fiction.* Bloomington: Indiana UP, 1978.

Fiedler, Leslie. *Love and Death in the American Novel,* rev. ed. New York: Stein, 1966.

Firmat, Gustavo Pérez. "Introduction." In *Do the Americas Have a Common Literature?* Durham: Duke UP, 1990: 1–5.

Fitz, Earl E. *Rediscovering the New World: Inter-American Literature in a Comparative Context.* Iowa City: University of Iowa Press, 1991.

Foucault, Michel. *The Order of Things: An Archaeology of the Human Sciences.* Rpt. *Les mots et les choses.* Editions Gallimard 1966. New York: Vintage, 1973.

Fowler, Alastair. *Kinds of Literature: An Introduction to the Theory of Genres and Modes.* Cambridge: Harvard UP, 1982.

French, Marilyn. "Joyce and Language." *James Joyce Quarterly* 19.3 (Spring 1982): 239–56.

Frye, Northrop. *Anatomy of Criticism: Four Essays.* Princeton, N.J.: Princeton UP, 1957.

——. *The Secular Scripture: A Study of the Structure of Romance.* Cambridge: Harvard UP, 1976.

Gaiser, Gottlieb. "Joyce and Joyceans: A Critical View on the Problem of Institutionalization." In *International Perspectives on James Joyce.* Ed. Gottlieb Gaiser. Troy, N.Y.: Whitston, 1986: 247–60.

Gasché, Rodolphe. Introduction. In Andrzej Warminski, *Readings in Interpretation: Holderlin, Hegel, Heidegger.* Minneapolis: U of Minnesota P, 1987.

Gates, Jr., Henry Louis. "African-American Criticism." In *Redrawing the Boundaries: The Transformation of English and American Literary*

Studies. Eds. Stephen Greenblatt and Giles Gunn. New York: The Modern Language Association of America, 1992: 303–19.

———. *Black Literature and Literary Theory*. New York: Methuen, 1984.

———. "'Ethnic and Minority Studies.'" In *Introduction to Scholarship in Modern Languages and Literatures*, 2nd ed. Ed. Jospeh Gibaldi. New York: Modern Language Association, 1992: 288–302.

———. "The Master's Pieces: On Canon Formation and the African-American Tradition." In *Loose Canons: Notes on the Culture Wars*. By Henry Louis Gates, Jr. New York: Oxford, 1992.

———. *"Race," Writing and Difference*. Chicago: U of Chicago P, 1985.

Geertz, Clifford. *The Interpretation of Cultures: Selected Essays*. New York: Basic, 1973.

Genette, Gérard. *Discours du récit*. Paris: Editions du Seuil, 1972. Rpt. *Narrative Discourse: An Essay in Method*. Trans. Jane E. Lewin. New York: Cornell UP, 1980.

Gibson, Donald B. "James Baldwin: The Political Anatomy of Space." In *James Baldwin: A Critical Evaluation*. Ed. Therman B. O'Daniel. Washington, D.C.: Howard UP, 1977: 3–18.

Gillespie, Michael Patrick. "Kenner on Joyce." In *Reviewing Classics of Joyce Criticism*. Ed. Janet Egleson Dunleavy. Urbana: U of Illinois P, 1991: 142–54.

Gilroy, Paul. *The Black Atlantic: Modernity and Double Consciousness*. Cambridge: Harvard UP, 1993.

Girard, René. *Deceit, Desire and the Novel: Self and Other in Literary Structure*. Trans. Yvonne Freccero. Baltimore: Johns Hopkins UP, 1965.

———. *Proust: A Collection of Critical Essays*. 1962; Westport, Conn.: Greenwood, 1977.

Godzich, Wlad. "Afterword." In *Institution and Interpretation*. By Samuel Weber. Theory and History of Literature, Vol. 31. Minneapolis: U of Minnesota P, 1987: 153–64.

Golden, Arthur. *Memoirs of a Geisha: A Novel*. New York: Random House, 1997.

Goldman, Arnold. Preface. *The Joyce Paradox: Form and Freedom in His Fiction*. Evanston: Northwestern UP, 1966.

Goldmann, Lucien. *Towards a Sociology of the Novel*. Trans. Alan Sheridan. Editions Gallimard, 1964. London: Tavistock, 1975.

Gossman, Lionel and Mihai I. Spariosu. *Building a Profession: Autobiographical Perspectives on the Beginnings of Comparative Literature in the United States*. Albany: State University of New York P, 1994.

Greenburg, Wendy N. "Les uns et les autres: La Différence chez Proust dans Sodome et Gomorrhe." *Studia Neophilologica: A Journal of Germanic and Romance Languages and Literature* 59.1 (1987): 103–07.

Grossberg, Lawrence, et al. *Cultural Studies*. New York: Routledge, 1991.

Grosskurth, Phyllis. "The Sickness and the Cure." *(London) Times Literary Supplement* 4080. 12 June 1981: 666.

Guenette, Mark D. "Le loup et le narrateur: The Masking and Unmasking of Homosexuality in Proust's *A la recherche du temps perdu*." *Romanic Review* 80.2 (March 1989): 229–46.

Guillén, Claudio. *The Challenge of Comparative Literature*. Trans. Cola Franzen. Barcelona: Editorial Crítica, 1985. Cambridge: Harvard UP, 1993.

——. *Entre lo uno et lo diverso: Introducción a la literatura comparada*. Barcelona: Editorial Crítica, 1985.

Guillory, John. *Cultural Capital: The Problem of Literary Canon Formation*. Chicago: U of Chicago P, 1993.

Harkness, Marguerite. *The Aesthetics of Dedalus and Bloom*. Lewisburg: Bucknell UP, 1984.

——. "The Separate Roles of *Language* and *Word* in James Joyce's *Portrait*." *Irish Renaissance Annual* 4 (1983): 94–109.

Harper, Margaret Mills. *The Aristocracy of Art in Joyce and Wolfe*. Baton Rouge: Louisiana State UP, 1990.

Hayashi, Tetsumaro. *James Joyce: Research Opportunities and Dissertation Abstracts*. Jefferson, N.C.: McFarland, 1985.

Heath, Stephen. "Joyce in Language." In *James Joyce: New Perspectives*. Ed. Colin MacCabe. Sussex: Harvester, 1982.

Hegel, G. W. F. *Phenomenology of Spirit*. Trans. A. V. Miller. New York: Oxford UP, 1977.

Heidegger, Martin. *Being and Time*. New York: Harper, 1962.

Herr, Cheryl. *Joyce's Anatomy of Culture*. Urbana: University of Illinois Press, 1986.

Herring, Phillip. "The Frankforall Symposium." *James Joyce Quarterly* 22.2 (Winter, 1985): 131–35.

Hicks, D. Emily. *Border Writing: The Multidimensional Text*. Theory and History of Literature, vol. 80. Minneapolis: U of Minnesota P, 1991.

Hindus, Milton. *The Proustian Vision*. New York: Columbia UP, 1954.

Hobsbawm, Eric and Terrence Ranger. *The Invention of Tradition*. New York: Cambridge UP, 1992.

Hodson, Leighton. *Marcel Proust: The Critical Heritage*. London: Routledge, 1989.

Houdebire, Jean-Louis. "De Nouveau sur Joyce: Littérature et Religion." *Tel Quel* 89 (Autumn 1981): 41–73.

Howe, Irving. *Decline of the New*. New York: Harcourt, 1963.

Hutcheon, Linda. "'Circling the Downspout of Empire': Post-Colonialism and Postmodernism." *Ariel: A Review of International English Literature* 20.4 (Oct. 1989): 149–75.

———. *The Politics of Postmodernism.* New York: Routledge, 1989. Jackson, Jocelyn Whitehead. "The Problem of Identity in Selected Early Essays of James Baldwin." In *Critical Essays on James Baldwin.* Ed. Fred L. Standley and Nancy V. Burt. Boston: G. K. Hall & Co., 1988: 250–67.

Huyssen, Andreas. *After the Great Divide: Modernism, Mass Culture, Postmodernism.* Bloomington, Indiana UP, 1986.

Ignatiev, Noel. *How the Irish Became White.* New York: Routledge, 1996.

———. *Race Traitor.* New York: Routledge, 1996.

Jameson, Frederic. *Marxism and Form: Twentieth Century Dialectical Theories of Literature.* Princeton, N.J.: Princeton UP, 1971.

———."Modernism and Imperialism." In *Nationalism, Colonialism, Literature.* Minnesota: U of Minnesota P, 1990: 43–66.

———. "Third World Literature in the Era of Multinational Capitalism." *Social Text: Theory, Culture, Ideology* 15 (Fall 1986): 65–88.

———. *Postmodernism, or the Cultural Logic of Late Capitalism.* Durham, N.C.: Duke UP, 1991.

JanMohamed, Abdul. *Manichean Aesthetics: The Politics of Literature in Colonial Africa.* Amherst: U of Massachuesetts P, 1983.

Jay, Paul. *Being in the Text: Self-Representation from Wordsworth to Roland Barthes.* Ithaca: Cornell UP, 1984.

Jephcott, E. F. N. *Proust and Rilke: The Literature of Expanded Consciousness.* London: Chatto & Windus, 1972.

Johnson, Richard. "What Is Cultural Studies Anyway?" *Social Text* 16 (Winter 1986/87): 38–80.

Jongh, James de. *Vicious Modernism: Black Harlem and the Literary Imagination.* Cambridge: Cambridge UP, 1990.

Jost, François. Introduction to Comparative Literature. Indianapolis: Bobbs-Merrill, 1974.

Joyce, James. "Ireland, Island of Saints and Sages." In *The Critical Writings of James Joyce.* Eds. Ellsworth Mason and Richard Ellmann. New York: Viking, 1959.

———. "Ivy Day in the Committee Room." In *Dubliners.* By James Joyce. Eds. Hans Walter Gabler and Walter Hettche. New York: Garland, 1993: 278–96.

———. *A Portrait of the Artist as a Young Man.* 1916. New York: Viking, 1976.

Kain, Richard M. *Fabulous Voyager.* Chicago: U of Chicago P, 1947.

———. "The Joyce Enigma." In *Portraits of an Artist: A Casebook on*

James Joyce's A Portrait of an Artist as a Young Man. New York: Odyssey, 1962: 3.

Kain, Richard M., and Robert E. Scholes. "The First Version of Joyce's *Portrait.*" *The Yale Review* 49 (Spring 1960): 355–69.

Kalaidjian, Walter. *American Culture Between the Wars: Revisionary Modernism and Postmodern Critique.* New York: Columbia UP, 1993.

Karl, Frederick. Foreword. In *Modern and Modernism: The Sovereignty of the Artist 1885–1925.* New York: Atheneum, 1988.

Kelly, Robert Glynn. "James Joyce: A Partial Explanation." *PMLA* 64 (March 1949): 26–39.

Kenner, Hugh. *Joyce's Voices.* Berkeley: U of California P, 1978.

———. "The Making of the Modernist Canon." In *Canons.* Ed. Robert von Hallberg. Chicago: U of Chicago P, 1984.

———. "The Portrait in Perspective." In *James Joyce: Two Decades of Criticism.* Ed. Seon Givens. New York: Vanguard, 1948: 132–70.

Kermode, Frank. *The Sense of an Ending: Studies in the Theory of Fiction.* New York: Oxford UP, 1968.

Kern, Stephen. *The Culture of Time and Space.* Cambridge: Harvard UP, 1983.

Kershner, Jr., R. B. "Time and Language in Joyce's *Portrait of the Artist.*" *English Literary History* 43.2 (Summer 1976): 604–19.

Kilmartin, Terence. *A Reader's Guide to Remembrance of Things Past.* New York: Random, 1983.

Kingston, Maxine Hong. *The Woman Warrior: Memoirs of a Girlhood Among Ghosts.* New York: Vintage, 1975.

Klein, Marcus. *After Alienation: American Novels in Mid-Century.* 1962, 1964. New York: World, 1970.

Knuth, A. M. L. *The Wink of the Word: A Study of James Joyce's Phatic Communication.* Amsterdam: Rodopi, 1976.

Koelb, Clayton and Susan Noakes. *The Comparative Perspective on Literature: Approaches to Theory and Practice.* Ithaca: Cornell UP, 1988.

Kolb, Philip. *Marcel Proust: Selected Letters, Vol. 2, 1904–1909.* Trans. Terence Kilmartin. New York: Oxford UP, 1989.

Kopp, Richard L. *Marcel Proust as a Social Critic.* Cranbury, N.J.: Associated UP, 1971.

Lauter, Paul. "Race and Gender in the Shaping of the American Literary Canon: A Case Study from the Twenties." In *Canons and Contexts.* Ed. Paul Lauter. New York: Oxford UP, 1991: 22–47.

Leeming, David. *James Baldwin.* New York: Knopf, 1994.

Lefebvre, Henri. *The Production of Space.* Trans. Donald Nicholson-Smith. 1974; Oxford and Cambridge: Blackwell, 1995.

Levin, David. "Baldwin's Autobiographical Essays: The Problem of Negro Identity." *Massachuesetts Review* 5 (Winter 1964): 239–47.

Levin, Harry. *James Joyce: A Critical Introduction.* Norfolk, Conn.: New Directions, 1941.

———. "Joyce's *Portrait.*" In *Portraits of an Artist: A Casebook on James Joyce's A Portrait of the Artist as a Young Man.* Ed. William E. Morris and Clifford A. Nault, Jr. New York: Odyssey, 1962: 31–44.

———. "Review." *New Directions* (1939). In *James Joyce: The Critical Heritage (1928–1941).* Vol. II. Ed. Robert H. Deming. New York: Barnes, 1973: 693.

Levin, Harry, and Justin O'Brien. "Proust, Gide, and the Sexes." *PMLA* 65 (1950): 648–53.

Levitt, Morton P. "Harry Levin's *James Joyce* and the Modernist Age." In *Reviewing Classics of Joyce Criticism.* Ed. Janet Egleson Dunleavy. Urbana: U of Illinois P, 1991: 90–105.

———. *Modernist Survivors: The Contemporary Novel in England, the United States, France and Latin America.* Columbus: Ohio State UP, 1965.

Lionnet, Françoise. *Postcolonial Representations: Women, Literature, Identity.* Ithaca: Cornell UP, 1995.

Litvak, Joseph. "Strange Gourmet: Taste, Waste, Proust." In *Novel Gazing: Queer Readings in Fiction.* Ed. Eve Kosofsky Sedgwick. Durham, N.C.: Duke UP, 1997: 74–93.

Lukacs, Georg. *Studies in European Realism.* New York: Grosset, 1964.

———. *The Theory of the Novel: A Historico-Philosophical Essay on the Forms of Great Epic Literature.* Cambridge: MIT Press, 1971.

Lyotard, Jean-François. *The Postmodern Condition: A Report on Knowledge.* Trans. Geoff Bennington and Brian Massumi. Theory and History of Literature, vol. 10. Paris: Minuit, 1979. Minnesota: U of Minnesota P, 1984.

MacCabe, Colin. Preface. *James Joyce: New Perspectives.* Sussex: Harvester, 1982.

MacDonagh, N. F. Mandle, and Pauric Travers. *Irish Culture and Nationalism, 1750–1950.* New York: St. Martin's Press, 1983.

McGee, Patrick. *Telling the Other: The Question of Value in Modern and Postcolonial Writing.* Ithaca: Cornell UP, 1992.

McGinnis, Reginald. "A propos d'Albertine." *Francofonia: Studi Ricerche Sulle Letterature di Lingua Francese* 9.16 (1989): 83–98.

McHale, Brian. *Constructing Postmodernism.* New York: Routledge, 1992.

Macebuh, Stanley. *James Baldwin: A Critical Study,* vol. I. New York: The Third Press, Joseph Okpaku, 1973.

Magalaner, Marvin. *A James Joyce Miscellany.* Second Series. Carbondale, Ill.: Southern Illinois UP, 1959.

————. *Time of Apprenticeship: The Fiction of Young James Joyce*. London: Abelard Schuman, 1959.

Mailloux, Steven. *Rhetorical Power*. Ithaca: Cornell UP, 1989.

Makkreel, Rudolf A., and Fithjob Rodi. Introduction. In "Poetry and Experience," *William Dilthey: Selected Works, Vol. V*. Princeton, N.J.: Princeton UP, 1985.

Manganiello, Dominic. *Joyce's Politics*. London: Routledge, 1980.

Marino, Adrian. "'Modernity' and the Evolution of Literary Consciousness." *Diogenes* 77 (Spring 1972): 110–137.

May, Derwent. *Proust*. Oxford: Oxford UP, 1983.

Mein, Margaret. *A Foretaste of Proust: A Study of Proust and His Precursors*. London: Saxon House, 1974.

Mehlmann, E. G. J. *A Structural Study of Autobiography: Proust, Leiris, Sartre, Levi-Straus*. Ithaca: Cornell UP, 1974.

Michaud, Guy. "The Personality of Marcel Proust." In *In Search of Marcel Proust: Essays from the Marcel Proust Centennial Colloquium at the Claremont Colleges*. Ed. Monique Chefdor. Claremont: Scripps College and The Ward Ritchie Press, 1973: 78–115.

Milly, J. "Autobiographie et littérature chez Proust." *Francofonia* 7.13 (1987).

Morganthau, Tom. "The Price of Neglect: America on Trial." Special Report. *Newsweek* May 11, 1992: 54–58.

Morrison, Toni. *Playing in the Dark: Whiteness and the Literary Imagination*. New York: Vintage, 1990.

Morse, J. Mitchell. *The Sympathetic Alien: James Joyce and Catholicism*. New York: New York UP, 1959.

Moseley, Virginia. *Joyce and the Bible*. De Kalb: Northern Illinois UP, 1967.

Mukarovsky, Jan. *Aesthetic Function, Norm and Value as Social Facts*. Trans. Mark E. Suino. Ann Arbor: The U of Michigan P, 1970.

Nelson, Emmanuel S. "James Baldwin's Vision of Otherness and Community." In *Critical Essays on James Baldwin*. Ed. Fred L. Standley and Nancy V. Burt. Boston: G. K. Hall, 1988: 121–25.

Newfield, Christopher. "What was Political Correctness? Race, the Right, and Managerial Democracy in the Humanities." *Critical Inquiry* 9 (Winter 1993): 308–36.

Newman, Charles. "The Lesson of the Master: Henry James and James Baldwin." *Yale Review* 56 (Autumn 1966): 45–59.

Noon, S. J., William T. *Joyce and Aquinas*. New Haven: Yale UP, 1957.

————. "*A Portrait*: After Fifty Years." In *James Joyce Today: Essays on the Major Works*. Ed. Thomas F. Staley. Bloomington: Indiana UP, 1966: 54–82.

Norris, Margot. *Joyce's Web: The Social Unraveling of Modernism*. Austin: University of Texas Press, 1992.

O'Brien, Justin. "Albertine the Ambiguous: Notes on Proust's Transposition of the Sexes." *PMLA* 64 (1949): 933–52.

Painter, George D. *Proust: A Biography.* 2 vols. 1959 and 1965. Rpt. London: Chatto & Windus, 1989.

Parrinder, Patrick. "The Strange Necessity: James Joyce's Rejection in England (1914–30)." In *James Joyce: New Perspectives.* Ed. Colin MacCabe. Sussex: Harvester, 1982: 151–67.

Peake, C. H. *James Joyce: The Citizen and the Artist.* Stanford: Stanford UP, 1977.

Perloff, Marjorie. "'Living in the Same Place': The Old Mononationalism and the New Comparative Literature." *World Literature Today* 69.2 (Spring 1995): 249–55.

———. "Modernist Studies." In *Redrawing the Boundaries: The Transformation of English and American Literary Studies.* Eds. Stephen Greenblatt and Giles Gunn. New York: The Modern Language Association of America, 1992: 154–78.

Peterson, Richard R. "A Reader's Guide to William York Tindall." In *Reviewing Classics of Joyce Criticism.* Ed. Janet Egleson Dunleavy. Urbana: U of Illinois P, 1991: 106–19.

Peyre, Henri. "The Legacy of Proust." In *Proust: A Collection of Critical Essays.* Ed. René Girard. 1962; Westport, Conn.: Greenwood, 1977: 28–41.

Pope, Deborah. "The Misprision of Vision: *A Portrait of the Artist as a Young Man.*" In *James Joyce: Modern Critical Views.* Ed. Harold Bloom. New York: Chelsea, 1986: 113–19.

Poulet, Georges. *Proustian Space.* Trans. Elliott Coleman. Baltimore: Johns Hopkins UP, 1977.

Powers, Lyall H. "Henry James and James Baldwin: The Complex Figure." *Modern Fiction Studies* 30.4 (Winter 1984): 651–67.

Proust, Marcel. "A Dinner in Society." In *Pleasures and Days and Other Writings.* Ed. F. W. Dupee. Trans. Louise Vanese, Gerard Hopkins, and Barbara Dupee. New York: Howard Fertig, 1978.

———. "Preface, *Contre Sainte-Beuve.*" In *Contre Sainte-Beuve précédé de Pastiches et Mélanges et suivi d'Essais et articles.* Paris: Gallimard, 1971.

———. *A la recherche du temps perdu.* Eds. Jean-Yves Tadié, Florence Callu, Francine Goujon, Eugene Nicole, Pierre-Louis Rey, Brian Rogers et Jo Yoshida, Bibliothèque de la Pléiade. 4 Tomes. Paris: Gallimard, 1987.

———. *Remembrance of Things Past.* 3 vols. Eds. C. K. Scott Moncrieff and Terence Kilmartin. New York: Vintage-Random, 1981.

Readings, Bill. *The University in Ruins.* Cambridge, Mass.: Harvard UP, 1997.

Redding, Saunders. "The Problems of the Negro Writer." *Massachusetts Review* 6 (Autumn/Winter 1964–65): 57–70.

Reilly, James P. "Non Ego—Non Serviam: The Problem of Artistic Freedom." In *Dedalus on Crete: Essays on the Implications of Joyce's Portrait*. Los Angeles: Immaculate Heart College, 1956: 45–52.

Revel, Jean-François. *Sur Proust: Une Lecture Con-Conformiste de A la Recherche du temps perdu*. Paris: Editions Donoe. Rpt. *On Proust*. Trans. Martin Turnell. New York: Library, 1972.

Rice, Thomas Jackson. *James Joyce: A Guide to Research*. New York: Garland, 1982.

Riva, Raymond T. *Marcel Proust: A Guide to the Main Recurrent Themes*. New York: Exposition, 1965.

Rivers, J. E. *Proust and the Art of Love: The Aesthetics of Sexuality in the Life, Times and Art of Marcel Proust*. New York: Columbia UP, 1980.

Robinson, David W. "'What Kind of a Name Is That?': Joyce's Critique of Names and Naming in *A Portrait*." *James Joyce Quarterly* 26.2 (Winter 1989): 325–35.

Rosello, Mireille. "L'Embonpoint du baron de Charlus." *French Forum* 10.2 (May 1985): 189–200.

Ross, Kristin. "The World Literature: Cultural Studies Program." *Critical Inquiry* 19 (Summer 1993): 666–76.

Rudinow, Joel. "Representation, Voyeurism, and the Vacant Point of View." *Philosophy and Literature*. 3.2 (Fall 1979): 173–86.

Rupp, Richard H. *Celebration in Postwar American Fiction 1945–1967*. Coral Gables, Fla.: U of Miami P, 1970.

Said, Edward W. *Culture and Imperialism*. New York: Knopf, 1994.

Samuel, Maurice. "The Concealments of Marcel: Proust's Jewishness." *Commentary* 29 (1960): 8–22.

Sansom, William. *Proust and His World*. London: Thames, 1973.

Sartre, Jean-Paul. *Being and Nothingness*. Trans. Hazel E. Barnes. New York: Washington Square, 1956.

Sayre, Robert F. "James Baldwin's Other Country." In *Contemporary American Novelists*. Ed. Harry T. Moore. Carbondale: Southern Illinois UP, 1964: 158–69.

Schlesinger, Arthur. *The Disuniting of America: Reflections on a Multicultural Society*. New York: Norton, 1993.

Scholes, Robert. *The Rise and Fall of English: Reconstructing English as a Discipline*. New Haven: Yale UP, 1998.

Schlossman, Beryl. *Joyce's Catholic Comedy of Language*. Madison: U of Wisconsin P, 1985.

Schorer, Mark. "Technique as Discovery." *Hudson Review* 1 (1948): 67–87.

Schraufnagel, Noel. *From Apology to Protest: The Black American Novel.* Deland, Fla.: Everett/Edwards, 1973.

Schultz, H.J. and P.H. Rein, eds. *Comparative Literature: The Early Years.* Chapel Hill: U of North Carolina P, 1973.

Schwarz, Daniel R. "Tell Us in Plain Words: An Introduction to Reading Joyce's *Ulysses.*" *Journal of Narrative Technique* 17.1 (Winter 1987): 25–38.

Scott, Bonnie Kime. *The Gender of Modernism: A Critical Anthology.* Bloomington: Indiana UP, 1990.

Seiden, Melvin. "Proust's Marcel and Saint-Loup: Inversion Reconsidered." *Contemporary Literature* 10 (1969): 220–40.

Senn, Fritz. "Joyce the Verb." In *Coping with Joyce: Essays from the Copenhagen Symposium.* Ed. Morris Beja and Shari Benstock. Columbus: Ohio State UP, 1989: 25–54.

Shattuck, Roger. *Marcel Proust.* New York: Viking, 1974.

Shorris, Earl. *Latinos: A Biography of the People.* New York: Avon, 1992.

Smithson, Isaiah. "Introduction: Institutionalizing Culture Studies." *English Studies/Culture Studies: Institutionalizing Dissent.* Ed. Isaiah Smithson and Nancy Ruff. Urbana and Chicago: U of Illinois P, 1994: 1–22.

Smithson, Isaiah and Nancy Ruff. *English Studies/Culture Studies: Institutionalizing Dissent.* Urbana and Chicago: U of Illinois P, 1994.

Soyinka, Wole. "Foreword." In *James Baldwin: The Legacy.* Ed. Quincy Troupe. New York: Simon & Schuster, 1989: 9–18.

Spagnoli, J. J. *The Social Attitude of Marcel Proust.* New York: Columbia UP, 1936.

Spillers, Hortense. *Comparative American Identities: Race, Sex, and Nationality in the Modern Text.* New York: Routledge, 1991.

Spivak, Gayatri Chakravorty. "The Making of Americans, the Teaching of English, and the Future of Culture Studies." *New Literary History* 21 (1990): 781–98.

———. "Who Claims Alterity?" In *Discussions of Contemporary Culture 4: Remaking History.* Ed. Barbara Kruger and Phil Mariani. New York: Dia Art Foundation, 1989.

Staley, Thomas F. *An Annotated Critical Bibliography of James Joyce.* New York: St. Martin's, 1989.

———. "Following Ariadne's String: Tracing Joyce Scholarship into the Eighties." In *James Joyce: An International Perspective.* Centenary Essays in Honour of the late Sir Desmond Cochrane. Ed. Suheil Badi Bushrui and Bernard Benstock. Gerrard's Cross, Buckinghamshire: Colin Smyth, 1982: 250–77.

———. "Notes and Comments." *James Joyce Quarterly* 22.2 (Winter, 1985): 109–11.

Stambolian, George, and Elaine Marks. *Homosexualities and French Literature*. Ithaca: Cornell UP, 1979.

Standley, Fred L. "James Baldwin: The Artist as Incorrigible Disturber of the Peace." In *Critical Essays on James Baldwin*. Ed. Fred L. Standley and Nancy V. Burt. Boston: G. K. Hall, 1988: 43–54.

———. "James Baldwin: The Crucial Situation." *The South Atlantic Quarterly* 15.3 (Summer 1965): 371–81.

Stephanson, Anders. "Regarding Postmodernism—A Conversation with Frederic Jameson." *Social Text: Theory, Culture, Ideology* 17 (Fall 1987): 29–54.

Strauman, Heinrich. *American Literature in the Twentieth Century*, 3rd rev. ed. New York: Harper, 1965.

Straus, Bernard. *Maladies of Marcel Proust: Doctors and Disease in His Life and Work*. New York: Holmes & Meier, 1980.

Sullivan, Kevin. *Joyce Among the Jesuits*. New York: Columbia UP, 1958.

Sundquist, Eric J. *To Wake the Nations: Race in the Making of American Literature*. 1993. Cambridge: Harvard UP, 1994.

Taylor, Gordon O. "Voices From the Veil: Black American Autobiography." *Georgia Review* 35.2 (Summer 1981): 341–61.

Thomas, C. "L'Allée Marcel Proust." *Poëtique* 63 (1985): 301–11.

Tindall, William York. *James Joyce: His Way of Interpreting the Modern World*. New York: Scribner's, 1950.

Torgovnick, Marianna. *Gone Primitive: Savage Intellects, Modern Lives*. Chicago: U of Chicago P, 1990.

Tratner, Michael. *Modernism and Mass Politics: Joyce, Woolf, Eliot, Yeats*. Stanford: Stanford UP, 1995.

Valente, Joseph. *James Joyce and the Problem of Justice: Negotiating Sexual and Colonial Difference*. New York: Cambridge UP, 1995.

van Ghent, Dorothy. "On *A Portrait of the Artist as a Young Man*." In *Portraits of an Artist: A Casebook on James Joyce's A Portrait of the Artist as a Young Man*. Ed. William E. Morris and Clifford A. Nault, Jr. New York: Odyssey, 1962: 65–76.

Vigneron, Robert. "Creative Agony." In *Proust: A Collection of Critical Essays*. Ed. René Girard. 1962; Westport, Conn.: Greenwood, 1977: 13–27.

Viswanathan, Gauri. *The Masks of Conquest: Literary Study and British Rule in India*. New York: Columbia UP, 1989.

Viti, Elizabeth Richardson. "Marcel and the Medusa: The Narrator's Obfuscated Homosexuality in *A la recherche du temps perdu*." *Dalhousie French Studies* 26 (1994): 61–68.

wa Thiong'o, Ngugi. *Decolonising the Mind: The Politics of Language in African Literature*. London: Currey, 1986.

Warren, Austin and Wellek, René. *Theory of Literature*. Harcourt, 1956.

Watt, Ian. *The Rise of the Novel: Studies in Defoe, Richardson and Fielding.* Berkeley: U of California P, 1957.

Weatherby, W. J. *James Baldwin: Artist on Fire.* New York: Bantam, 1989.

Weisstein, Ulrich. *Comparative Literature and Literary Theory.* Bloomington: Indiana UP, 1974.

Wellek, René. *Concepts of Criticism*. New Haven: Yale UP, 1963.

———. *Discriminations: Further Concepts of Criticism*. New Haven: Yale UP, 1970.

Werner, Craig. "Bigger's Blues: *Native Son* and the Articulation of Afro-American Modernism." In *New Essays on Native Son*. Ed. Kenneth Kinnamon. Cambridge: Cambridge UP, 1990: 117–52.

West, Cornel. "Minority Discourse and the Pitfalls of Canon Formation." *The Yale Journal of Criticism* 1.1 (Fall 1987): 193–201.

White, Hayden. *Metahistory: The Historical Imagination in Nineteenth-Century Europe*. Baltimore: Johns Hopkins UP, 1973.

———. "The Rhetoric of Interpretation." *Poetics Today* 9.2 (1988): 253–274.

Williams, Raymond. *Marxism and Literature*. Oxford: Oxford UP, 1977.

Wilson, Edmund. *Axel's Castle: A Study in the Imaginative Literature of 1870–1930.* New York: C. Scribner's Sons, 1931.

Wimsatt, W. K., and Cleanth Brooks. *Literary Criticism: A Short History.* New York: Random House, 1957.

Wimsatt, Jr., W. K., and Monroe C. Beardsley. *The Verbal Icon: Studies in the Meaning of Poetry*. Lexington, Ky.: U of Kentucky P, 1954.

Wolitz, Seth L. *The Proustian Community*. New York: New York UP, 1971.

Wright, David G. *Characters of Joyce*. Totowa, N.J.: Barnes & Noble, 1983.

Zahorski, Kenneth J. "James Baldwin: Portrait of a Black Exile." In *James Baldwin: A Critical Evaluation*. Ed. Therman B. O'Daniel. Washington: Howard UP, 1977: 199–204.

Zenou, Gilles. "Proust et la judéité." *Europe: Revue Littéraire Mensuelle.* 705–706 (Jan.–Feb. 1988): 157–64.

INDEX